RORSCHACH'S
TEST

THE SERIES IN CLINICAL AND COMMUNITY PSYCHOLOGY

CONSULTING EDITORS
Charles D. Spielberger and Irwin G. Sarason

Auerbach and Stolberg Crisis Intervention with Children and Families
Burchfield Stress: Psychological and Physiological Interactions
Burstein and Loucks Rorschach's Test: Scoring and Interpretation
Cohen and Ross Handbook of Clinical Psychobiology and Pathology, volume 1
Cohen and Ross Handbook of Clinical Psychobiology and Pathology, volume 2
Diamant Male and Female Homosexuality: Psychological Approaches
Froehlich, Smith, Draguns, and Hentschel Psychological Processes in Cognition and
    Personality
Hobfoll Stress, Social Support, and Women
Janisse Pupillometry: The Psychology of the Pupillary Response
Krohne and Laux Achievement, Stress, and Anxiety
London Personality: A New Look at Metatheories
London The Modes and Morals of Psychotherapy, Second Edition
Manschreck and Kleinman Renewal in Psychiatry: A Critical Rational Perspective
Morris Extraversion and Introversion: An Interactional Perspective
Muñoz Depression Prevention: Research Directions
Olweus Aggression in the Schools: Bullies and Whipping Boys
Reitan and Davison Clinical Neuropsychology: Current Status and Applications
Rickel, Gerrard, and Iscoe Social and Psychological Problems of Women: Prevention
    and Crisis Intervention
Smoll and Smith Psychological Perspectives in Youth Sports
Spielberger and Diaz-Guerrero Cross-Cultural Anxiety, volume 1
Spielberger and Diaz-Guerrero Cross-Cultural Anxiety, volume 2
Spielberger and Diaz-Guerrero Cross-Cultural Anxiety, volume 3
Spielberger and Sarason Stress and Anxiety, volume 1
Sarason and Spielberger Stress and Anxiety, volume 2
Sarason and Spielberger Stress and Anxiety, volume 3
Spielberger and Sarason Stress and Anxiety, volume 4
Spielberger and Sarason Stress and Anxiety, volume 5
Sarason and Spielberger Stress and Anxiety, volume 6
Sarason and Spielberger Stress and Anxiety, volume 7
Spielberger, Sarason, and Milgram Stress and Anxiety, volume 8
Spielberger, Sarason, and Defares Stress and Anxiety, volume 9
Spielberger and Sarason Stress and Anxiety, volume 10: A Sourcebook of Theory and
    Research
Spielberger, Sarason, and Defares Stress and Anxiety, volume 11
Strelau, Farley, and Gale The Biological Bases of Personality and Behavior, volume 1:
    Theories, Measurement Techniques, and Development
Strelau, Farley, and Gale The Biological Bases of Personality and Behavior, volume 2:
    Psychophysiology, Performance, and Applications
Ulmer On the Development of a Token Economy Mental Hospital Treatment Program
Williams and Westermeyer Refugee Mental Health in Resettlement Countries

IN PREPARATION

Spielberger and Diaz-Guerrero Stress and Anxiety, volume 12
Spielberger, Sarason, and Strelau Cross-Cultural Anxiety, volume 4
Spielberger and Vagg The Assessment and Treatment of Test Anxiety

RORSCHACH'S TEST:
SCORING AND INTERPRETATION

Alvin G. Burstein, Ph.D.
Department of Psychology
University of Tennessee at Knoxville

Sandra Loucks, Ph.D.
Department of Pediatrics
University of Tennessee Medical Center,
and Department of Psychology
University of Tennessee at Knoxville

⬤HEMISPHERE PUBLISHING CORPORATION
A member of the Taylor & Francis Group

New York   Washington   Philadelphia   London

RORSCHACH'S TEST: Scoring and Interpretation

1 2 3 4 5 6 7 8 9 0   E B E B   8 9 8 7 6 5 4 3 2 1 0 9

This book was set in Melliza. The editor was Diane Stuart; the designer was Sharon DePass; and the typesetter was General Graphic Services.
Cover design by Debra Eubanks Riffe.
Edwards Brothers, Inc. was the printer and binder.

Library of Congress Cataloging-in-Publication Data

Burstein, Alvin G. (Alvin George), date.
  Rorschach's test.
  (The Series in clinical and community psychology)
  Bibliography: p.
  Includes index.
  1. Rorschach's test.   I. Loucks, Sandra.   II. title.
III. Series. [DNLM: 1. Rorschach Test. WM 145 B972r]
RC473.R6B87   1989   155.2′842   88-34737
ISBN 0-89116-771-4
ISBN 0-89116-780-3 (pbk.)
ISSN 0146-0846

To Sam Beck and Alan Rosenwald,
courageous pioneers, inspiring mentors,
and generous colleagues

CONTENTS

7.   INTERPRETATION OF THE STRUCTURAL
           SUMMARY   273

PREFACE

Like any work of this kind, this effort has multiple historical roots. Part of its origin lies in one of the author's experiences some 30 years ago as a student of Sam Beck and, later, as a collaborator with Sam in teaching graduate courses at the University of Chicago. Another point of origin lies in the formation by the authors of a Rorschach study group in San Antonio, Texas, in the mid-seventies. What coalesced was a realization that extant scoring systems involve irrationalities and omissions that severely limit them. What has emerged is this book, designed for graduate level assessment courses and doctoral level psychologists. The system is clearly linked to psychoanalytic theory and should be taught in the context of supporting course work or previous knowledge of psychoanalytically informed personality theory and psychopathology. The system gives careful attention to the systematic and formal scoring of content from the point of object relations and psychosexual theory and provides not only clear scoring variables, which are theoretically and logically informed, but also multiple examples and illustrative normative data from hundreds of pathological and nonpathological individuals.

There are two other introductory comments we should make. When we were discussing our work with Alan Rosenwald, he pointed out that no scoring system can be mechanically applied and that the merit of any system lies in its ability to facilitate disciplined analysis of an individual's cognitive processes as reflected in Rorschach's test.

Our system is not complete; any Rorschach system should continue to grow with its application and with the elaboration of psychological theory.

Alvin G. Burstein
Sandra Loucks

ACKNOWLEDGMENTS

The students and colleagues who contributed their time, thought, and energy have made our efforts possible. We would like especially to mention Lance Apple, Jon Barrett, Bonnie Blankmeyer, Rochelle Lefton, Karen Fiducia, Melanie Fitzgerald, Joe Kobos, Kathryn White, Pete Young, Chuck Jones, Cheri Kenna, Charisse Chapelle, Joanna Williams, Nan Hawkes, David Winecoff, Betsy Gertz, Mark Zitlin, Laura Saxton, Karen Josvanger, Julie Shaing, Pat Marterer, John House, Helen Mugg Worsham, Carol Atwater, Mavis Bryant, Wayne Coursol, Susan Justice, Charlie Kimbell, Mary Lou Murray, and Sheila Stack. Special thanks to Don Broach, Merle Bragdon, Kathryn White, Joyce Cartor, Mike Bertenthal, Scott Glass, Janet Carnes, and Lisa Blair. We would also like to thank the staff and administrators of the Northside Independent School District in San Antonio, Texas, and the Knox County and Blount County School Districts in Tennessee, who helped us collect the child data.

1
HISTORY AND THEORETICAL CONTEXT

The doyen of psychology's historians, E. G. Boring (1950), begins his history with Ebbinginhaus' comment that psychology has a long past, but a short history. The same might be said of projective testing, and of Rorschach's test.

The notion that what one "sees" in ambiguous stimuli reveals mental status is implied in the cloud game played by Shakespeare's Hamlet and Polonius. Although Binet thought of inkblots as stimuli in a test of imagination (1895), it was Herman Rorschach that formalized that game as a psycho-diagnostic technique three centuries later, with the publication of his 1922 monograph.

One of the most curious features of the test has been the degree to which its development has been independent of an explicit theoretical context. Rorschach, a Jungian analyst, referenced both Freud and Jung in his original monograph. Despite the implications of these references and the fact that the first two decades of the century were times of great activity and interest in psychoanalysis, the test as described by Rorschach was only minimally related to or informed by psychoanalytic theory, and the works of Rapaport (1946), Schafer (1954), and Holt (1970) not withstanding, that remains largely the case today.

As the test became known in the United States with publications in the 1930's and 1940's by Beck (1930), Hertz (1935), Klopfer (1942), Piotrowski (1936) and Rapaport (1945, 1946), it *did* get assimilated, not into a theoretical context, but into the psychometric tradition, exemplified by Binet. The psychometric tradition has been rooted in educational settings, and was historically fueled by the vocational/classificational needs emerging during World War II and the aftermath of veteran rehabilitation. Perhaps for this reason, the explosion of research activity using the test, from a few hundred studies in the 1930's to thousands yearly in the forties and fifties (Klopfer, 1973), was typified by approaches focusing on predictive or concurrent validity. Scores or combinations of scores on the Rorschach were related to concurrent diagnoses, to treatment outcomes, and the like. Hence, the focus of the test shifted from the psychological processes thought to be reflected in the test to the Rorschach scores and their psychometric "validity."

The outcome of this burst of research was not promising. The results were unimpressive, in part because, as Chronbach pointed out (1949), the studies were statistically naive and/or careless, and in part because the variables being predicted to (e.g., diagnosis) were not very reliable. In any event, a negative scientific climate for Rorschach's test developed, typified and epitomized by Meehl's sweeping critique (1954) of "clinical" prediction.

This climate must be interpreted in context, and, in particular, with respect to four points. First, despite the accretion of dreary failures to replicate predictive validity in narrowly conceived psychometric experiments, Rorschach's test has proved hardy in clinical settings, and in the academic settings committed to training clinicians. Piotrowski has documented the degree to which Rorschach's test continues to be among the most commonly given of psychological tests. It continues to be taught, despite a reported perception that its importance is declining, in academic and practicum settings (1984a, b, c; 1985). The extent to which skeptical educators acknowledge the pragmatic demand for the test was illustrated when one of the authors recently paid an accreditation visit to a doctoral program known for its exclusively behavioral orientation, to find Rorschach training required of students—and taught by behavioral faculty!

Second, the lack of consensus within psychology on basic theoretical issues—psychology's failure to generate a dominant theoretical view—led Rorschach teachers and practitioners to focus on matters of convention and technique rather than of theory. Controversies were cast in terms of whether animal movement should be scored, whether it was "really" movement, rather than on the inferred psychological processes. Rorschach scoring systems—Beck's (1961), Piotrowski's (1957), Klopfer's (1954, 1956), Rapaport's (1945, 1946) and lately, Exner's (1974), et al.—compete without reference to their ability to contribute to the useful elaboration of mentalist constructs, despite the fact that the test is rooted in assumptions about the mind and how it works.

The recent reawakening of experimental psychology's interest in cognition (Pribram, 1986) is a hopeful development that resonates with the Wundtian origins of scientific psychology, as well as with the Jamesian domestication of it and the more recent cognitive style work of Klein (1970), Witkin (1954) and their followers. The cognitive reaction to radical behaviorism may generate an academic-scientific context in which Rorschach behavior is seen as non-trivial, and for which Rorschach's experiment may prove to be one useful experimental paradigm.

Finally, classical psychometrics is a tool devised for the kinds of gross but reliable classifications which characterize educational and industrial work. Recent developments in psychometrics, for example, latent trait theory (Weiss, 1983; Lord, F. M. 1968), are more geared to evaluating and refining the ability to measure constructs as opposed to behaviors, and may therefore offer more useful ways of characterizing Rorschach's test.

The basic notion of Rorschach's test (or experiment) is straightforward. The subject is presented with a stimulus known to be non-representational and asked what it looks like. He or she later is asked to elaborate. Each comment is reduced or scored by noting a number of dimensions thought to be relevant, for example, how complicated the "percept" is, how much of the stimulus is accounted for, the ways in which the percepts are justified, etc.

Much attention has been paid to spelling out the specific rules by which responses are to be scored or reduced. The most widely known systems for scoring are those of Beck (1961), Piotrowski (1957), Klopfer (1954), Rapaport-Schafer (1945), and Exner (1974). The test's underlying assumption is that each of us induces order and clarity into our experiential world on the basis of a grammar that is individual and related to fundamental consistencies of behavior. The implications of this assumption depend upon how the mind is understood.

In the study of mind, the dominant trend has been to separate considerations of cognitive or intellectual function from those of emotional or motivational concerns. This tendency is in part due to the historical relationship between intelligence testing for the educational enterprise, with its necessary emphasis on aptitudes and achievement testing, in contrast to the psychopathological interests of clinical psychology. Such emotion-intellect distinctions perhaps find their fullest expression in some of the neuromythology surrounding right brain-left brain differences, and in some of the speculations about artificial intelligence and thinking machines. Whatever the history of this division, it is highly likely that, in practice, any psychological test report selected at random will contain a section on intellectual abilities and a parallel section on personality factors, as though these subjects are usefully separated.

Despite the dominance of this separatist trend, a hardy counterculture has always existed. For example, Binet not only studied imagination (1905), but mentioned the faculty of "application" to work as interacting with aptitudes; further, the main thrust of the cognitive style research of the 1960's, (Witkin, 1954; Klein, 1970) focusing on such factors as field dependence-independence, and sharpeners-levelers, was that questions of personal style and intellectual ability are mutually relevant and perhaps inseparable.

Although much of what has been written and taught about Rorschach's test has been colored by the dichotomization of intellect and emotion, the test, properly understood, belongs solidly in the countercultural tradition of interactionist considerations of these psychological functions. Despite the generally bad press in the psychometric research literature and a general antidynamic bias in graduate training, Rorschach's test has proven to be remarkably popular and useful in practice settings. This resilience is due to the central interactionist assumption underlying the test, which embodies a core notion whose vitality transcends the weaknesses of scoring and the trivialities of training that have hampered the test.

Intrinsic to the study of mind is the notion of humankind as seekers of meaning. Our species is styled *homo sapiens*. In this sense cognition is central to psychology. Rorschach's test is a test of cognition. The subject is handed a stimulus known to be non-representational or ambiguous ("a picture of an inkblot"), and asked what it looks like. Later he or she is asked to elaborate, and his or her reactions scored by noting the factors thought to be relevant. The task which Rorschach's test sets the subject is: "make sense of this," "recognize this stimulus." The task is paradoxical and prototypical—recognizing the unfamiliar, making sense of the novel, assimilating new experience into the apperceptive mass. This is an effort in which affective-motivational and intellectual-cognitive systems must participate.

The key assumption is that making sense of experience is an effortful task that is largely invisible to us, because it is so over-practiced. It is effortful, not automatic, and involves a grammar which is for each of us, individual and as much affective/motivational as it is cognitive.

It was a brilliant intuition on Rorschach's part that cognition, the act of making sense, would become more amenable to study by asking subjects to recognize stimuli that were entirely novel, and were, in fact, nonrepresentational. Most recognitions are rapid, and, therefore, hard for the subject to analyze retrospectively. Rorschach recognitions, in contrast, are often both slow and difficult, making the psychologist's request for an explanation more likely to be productive.

In summary, then, Rorschach's test assumes making sense of the world to be a cognitive, affective, motivational act that can be productively studied by a phenomenological exploration of a paradoxical situation: insisting that the subject "recognize" non-representational stimuli.

One of the serious weaknesses in the teaching of Rorschach's test is the tendency to present it as a relatively theory-free technique. As noted earlier, this tendency may be rooted in the absence of a single dominant theory of personality in psychology, and in a wish to avoid controversies that cannot be quickly resolved by a crucial experiment. Nevertheless, one cannot have a theory-free view of personality or of Rorschach's test.

Our view of the test is deeply rooted in psychoanalytic theory, especially Otto Kernberg's view (1966, 1980), that native experience is transactional in nature, consisting, as it were, of initially undifferentiated self-other-affect packets. The differentiation and integration of these packets into one's identity, one's interpersonal and objective world, and one's motives constitutes psychological development. That development gone awry is the basis for psychopathology. It is this process of differentiating experiential activity that Rorschach's test seeks to recreate and to study.

Interpretation of the results of Rorschach testing is possible only in the context of theoretical expectations about the functions of the mind, the origins of psychopathology and the psychotherapeutic implications of such factors. Of course, theoretical points of view alternative to ours are possible, but the point is that an attempt to find a theory-free meaning for test results condemns one to a trivial correlational sign approach that has proven relatively barren. The theoretical matrix for the test should be explicit.

DIMENSIONS OF SCORING

Dimensions of Scoring Rorschach Responses

As explained above, a great deal of attention has been given to noting the ways in which the subject deals with the cognitive problems posed by Rorschach's test. At least five major systems are in common use: those of Beck (1961), Piotrowski (1957), Klopfer (1954, 1956), Rapaport-Schafer (1945, 1946), and Exner (1974).

These current major scoring systems share three major shortcomings: a) conceptual gaps in the scoring categories employed, b) lack of attention to the specific nature of the "recognitions" and to nuances of cognitive functions, and c) lack of clear articulation with personality and psychopathological theory. This author's scoring system attempts to address each of these shortcomings.

For example, most approaches do not systematically distinguish between "determinants" that are attempts by the subject to justify his percept by referring to physical aspects of the blot (form, color, etc.) and, on the other hand, attempts by the subject to impart some subjective interpretation of the blot (references to movement, texture, etc). In our system this distinction is recognized by dividing so-called "determinants" into "Justifications" and "Imaginal Aspects."

As another example, we have given much attention to what we call "Perceptual-Cognitive Characteristics." An attempt has been made to provide an extensive set of categories for classifying notable ways of approaching the task of "recognizing" the stimuli. Figure-ground reversals (usually scored as "S" in the location sector), predicate thinking (often called confabulation), use of very common stereotypes (populars) and other modes of cognition are systematically noted.

As a final example, the content of each response is also assessed, not only to label its conceptual class, but also to determine the precision and tone of interpersonal expectations. Responses are also assessed from a psychoanalytic psychosexual point of view to determine the extent to which oral, anal, or phallic material is represented and defended against.

To highlight the differences between our approach and those in current use, we will present a précis of our system in the context of a review of the conventional categories and their shortcomings.

Conventional Dimensions of Scoring and Interpretation

In Rorschach's original work (1969), four basic dimensions within each response were noted: mode of apperception (location and derived scores); form, movement and color (later called determinants); content; and noting of original answers (later expanded to include noting popular responses and other qualitative observations). Beck (1933) introduced the notion of an additional dimension, organizational activity, an idea also implemented in various ways by Klopfer (1973), Hertz (1935), Rapaport (1945, 1946), Exner (1974), Holtzman (Hill, 1972) and others. Hence, the five basic dimensions can be designated: location, organization, determinants, content, and qualitative observations. We will consider each of these dimensions serially.

Location

This dimension of scoring involves noting which area of the blot was utilized, its size, and the frequency with which it tends to be chosen by individuals taking the test. Derivative observations are also made, such as noting the relative preference he or she may have for using the whole blot as opposed to using smaller areas (often called approach) and the degree of orderliness with which the person searches for responses (often called sequence). The kinds of psychological inferences conventionally based on location scores have to do with the vigor and orderliness of problem solving strategies.

A number of problems plague the scoring and interpretation of location. Some of the confusion stems from the way in which Rorschach put the original question: "Is the figure conceived and interpreted as a whole or in parts? Which are the parts interpreted?" (1969, p. 19). This disjunction implies that all wholes are alike, but that all parts are not. Accordingly, many scoring systems sort out parts by size or by frequency, but most do not systematically sort out whole responses in the same way. Clearly, if the frequency with which an area is chosen is important, it should be noted for all responses, including whole responses. To put it another way, some whole responses, like some part responses are frequently chosen and some are not.

In our system we take separate note of size and of frequency. With respect to size we score whole responses, whole responses with minor qualifications, large areas, and small areas. Detailed rules for scoring these variables are found on page 29 ff.

The tables on page 81 ff indicate for each card which specific locations are to be scored as large areas and which are to be scored as small. Each area of each blot has been assigned a number by Beck, and we have retained these numbers. In Beck's system, the numbers reflected the frequency with which specific areas were utilized. Our data indicates some significant shifts in frequency. The tables on page 81 ff list for each card the locations in order of the frequency with which they are used in our initial sample of more than 250 subjects. The tables also indicate which locations are to be considered rare. It is interesting to note that the whole location is that most commonly used for Cards I, II, IV, V, VI, and VII; it is rare in card III, but relatively frequent in VIII, IX, and X. Areas (large or small) which are rarely chosen (e.g., represent less than about 10% of the responses) are underlined in our scoring system.

Another complication of scoring location has resulted from the inclusion in the location sector of the scoring of other considerations. For example, both Rorschach and Beck assumed a necessary connection between whole responses and the tendency to give responses which are highly organized. Our data suggest that there is a weak correlation between the two tendencies, but not a causal relationship. In fact, some whole responses (e.g., the "bat" to Card V) can be quite "easy." Accordingly, in evaluating organizational activity (See below), it is important to do so *independently* of location.

The meaning of location scores seems to derive from the likelihood that subjects interpret the test's instructions to mean that they are to use the whole blot. We infer this from the fact that subjects often ask permission to use a part of the blot, but never, in our experience, ask permission to use the whole blot; in addition we have already noted the relatively high frequency with which whole responses are given in comparison with other unique areas. In other words, the failure to produce a fair number of whole responses is a deficiency that needs to be accounted for—as is the failure to produce a fair number of other large area responses.

Other extraneous intrusions into location scoring in conventional systems include noting figure ground reversals (use of white space) as well as other cognitive tendencies, such as inferential failures (usually called confabulated responses: DW, DdD, or DD), and failures to see easy wholes (oligophrenic details, Do).

Such cognitive tendencies are important and meaningful, but not really related to location scoring. We deal with them in a separate sector of scoring, Perceptual Cognitive Characteristics (p. 59 ff), because attempting to do so in the location sector multiplies the symbols used in that sector in a way which blurs the basic questions to be considered: the size and the rarity of the area used by the subject for a particular response. Detailed rules, specific symbols, and examples relevant to the scoring of location are presented on pages 29 ff.

The Meaning of Location Scores

Basically to be considered here are the issues of the size of the area used and the frequency with which a particular area is selected. Overall, approximately 10% of an individual's responses can be expected to be rarely selected (underlined) areas, whether W, D, or Dd. Where this percentage is significantly exceeded, in excess of 20%, the subject is demonstrating an ability to focus on unusual, original, or idiosyncratic aspects of his experiential field. Such a capacity may reflect a failure of socialization, creative individuality, or inability to focus, depending upon other aspects of performance.

In the older Rorschach literature, the relative preference for whole responses, large areas and small areas is often called the approach type. Our data suggest that the percentages of large areas (D) tends to be relatively stable, with the consequences that W% and Dd% tend to be reciprocal. In other words, the tendency to use the whole blot or a very small portion are stylistic alternatives, the former being either impressionistic or integrative, the latter analytic. Variations in the D%, tend to be much rarer. Generally, as Exner suggested (p. 237) D answers appear easier to give. In other words, both W's and Dd's are more likely to require mental energy, and notably high levels of D% seems to reflect conservatism, guardedness or lack of capacity.

A second aspect of location scoring has to do with noting the sequence of the kinds of locations used by subjects. As mentioned above, the standard instructions for Rorschach's test, and perhaps the nature of the first blot seem to predispose subjects toward initial W responses. Frequently subjects ask whether they can use part of the blot; never do they ask whether they can use the whole blot. Most subjects develop a strategy of giving any whole response which occurs to them, then D responses and last, Dd responses. When this sequence becomes invariable and stereotyped, Rorschach suggests pedantry, depression, or anxiety and low self-esteem (p. 43). Failures to develop a strategy of where to look produce a confused sequence and suggests an inability to exert mental discipline. In practice, it is even more useful to examine each protocol for evidence of disruption in the subject's typical strategy, and to consider whether the disruption might be due to transient anxiety. Where this is the case, it is often accompanied by other signs of cognitive inefficiency, such as an increase in socially unconventional content, and is called "shock."

Organization or Cognitive Complexity

Cognitive Complexity reflects the subject's tendency to see the world in complex, as opposed to simple terms. It reflects, for example, the difference between seeing on Card I, "a bat" as opposed to "two winged creatures holding on to a third person." It is a factor highly related to intelligence. Evaluating this factor in Rorschach responses has been complicated by two issues. The first is a bias toward thinking of intelligence as a undimensional factor, with a consequent tendency to force varying styles, talents, or deficiencies into a simple ordinal scale. Beck, for example, weights the organizational values assigned to each response and then adds them to obtain a weighted sum. This tendency is at variance with views of intelligence or talent as irreducibly multifaceted.

A second problem has to do with the tendency to confuse issues of location (e.g., whether or not a whole response is given) with issues of whether a response is a complicated one, which was discussed above. The best solution to the second problem is to score location and organization without making assumptions about their relationship, the approach we adopt.

Recognizing some of the subtleties of intellectual operations and their deficiencies involves categorizing them in a fairly complicated way.

We have adopted a procedure similar to that of Rapaport, classifying each response as "integrated," if it displays the synthetic ability to see distinct things in relationships; "arbitrary" if synthetic ability is misused; "articulated," if it displays the ability to analyze objects into component parts; "simple," if neither integrative or articulatory abilities are displayed; and "diffuse" if the objects seen are inherently shapeless. Arbitrary and diffuse responses are thought to represent psychopathological intrusions into potential ability, emphasis on simple responses may reflect guardedness or represent intellectual limitations. Synthetic and analytic cognitive approaches are nominal, not ordinal, stylistic variants of cognition.

Specific symbols, rules, and examples of scoring responses are given below on page 30 ff, under the heading Cognitive Complexity.

Determinants

Rorschach originally noted whether responses depended on form or color or seemed to involve human movement. He said (1969, p. 22), "Most interpretations are determined by form alone . . . (but) in contrast to these we have 'Movement' and 'Color' responses." Evaluating this sector of Rorschach behavior is usually called scoring for determinants, probably because of Rorschach's use of the word "determined." Over the years the list of determinants has been expanded, adding use of the black-white dimension, spatial dimensionality, and distinguishing among human, animal, and object movement.

The scoring and interpretation of these variables has been plagued by two difficulties. The first is an ambiguity about the basis for scoring a determinant. Is it to be scored when the subject reports it or when the examiner is convinced it "determines" the response? Out of this ambiguity have grown elaborate schemes for "testing the limits" of whether a determinant is "really" involved, asking, for example, "would this look as much like blood if it weren't red?" The problem with leading questions is that they lead, informing the subject as much as they do the examiner. We prefer to act on the assumption that we are scoring not what determines the response, but how the subject spontaneously justifies it. For that reason, we call these scores Justification scores.

This resolution helps to highlight and resolve the second difficulty. Close reading of the relevant section of *Psychodiagnostics*, makes clear that Rorschach is contrasting the use of movement, on the one hand, with color and form on the other. He points out that for movement responses, "the subject imagines the object 'seen' as moving."

In other words, in the case of movement the "determinant" is imagined; in the case of form and color the "determinant" is perceived in the blot. Accordingly, our system distinguishes between Justifications, or blot characteristics seen in the blot to which the subject alludes in order to justify the response, and "Imaginal Aspects," references made by the subject, not to perceptual qualities of the blot, but to events or objects he or she knows to be in his or her memory or imagination.

We believe that Justifications and Imaginal Aspects are two distinct realms, and that the clinical importance of the relative use of each is what gives weight to the traditional experience balance measure, the ratio of color (a common justification) to movement (a common imaginal reference). Unfortunately, the experience balance is a very flawed measure: its shortcomings include arbitrary weights assigned to various color usages, and the exclusion of some common justifications and some common imaginal aspects. Our system will hopefully provide a means of developing a sounder, empirically justified analogue of the traditional experience balance.

The psychological meaning of the "determinant" scores is necessarily complicated. In the older literature, singular meanings were often ascribed to each. For example the use of F denoted an objective approach, the use of color denoted impulsive or instinctual discharge, the use of shading, anxiety, etc. In our view, the major distinction to be made has to do with the relative tendency to justify responses in "objective terms" (via use of Justifications) as opposed to imparting one's subjective reactions (via use of Imaginal Aspects). As mentioned above, this is the contrast that gives meaning to the traditional comparison of movement scores and color scores, often called the experience balance. In our view the contrast is not between seeking satisfaction in fantasy as opposed to seeking it in action. Rather it is in self-revelation as an interpersonal mode, in contrast to appealing to external reality. In the former mode, one creates his or her reality and then shares it, in the latter one seeks to discover an external reality. At present this view constitutes a speculation grounded in clinical experience; clarifying Rorschach scoring in the way that we have should provide a means for validating this notion clinically and experimentally. In general, the meaning of individual Justification scores is contextually derived. The use of color without other justifications often involves reliance on a noncriterial attribute (e.g., "a bear because it's brown"). When this is the case we are dealing with predicate thinking, the impulsive, poorly reviewed drawing of inferences. Our system also provides for clear notation of other uses of color as a justification, when it is unrealistic (e.g., "green sheep"), arbitrary (as in a diagram or map), or invoked when it is not present in the blot. Clear and consistent notation of such usages will permit clarification of their meaning. Our experience to date suggests that the first is often correlated with affective dissociation,

the second with intellectualization rather than emotional display, and the
last the possibility of seizure activity. The use of the black-white dimension (achromatic color) and of the intensity or saturation dimension (shading) is usually associated with painful feelings, respectively depression
and anxiety. Applebaum (1968) has noted the correlation between the
simultaneous use of color and shading (or achromatic color) and suicide;
in our experience that co-occurrence is also associated with assaultive
behavior.

The Imaginal Aspects as a group can be regarded as reflecting imagination or fantasy in the broadest sense. Human movement responses
denote the imagination of a world informed by human motives and feelings; animal responses a world in which the conflict inherent in human
interaction is diffused by the Disneyesque defenses of symbolization,
repression, and displacement, and object movement responses a world
which unconsciously reflects the failure of preoedipal parents adequately
to modulate environmental and instinctual pressures. References to an
imaginal tactile quality (Texture responses) are said to be associated with
excessive frustration of needs during the earliest months of life for contact
stimulation. An impressionistic confirmation of this possibility is found
in the frequency with which individuals alluding to Texture finger or
stroke the blot. References to imaginal dimensionality in which the psychological center of the percept is at a distance or difficult to access (Vista
responses) are thought to be associated with the inner experiences of being
weak, overwhelmed and/or without resources, a complex of feeling associated with the old diagnostic category of psychoasthenia.

A derived score of some importance is the proportion of responses
justified by form alone, and without Imaginal Aspects (pure F responses).
Almost all writers assume that the proportion of such responses reflects
the degree of the individual's investment in the denotative, "out-there"
world; this relationship probably flows from the fact that Form like the
other justifications (color, shading, and achromatic color) involves the
convergence of two sense modalities, vision and touch. In other words,
shape can be perceived by either modality and can be confirmed by their
convergence. Hence a reliance on that Justification reflects a predisposi-
tion to live in an "out there" world that is assembled to validational
experiment.

To review, we score as Justifications allusions to shape, size, color,
and intensity or saturation. We score as Imaginal Aspects references to
movement, emotion, dimensionality, or tactile qualities. Specific symbols,
rules and examples are given on page 35 ff under the heading Justifications
and page 41 ff under the heading Imaginal Aspects.

Form Quality

An issue usually treated as related to determinants is that of form level or quality. In Rorschach's discussion of Form quality (1969, p. 23) two issues are confused: frequency of occurrence of a particular percept in normal subjects, and sharpness or clarity of form. To this confusion has been added over the years a third element: the goodness of fit between the blot and the thing named.

As might be expected this confusion has generated a certain amount of controversy, with some writers emphasizing the need for norms, and others emphasizing basically subjective judgments of clarity or precision of form. Almost all writers associate this dimension of the percept with the form "determinant" although Beck, committed to normative distinctions, acknowledges the dubiousness of that relationship, referring (1961, p. 30) to the role of "'good form' in the social sense."

Our view is that issues of clarity and precision overlap with judgments of cognitive complexity, and the typology we present there (q.v.), permits adequate treatment of them in that sector of the scoring system. Attending to normative distinctions, or, more precisely, to the likelihood that healthy vs psychotic individuals will associate a given content to a given area is a content issue determined by a host of variables, including the subject's perception of the goal of the testing. Form plays a role, but not an exclusive one.

Because the normative judgment of "form quality" is more accurately understood as the social appropriateness of specific context to a specific area in the context of the test, we have redesignated that variable "Response Appropriateness." Also unlike other systems, ours makes the judgment of appropriateness for each response, not only those involving form.

Beck's tables, revised by him on the basis of survey responses from several hundred practitioners, permit such a judgment. With the permission of Grune and Stratton and the authors of *Beck's Vol. I Rorschach's Test: Basic Processes*, these tables are reproduced here on p. 81. They have been modified by grouping separately the + and − responses to each area. Specific procedures for using these tables are presented on pages 82 ff.

Judging the response appropriateness for pure Form responses leads to the development of a derived score, the proportion of the pure Form responses that are socially appropriate (F + %). This proportion reflects the degree to which the denotative world lived in by the subject is consensually validated. Our system permits, too, the development of a parallel score, the proportion of the remaining responses—those more related to inner states and the connotative world—that are socially appropriate (B + %). This score is thought to reflect the degree to which the individual's connotative world is consensually validated.

Content

Despite the contemporary identification of Rorschach's test with psychodynamic personality theory, Rorschach held the view that the test is "not a means for delving into the unconscious" (1969, p. 123) because it seemed too influenced by reality considerations. This view is especially paradoxical in light of the emphasis placed on "content interpretation" by many contemporary working clinicians, some of whom treat the test almost as they would a dream. Rorschach does suggest that the test can be useful in ruling out schizophrenia, in predicting the outcome of a psychoanalysis, or in estimation of investment and adaptability in work situations.

One reason for the shift from Rorschach's view to the more contemporary ones is the intervening developments in psychoanalytic theory. What Rorschach appeared to have had in mind by the contents of the unconscious are specific repressed traumatic events, consistent with the psychoanalytic view circa 1900. With the movement of psychoanalytic theory away from individual pathogenic events toward an elaborated view of transference and the repetition compulsion as reflected in repetitive patterns of relationship with historical meanings, and with the elaboration of structural psychoanalytic theory with its emphasis on ego-function and patterns of defense and adaptation, the concept of an unconscious domain became less figural and the purpose of projective testing expanded.

Despite the emphasis that working clinicians place on content interpretation, the best known scoring systems, following Rorschach, treat this sector in relatively casual terms. Usually there is a list of content categories that can be judged as good or bad form (vide supra). In addition, these are usually categorized in some way to provide a rough measure of the number or proportion of human responses, animal responses, and breadth of real world interests, permitting inferences of the sort described by Rorschach of the subject's *conscious* concerns and interests. We have retained such a list using broad content categories of obvious relevance. The specific symbols and rules for the conceptual categorization of content are listed on pages 49 ff.

In addition, we have expanded the formal scoring of content in two basic ways related to psychoanalytic theory and in a third way related to experimental and clinical work on thought pathology, a central issue because this is a cognitive test. These three dimensions are called, respectively, Interpersonal Expectations, Psychosexual Drive and Defense, and Perceptual-Cognitive characteristics. The first borrows heavily from the work of Blatt (1976, 1984) and his colleagues, the second from Holt (1970) and his co-workers, and the third from a host of work done by experimental and clinical researchers, especially in the 1950's and 60's (Chapman & Chapman, 1973; Holt, 1970; Kasanin, 1944). Each dimension will be summarized below.

INTERPERSONAL EXPECTATIONS

This sector of response evaluation draws heavily on the work done by Blatt (1976), Mayman (1974), and others on a topic called, variously, object relations and/or object representations. This work is in the tradition of an ego-psychological view that the sophistication with which mental representations of the external world, including the mental representations of self and self-relevant others, plus the affective quality associated with those representations, is a crucial element in psychological development.

In this sector of our system four components are evaluated, one characterizing human percepts, two characterizing percepts involving imagining human movement and/or human emotions, and a final one evaluating the affective tone or ambience of non-human percepts. These variables are called, respectively, "Human Articulation," "Motivational Articulation," "Motivational Valuation" and "Implicit Motivational Valuation." Symbols, rules, and examples relevant to the scoring of these variables are provided (p. 55 ff).

These scores are an index of the individual's capacity to conceptualize sharply his or her interpersonal world in terms of social roles and interpersonal motivations, and the degree to which the environment is seen as welcoming or threatening. Such characterizations are central to psychoanalytic formulation of individuals from an object relations or self-psychology point of view.

PSYCHOSEXUAL DRIVE AND DEFENSE EFFECTIVENESS

Another aspect of Rorschach content that is not dealt with explicitly by current scoring systems is related, not to object relations, but to psychoanalytic drive theory. The notion is that all behavior is driven by primitive drives whose early foci are the familiar oral, anal, and phallic ones. From a classical psychoanalytic view the story of psychopathology and development involves resolving the inevitable conflicts attendant on drive discharge. Much of the originally instinctual behavior becomes neutralized, and freely available to the ego, its psychosexual origins no longer evident in behavior. Some behavior retains traces of its origins and continues to stir up conflict, which can be defended against flexibly or clumsily.

Robert Holt's primary process scoring scheme (1970) represents a very sophisticated and detailed means of assessing each Rorschach response to determine the extent to which its psychosexual origins are identifiable, and if they are, the quality of the defense deployed against it.

Drawing heavily on Holt's notions, we have developed a simplified scheme for making such assessments. As one would predict, use of this scheme indicates that the Rorschach responses of healthy adults are largely conflict-free. As would be predicted, children show higher levels of drive expression with younger children evidencing more than older children. These data are in the child norms presented on pages 192 ff. One would assume that structural neurotics would have focalized areas of conflict, and that more primitive pathologies would involve more diffuse patterns of drive derivative expression, i.e. across two or more psychosexual areas.

Specific symbols, rules, and examples relevant to scoring Psychosexual drive and defense are found on pages 56 ff under that heading.

PERCEPTUAL COGNITIVE CHARACTERISTICS

Qualitative observations, Rapaport's "fifth column," traditionally includes the noting of popular and/or original responses, as well as significant forms of thought pathology or cognitive slippage, especially of the kind associated with psychosis.

Two problems with current practice are apparent. The first is that many systems score some forms of perceptual/cognitive slippage in this sector while others are confused with other sectors of scoring. For example, figure-ground reversal is usually scored as a location variable, as is the tendency to engage in certain faulty inferences (e.g., "a cat because it has whiskers" usually called a confabulation). On the other hand the primary process condensations usually called contaminations, in which two unrelated percepts are fused, are almost always scored in the fifth sector. The second problem is that a large and unsystematic set of conventions has developed, with many duplications, omissions, and unclear definitions.

In our system, we have tried to develop a comprehensive, relatively nonredundant taxonomy for noting perceptual-cognitive characteristics. Some are common in healthy individuals, others are pathognomonic. Detailed symbols, rules and examples for scoring this material are presented on pages 59 ff.

2

ADMINISTRATION AND SCORING SYMBOL SYNOPSIS

As is the case with any test, Rorschach's test is more than a bundle of materials. It consists of ten cards presented to a subject in the context of certain instructions and procedures, as well as rules for scoring. The subject's perceptions of the examiner's wishes and motives, as well as the goals and motives of the subject helps form the content of the testing and will also help determine what the subject says.

For these reasons, the variability in instructions among the common systems is unfortunate. Obviously, instructions and procedures must be consistent with one's ethical and professional responsibility to respect the patient's autonomy; beyond that the administrative procedures should be minimally intrusive in order to avoid establishing expectancies beyond the most complete possible reporting of the subject's thoughts.

For these reasons, the examination should begin by clarifying its purpose. When the testing is based on a referral, the identity and role of the referring professional should be explicitly clear, as should the nature of the report and the party or parties to whom it will be accessible.

When subjects are being tested for training purposes within a service setting—a school, clinic, or hospital—it is important to clarify to what extent a report will become part of the subject's record, and what access he or she will have to it. It is also important to provide a means for such subjects to have retrospective questions answered about themselves or about the procedure.

For example, a graduate student might say,

> Hello Ms. Smith, I'm John Jay, a graduate student in clinical psychology. As part of my training I have to learn to give certain psychological tests, and I appreciate your volunteering your time in this way. Because this is a training exercise, there won't be any report of the results in your school/clinic/hospital records. Before we start, are there any questions you have? If questions occur to you later you can call Dr. Jones at 977-7777.

Because we believe in keeping the various sources of clinical inferences as separate as possible, we do not begin testing sessions with a clinical interview. Such interviews can be very informative, but are best done by someone other than the tester whenever possible.

INSTRUCTIONS FOR ADMINISTRATION

Seating Arrangement

It is recommended that the examiner position him or herself so that the subject's handling of the card can be observed and so that the examiner may comfortably write down the subject's responses and note behaviors. The position we generally use is one in which the examiner and subject are approximately side by side, at an angle of approximately 45 degrees. We feel this allows the examiner to observe accurately while affording some privacy in recording.

Instructions

The purpose of the instructions is to establish a consistent set in the minds of the subjects being tested. The basic points to be covered are that the patient will be shown ten non-representational stimuli and asked to report all associations to them. The form we use is approximately as follows:

"I'm going to show you ten cards, each containing a picture of an inkblot. I'll give them to you one at a time. I'll ask you to look at each card and tell me what it looks like. Spend as much time as you like on each card but be sure to tell me everything that occurs to you."

If the subject fails to give an association and tries to return the first card in less than two minutes, the examiner is to say, "Give yourself plenty of time. Most people see several things on each card."

If the subject gives only one response to the first card and spends less than two minutes searching for additional responses, the examiner is to say:

"Give yourself plenty of time. Most people see more than one thing on each card."

This urging procedure is to be repeated, if necessary, on the second card, but not subsequently.

Response to Questions

Requests by the subject for permission to turn the card or to respond to only a part of the blot are acceded to as simply as possible. A "yes" will usually suffice. The principle of minimal intrusion by the tester holds true for most questions subjects pose about administrative procedure.

Inquiry

The purpose of the inquiry is to obtain any necessary further information about the subject's responses for the purpose of scoring the record after associations have been obtained to all ten cards. We choose to defer the inquiry until after the free association phase is complete because to introduce it after the first card tends to make subjects more cautious.

It is usually best for the tester to minimize any defensiveness or anxiety the patient might feel by taking on the responsibility for needing additional information and by carefully avoiding the implication that the patient's performance has been inadequate or faulty. A second principle is to obtain any necessary additional information with a minimum of biasing structure being introduced; avoid suggesting or encouraging the use of specific justifications. At the same time, do be sure to inquire about each element of the percept.

In general, we begin the inquiry as follows:

"Okay. Now that we're done, I'd like to go back over the cards with you to make sure I got your responses straight. Let's see. The first thing you saw on this card was (verbatim response)."

The tester then looks up expectantly, providing an opportunity for the patient to talk further about the response. This opportunity will usually elicit sufficient additional information. If the patient does not respond at all, the tester should say, "Tell me more about that."

If sufficient information still is not elicited at this point, the tester should say, "What about the blot brought that to mind?"

If sufficient information still is not available, we conclude that it will not be forthcoming without the introduction of biasing structure.

Be sure to inquire about every salient aspect of the response, indicating in your notes in parentheses what you asked about. For example, Free Association: "A scary bat"; Inquiry: "Why a bat?" . . . "Why scary?"

The tester should specifically avoid asking the patient to trace the outline of the percept (biasing toward form), and asking about the importance of specific variables (e.g., "Was the color important?").

Testing Children

Modifications in testing procedure are used in testing children five and six years old. Because this age group usually has not been well socialized into structured task performance and because social expectations are less clear, it is necessary to be more explicit in informing these subjects of what is desired from them during the Inquiry phase. Therefore, if sufficient scoring information is not forthcoming following the standard inquiry procedure, the examiner should ask directly for location and should repeat instructions such as "But, what about this inkblot makes it seem like a bat? Exactly where did you see the bat?" Very young children will often have difficulty justifying their responses by objective criteria and may have only a vague notion of where the response is located. Further pushing is, therefore, not fruitful and runs the risk of suggesting "correct answers."

Materials for Noting Rorschach Responses

The final test protocol will consist of three parts: the response sheets, the scoring sheet(s), and the summary sheet(s).

Response sheets

Use plain white $8\frac{1}{2}''$ by 11" paper turned sideways with three columns marked off on each sheet (Fig. 1). The first column should be about $\frac{3}{4}''$ wide to record the card numbers and the latency. Latency is the time that elapses between receiving the card and the first response to that card. Count with seconds in your head; do *not* use a watch. The notations need not be exact.

The second column should be about 4" wide to record the free-association. Record only three or four responses per sheet, leaving space between them. Number each response in succession. Be prepared with 10 or 12 sheets for each administration. For each response, note in which position the card was held when the response was given. Use "carets" with the point of the caret in the same position as the top of the card. For example, ∧ would indicate the card was held in the normal position, ∨ would indicate it was held upside down, and < and > would indicate it was rotated a quarter turn. All card turning should also be indicated. A circular arrow is usually used for this purpose, e.g., ↻.

The third column should also be about 4" wide to record the inquiry. Put each response *directly across* from the free-association response to which it corresponds, labeling it with the same number.

It is suggested that ink be used in recording the free-association and inquiry. The response sheets must be written so that others can read them.

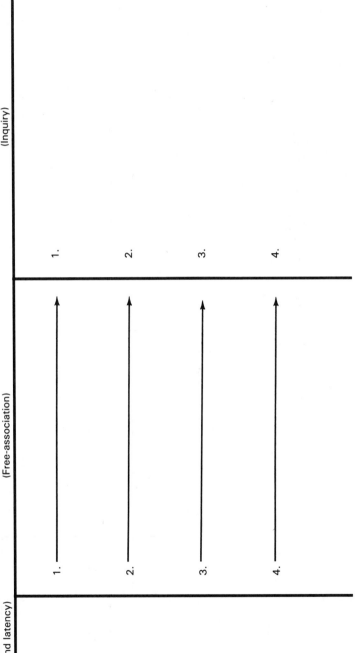

Subject's Name:

(Inquiry)

(Free-association)

(Card numbers and latency)

1.
2.
3.
4.

1.
2.
3.
4.

FIGURE 1. Response sheet

21

NAME: AGE: SEX: EXAMINER: DATE:

Card	Response	Latency	Position	Location	Cognitive complexity	Justifications	Imaginal aspects	Response appropriateness	Content	HA = Articulation of human percepts	MA = Motivational articulation	MV = Explicit motivational valuation	(MV) = Implicit motivational valuation	Inferred psychosexual drives	Defense effectiveness	Perceptual cognitive characteristics

FIGURE 2. Burstein-Loucks scoring sheet

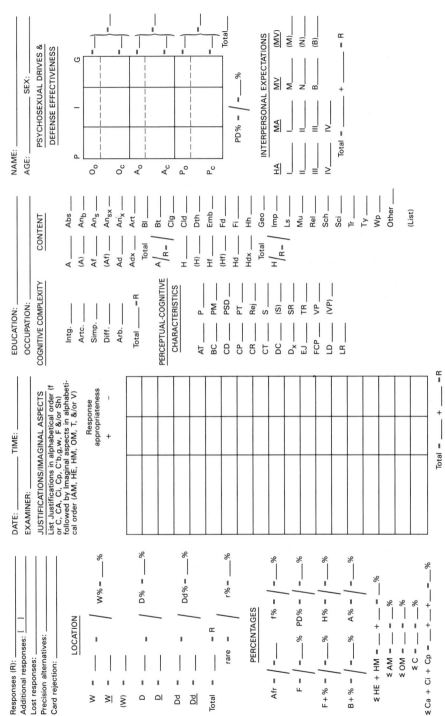

FIGURE 3. Burstein-Loucks summary sheet

23

The subject's name should be written on each sheet. It is helpful to train oneself to write legibly during the administration so that one need not use time recopying.

Scoring sheets and summary sheets

A sample of each of these forms is shown in Figs. 2 and 3. All scoring may be done in pencil. After the scores are completed on the scoring sheets, they are tallied and are then recorded on the summary sheet. Instructions for using the summary sheet are found on p. 72 ff.

PRÉCIS OF SCORING, CATEGORIES, SYMBOLS AND CRITERIA

Because of the complexity of Rorschach scoring, the précis below may be helpful:

The scoring system is divided into the following categories:

Location: Blot Area and Frequency (p. 29–30).
Cognitive Complexity: Perceptual Approach and Organization (p. 30 ff).
Justifications: Blot Attributes alluded to (p. 35 ff).
Imaginal Aspects: Imaginary Attributes (p. 41 ff).
Social Appropriateness: The degree to which the response is characteristically found in grossly disturbed individuals (p. 46 ff).
Conceptual Content: Type of Percept: animal, vegetable, mineral (p. 49–50).
Interpersonal Expectations: Complexity and Quality of Conscious Human-related Fantasies and Less Conscious General Expectations (p. 51 ff).
Psychosexual Drive and Defense Effectiveness: Psychoanalytically-derived (p. 56 ff).
Perceptual-Cognitive Characteristic: Thinking Style not scored elsewhere (p. 59 ff).

These nine areas form the Burstein-Loucks Scoring System. These are the areas important to the assessment of the psychological functioning of the subject. The various scores which fall under each of these headings are simply elaborations of these concepts. An overview of all categories and scores is provided on pages 25–26.

Scoring Overview

*Position	*Location	*Cognitive Complexity	*Justification	Imaginal Aspects	*Response Appropriateness	*Conceptual Content			Human Articulation (scored only for human responses)
	W	Intg	C	AM	+	A	Bl	(Hd)	HA1
	(W)	Arb	Ca	HE	−	(A)	Bt	H_f	HA2
	D	Artc	Ci	HM		Abs	Cld	(H_f)	HA3
	Dd	Simp	Cp	OM		Ad	Clg	Hh	HA4
	_(rare)	Diff	C'b	T		(Ad)	Dth	Imp	
			C'g	V		A_f	Emb	Ls	
			C'w			(A_f)	Fd	Mu	
			F			An_b	Fi	Rel	
			Sh			An_s	Geo	Sch	
			f			An_{sx}	H	Sci	
						An_x	(H)	Tr	
						Art	Hd	Ty	
								Wp	

25

Scoring Overview (*Continued*)

Motivational Articulation	Motivational Valuation Explicit	Motivational Valuation Implicit	Psychosexual Drive	Defense Effectiveness	Perceptual-Cognitive Characteristics
(scored only for HM and HE responses)	(scored only for HE and HM responses)	(scored for responses without HM or HE)	(scored only for those indicated)	(scored only for psychosexual responses)	(scored only when indicated)
MA1	M	[M]	Oo	P	AT	P
MA2	N	[N]	Oc	I	BC	PM
MA3	B	[B]	Ao	G	CD	PSD
MA4			Ac		CP	PT
			Po		CR	Rej
			Pc		CT	S
					DC	(S)
					D$_x$	SR
					EJ	TR
					FCP	VP
					LD	(VP)

* Always scored

26

PREFACE TO SCORING

The following section will present the criteria for all possible Rorschach scores, category by category and score by score within each category. Whenever possible, criteria have been listed. In some cases all criteria must be met for a response to receive a score; in other cases, only one or two criteria must be met. When all criteria must be met, the word "ALL" is placed above the criteria list.

In giving sample responses, a number of common abbreviations are used: l.l. or ll = looks like; b.f. or bf = butterfly; a.e. or ae = anything else; ? or Q = question asked; I or Inq. = inquiry.

Scoring Exceptions

Scoring exceptions consist of those cases where the subject gives a response, but it is not scored in the usual way. Exceptions are listed below.

1. *Precision Alternatives* are second responses to exactly the same area, utilizing exactly the same justification, imaginal aspects, content, psychosexual drive, and motivational valuation with no intervening responses and no card turning. These precision alternatives are designated PA under the Perceptual-Cognitive Characteristics column of the previous response and not scored otherwise.
2. Responses which are elicited for the first time in the inquiry are called *additional responses*. They are scored in brackets and not included in computing ratios and totals on the summary sheet.
3. Occasionally in the inquiry phase, a subject will be unable to remember having given a response or where it was seen. This *lost response* is not counted as a response but is scored LR in the Perceptual-Cognitive Characteristics Category column of the previous response.
4. One exception consists of a free association process in which responses are given by the subject but then later combined into a global, larger response. In this case, the larger, global response is scored rather than the separate scorings of each response element. Scoring Examples: "a tree," "a flower," "a waterfall," "a girl," "Oh, it's a forest scene with a native girl bathing." In this case the overall synthesized response is the one scored.

3
DETAILED SCORING RULES

LOCATION: W, (W), W̲, (W̲), D, D̲, Dd, D̲d̲

Two characteristics of the location of the percept are scored, the *portion* of the blot utilized and the *frequency* with which that portion is used in a "normal" population. Infrequently used areas are called "rare," denoted by underlining the location symbol.

Location Scoring Criteria	Scoring Symbol	Rare Scoring Criteria (r)
Entire blot is used.	W or W̲	W is underlined only when it occurs on Card III.
All of the blot (95%) is used, but some small, minor area is excluded, almost always as an afterthought.	(W) or (W̲)	(W) is underlined only on Card III.
A large, blot area is utilized, but not the whole blot.	D or D̲	Large areas are identified in the array that precedes the social appropriateness table for each card (p. 81); underlining indicates that the area is rarely chosen, as shown in the table preceding each array.
Only a small portion of the blot area is used.	Dd or D̲d̲	Small areas are identified in the array that precedes the response appropriateness tables for each card; underlining indicates the area is rarely used, as shown in the appropriate table preceding the array.

The specific portion of a blot used by a subject should be designated by a numerical subscript to the above symbols. The numerical subscripts to be used are those developed by Beck (1961) for denoting particular areas of each blot. They are indicated in the arrays that precede the social appropriateness tables for each card, to be found on page 82 ff.

A problem arises when the subject uses a rare area that includes one or more commonly selected areas. Our convention is to score this as rare if it is a single object and to regard it as common if the included common area(s) are seen as distinct object(s).

COGNITIVE COMPLEXITY: Intg, Arb, Artc, Simp, Diff

The ability to perceive and understand complex relationships is an important aspect of intellectual and general psychological functioning. The extent to which an individual invests in this kind of cognitive activity may be conceived as a stylistic variable, which is correlated with intellectual ability, as well as affective function. Thus, the cognitive complexity scores measure the organizational energy invested by the individual in formulating responses to the inkblots. These scores capture an individual's intellectual approach toward the world, i.e. the quantity and quality of an individual's attempts to synthesize and analyze in perceptual-cognitive interaction with the environment.

General Scoring Principles

Integrated is scored when the subject perceives parts of the inkblot as distinct units and then draws them into relationship with each other to form a larger, complex response, the elements of which could stand alone as separate percepts. *Articulated* is scored when the subject perceives a single unit and then analyzes it into parts. It is important but not always easy to discern during the free association and inquiry which of these two processes the subject has experienced. *Simple* is scored when the subject perceives a gestalt without analyzing it into parts. *Diffuse* is scored for simple responses which inherently have no distinctive shape, either because they are fluid or multi-shaped or because the response concept itself is so abstract that many different percepts and different shapes fit the response.

Category	Scoring Symbol	Scoring Criteria: ALL
Integrated	**Intg**	1. More than one unit is seen. 2. The units could be seen separately, i.e. are independent of each other. 3. There is a reasonable relationship posited among the units. 4. The units are interrelated but do not themselves compose a larger single unit with concrete boundaries.

Note: The criteria of a reasonable relationship (3) requires careful consideration and is related to the criteria for several of the Perceptual-Cognitive scorings, e.g. Contradiction of Reality (CR). The relationship between units may be unreasonable for many reasons; some of the most frequent reasons are that the relationship posited does not or could not exist in reality due to:

1. Violations of size and proportion—"a man squeezing through the eye of a needle"
2. Impossible feats—"a woman walking through a wall"
3. Extremely unlikely events—"a penguin with a bow tie going to a ball." Animals engaged in human-like activities are excepted from the unreasonable relationship category due to the frequency of these responses in normal records. However, the elaboration of this type of response may receive an unreasonable judgment, e.g. the bow tie on a penguin.

Scoring Examples

CD II, D6	"Two bears dancing in the circus—they're touching their paws together."	Intg
CD VIII, W	"Two panthers climbing a mountain in search of prey."	Intg
CD V, W	"A bat—here are its wings and here's it's body."	Not Intg (Artc)
CD VIII, W	"A bag of candies, different flavors." I— "It's a bag of candies—the shape (flavors?) the different colors reminded me."	Not Intg (Artc)

Category	Scoring Symbol	Scoring Criteria: ALL
Arbitrary "Spoiled Intg"	**Arb**	1. More than one unit was seen. 2. A relationship was posited among the units. 3. Either: a. the relationship posited is unreasonable or; b. One or more of the units themselves are not consensually validatable, socially appropriate percepts and, thus, are scored minus. c. The attempt to integrate was chaotic, fluctuating, or elusive.

Category	Scoring Symbol	Scoring Criteria: ALL (*Continued*)	

Scoring Examples

	CD III, W	"Two people catching a butterfly." I—"Here's the face, here's one arm, and here's the other arm—the butterfly is bleeding."	Arb (3&4)
	CD VIII, W	"Two dogs climbing on the back of a beautiful butterfly."	Arb (3)
	CD I, D2 + 7	"That ll a scary one. It's sort of like a scary movie with bat wings and a lady looking like she's going to die and hands coming out of the ground." I—"Just put it together—you see a dark ground with hands coming, bat wings up here, a grave down here, etc."	Arb (3&5)
	CD II, D6	"Two bears dancing a hula." *Due to the frequency of these responses, animals seen in human interaction are scored integrated rather than arbitrary unless the response violates the criteria for some other reason.	Not Arb
Articulated	**Artc**	1. One or more units are seen in which parts of the unit itself is identified and labeled; the elaboration of the unit must not consist merely of a description of its blot characteristics, e.g. shape or color. 2. There is no relationship posited among the units if more than one is seen. 3. The parts of the unit that are labeled are integral to the unit rather than separate from it, i.e. within the concrete boundaries of the overall unit. 4. Clothing worn on the bodies of humans is considered integral to the percept but articles of clothing carried are not.	

Scoring Examples

	CD I, W	"Kind of ll (looks like) a moth or a BF." I—"cuz it ll it has wings."	Artc
	CD VI, W	"LL an alligator." I—"cuz it has eyes like an alligator, and a long mouth, and teeth."	Artc
	CD II, Dd31	"Two little bones." I—"Cuz they're straight and they have these bumps* on them."	Not Artc (Simp)

*Bumps are not parts of bones, but are rather a description of shape.

	CD VII, W	"That ll a 'U'." I—"Cuz it goes up and then it goes down."	Not Artc (Simp)

Category	Scoring Symbol	Scoring Criteria: ALL (*Continued*)	
		Scoring Examples	
	CD II, D5	"A rocket ship." I—Because it has a point* on top and it goes around here.	Not Artc (Simp)
*Point is a shape characteristic.			
	CD II, D5	"A rocket ship." I—"Because this pointed area is the cockpit and these are the wings."	Artc
Simple	**Simp**	1. One or more units are seen which have structural unity and definite physical form. 2. If more than one unit is seen, there is no relationship posited among them. 3. The unit(s) seen is not further elaborated, i.e. broken down into parts.	
		Scoring Examples	
	CD III, D3	"That ll a red bow." I—"Cuz it's made like a bow."	Simp
	CD IV, Dd4	"That looks like arms." I—"Cuz of the way they hang down."	Simp
	CD X, W	"Flowers." I—"because of all the pretty colors."	Simp
	CD V, W	"That ll a bat." I—"Cuz it's black and it has wings."	Not Simp (Artc)
	CD VI, D8	"An Indian on a rock."	Not Simp (Intg)
Diffuse	**Diff**	1. One or more units are seen but are not seen in relationship to each other. 2. The unit(s) is not broken into parts. 3. The unit(s) has no distinctive shape, either because it is an amorphous matter or because it can take on many different configurations.	
		Scoring Examples	
	CD I, W	"Mud." I—"Cuz it's kind of splattered out and black."	Diff
	CD IX, D6	"Pretty, soft, pink clouds." I—"They look all pink and fluffy."	Diff
	CD II, W	"A little toy." I—"Toys can be anything, like a bat or doll, but they're not real, so you could make it ll anything 'cuz anything could be a toy'."	Diff

Category	Scoring Symbol	Scoring Criteria: ALL (*Continued*)

Scoring Examples

CD II, D1   "A monster*." I—"It's a monster all here."   *Not Diff* * (Simp)

*Monster usually connotes a scary or distorted human or animal form, not vague or amorphous enough to be scored diff unless "blob," "slime," or some other amorphous creature is specified.

CD IX, W   "A picture of a beautiful landscape*." I— "Here's a lake, here are the trees, here's the reflection in the water."   *Not Diff* * (Intg)

*Landscape implies a certain minimal shape even if the subject did not elaborate.

Other Examples of Diffuse Content

Fog, fire, smoke, explosion, colored rocks, dirt, art, party, anger, sky, blood.

Scoring Overview—Cognitive Complexity

Intg	Integrated	More than one unit, plus response overall, reasonable relationship posited.
Arb	Arbitrary	Spoiled attempt at an integrated response.
Artc	Articulated	One or more units, unit given identified parts not an integrated response—no relationship with other units.
Simp	Simple	One or more units, no parts identified, no relationships specified.
Diff	Diffuse	A simple response that has no distinctive shape.

Scoring Complexities

Occasionally, a response will be given which qualifies for more than one cognitive complexity scoring. By convention, double scorings are not given. The most frequent occurrence is when integrated responses are also articulated. The scoring for this type of response is Intg, integrated. When an otherwise diffuse percept is seen in a specific shape, e.g., a cloud in the shape of a necklace, the response is scored according to the criteria based on the shape. If necklace is not given in parts, the response is scored Simp. If a clasp and pendant are denoted, the response is scored Artc. Were the necklace of clouds seen in relationship to a woman-shaped cloud holding the necklace, then the response would be scored Intg.

Scoring Exercise: Cognitive Complexity

The following exercise takes you through the essential differences among the cognitive complexity scorings.

CD VII, W	Scoring
1. "A cloud."	Diff
2. "A cloud shaped like a bunny."	Simp
3. "A bunny-shaped cloud with long ears and a tail."	Artc
4. "Two bunny-shaped clouds with long ears and tails."	Artc
5. "Two bunny-shaped clouds being blown atop two other little clouds—they're being pushed together."	Intg
6. "Two bunny-shaped clouds hopping atop a cabbage."	Arb

CD IX, W	Scoring
1. "A weird medical drawing." I—"IDK—could be of anything—the way its colors are so bright and in different sections."	Diff
2. "A drawing of a cross section of a brain." I—"This middle part is light and this part is bumpy." (?) "That's all."	Simp
3. "A drawing of a cross section of a brain." I—"This light part is the ventricles and this is the outer cortex here."	Artc
4. "A drawing clipped on a clipboard." I—"Here's the light part that's the ventricle and this is the cortex." (clipboard?) "This pink thing (D9) is holding it down."	Arb

JUSTIFICATIONS: C, C', F, Sh, f

The way in which a subject justifies the reported percept is scored in terms of the stimulus features of the blot he or she refers to as providing the basis or rationale for the percept. The major justifications are color (C), blackness/whiteness (C'), form (F) and translucence/saturation (Sh). A failure to justify is noted by the symbol (f). When more than one justification is given, they are all scored as blends. There is no limit on the number of justifications which can be scored as a blend. The "blended" scores are arranged in the following alphabetical order and are separated by a dot, (e.g. C·F·Sh).

Category	Scoring Symbol	Scoring Criteria: ALL
Color	C	1. The percept is justified by reference to the chromatic quality of the blot area used. 2. The color referred to must be consistent with the color of the reported percept as it would occur in nature. 3. Note: If the subject justifies a response to an achromatic card saying, e.g., "Just the color," inquire by saying, "Color?" This will usually elicit a response of black, grey, or white which is scored C'.

Category	Scoring Symbol	Scoring Criteria: ALL (*Continued*)

Scoring Examples

	CD X, W	"A bouquet of flowers." I—"all the pretty colors."	C
	CD IX, W	"A sunset." I—"the orange, pink, blue."	C
	CD III, D3	"A red bow tie." I—"it's shaped like a bow tie and it's red."	C·F
	CD II, D3	"This red* part reminds me of a moth." I—"the way it's shaped" (AE?) No.	Not C*

*The color is used only to denote location.

Artificial color	**Ca**	1. The subject refers to the chromatic color of a blot area to justify a percept. 2. The colors are used merely to distinguish areas having specific form connotations, e.g. in maps, charts, or diagrams.

Scoring Examples

CD VIII, W	"a medical chart" I—"the different colored areas just remind me of the ones I've seen in textbooks."	Ca
CD IX, W	"a map of a continent." I—"these colored areas show the different countries. It must be Europe because this one looks like Spain."	Ca
CD VIII, W	"a dissection showing sections of the human." I—"The pink here is the lungs— pink because bloody, the blue here is the spleen, the green is the liver."	Ca

Inappropriate	**Ci**	1. In reporting or justifying a color, the subject refers to the chromatic quality of the blot area used. 2. The color referred to is inconsistent with the color that the percept would have in nature, e.g. "green sheep."

Scoring Examples

CD III, D2	"red lions" I—"they have big necks and manes, here's the mouth, eyes, and legs" (?) "Yes, they're red."	Ci·F
CD X, D9	"two pink men swimming in a lake" I— "here's the lake, here are the men—here are their legs" (?) "pink men"	Ci·F
CD X, D1	"blue crabs" I—"all the legs, the body."	Ci·F

Category	Scoring Symbol	Scoring Criteria: ALL (*Continued*)
Projected color	**Cp**	1. The subject uses color to *justify* a response to an achromatic area. 2. The subject must do more than think of the blot area as a colored percept but must actually attribute the color to the blot.

		Scoring Examples	
	CD II, W	"a hurricane with lightening going off." I— "it's all grayish green like a hurricane and there's lightening" (lightening?) "the red looks like it." (D2&3)	Cp·C
	CD I, W	"This is a blue bird."	Cp·F
	CD VI, D8	"a beautiful sunset." I—"Well, this looks like the sun, these are it's rays going out, it's going behind this mountain, sunsets are real pretty—orange and pink, at all." (see it as orange and pink?) "no, but it would be in real life."	Not Cp

Category	Scoring Symbol	Scoring Criteria: ALL (*Continued*)
Achromatic color	**C'**	1. The subject refers to the black, grey, or white quality of the blot area as a color which justifies the reported percept. 2. This score may be further differentiated by subscripts to indicate whether black, grey, or white is involved, e.g. C'_b for black, C'_g for grey, and C'_w for white. 3. Combinations may also be used such as C'_{gw}.

		Scoring Examples	
	CD II, D5 & 6	"that famous light at the end of the tunnel." I—"just the white next to the black tunnel."	$C'_{w,b}$
	CD II, D5	"a church with a steeple." I—"it has a long, pointed area at the top here, it's just shaped like one (Ae?) well, it's white like those wood frame churches in New England."	C'_w·F
	CD V, W	"It's a bat" I—"here are its wings, its antenna, it's black like a bat."	C'_b·F
	CD VI, D1	"it's a fur rug" I—"the gray and it looks like these were paws."	C'_g·F
	CD III, D1	"These are people doing something on the sides." "Maybe they're trying to pull something apart and are helping each other."	Not C'

Category	Scoring Symbol	Scoring Criteria: ALL (*Continued*)

Scoring Examples

I—"It's this whole black* part here." (people?) head, arms, torso, and legs. (ST?) I don't know what it is and it looks like they are succeeding (?) because there are 2 darker parts and a lighter part in the middle.

*Black is used only to denote area.

Form	**F**	The subject justifies the percept by verbalizing or pointing to the: 1. Spatial configuration; 2. Elongation or extension in space; 3. Contour or outline; 4. Or general shape of the blot area selected.

Scoring Examples

CD III, D3	"Looks like a butterfly in the middle." I— "It has a body and wings."	F
CD III, D2	"The red things on the sides are perhaps guitars. I just saw *Spinal Tap* and got that on my mind." I—"The neck, a bit bent." Turning screws and the body."	F
CD V, W	"It's a bat." I—"It just looks like a bat." "We cut one out in class today."	Not F

Shading	**Sh**	1. The light-dark dimension is used to justify the response. 2. The justification may reference gradations of lightness or darkness alone or 3. The justification may reference variations in lightness-darkness; this may involve variations in lightness along the black to white dimension in achromatic areas or variations in color saturation in chromatic areas in which cases a blend would be scored. 4. Transparency or opaqueness is usually based upon a light quality, i.e. the light shining through.

Scoring Examples

CD VI, W	"a fur rug." I—"It looks so soft and furry— (fur?) It's sort of wavy—light and dark (AE?)—the shape."	F·Sh
CD VII, W	"Smoke." I—"Because you can almost see through it."	Sh

Category	Scoring Symbol	Scoring Criteria: ALL (*Continued*)	

		Scoring Examples	
	CD X, Dd12	"It looks like a plant in the Springtime." I—"Because the green is so light and delicate."	C·Sh
Failure to Justify	f	1. The subject does not refer to any of the listed stimulus features of the blot to justify the reported percept.	
		2. This will most frequently occur when in response to the inquiry the subject says, "I don't know" or "It just looks like it" or simply paraphrases the original responses.	
		3. No other justifications are to be used with f.	
		4. Note: For example, for the inquiry response, "I don't know, it just looks like a fish, maybe the color," score C. However, f may be used with the imaginal aspects (Section C). For example, if the response, "A boy running" received in the inquiry, "I don't know, it just looked like it to me," the score would be f·HM.	

		Scoring Examples	
	CD I, D4	"a woman." I—"It's a woman standing up very straight." (Tell me more) "She's standing there."	f
	CD V, W	"a bat" I—"It just looks like a bat, that's all." "I drew one in school today."	f
	CD III, D1	"A boy bending over to pick something up." I—"I don't know. It just reminded me of it."	f
	CD I, D4	"A woman." I—"It's a woman standing very straight." (Tell me more) "She's got a tiny waist, her arms are uplifted, and her head's bent over."	Not f
	CD X, D4	"green worms" I—"They just look like green worms, that's all?" (AE?) "No."	Not f*

*Even though the subject does not explicitly present color or a justification, the use of color strongly implies color as an implicit justification.

Scoring Overview—Justifications

C	Color	Chromatic nature of the blot used as part of the free association or to explain the response.
Ca	Artificial Color	Color used merely to demarcate sections of response, as in maps.

Scoring Overview—Justifications (*Continued*)		
Ci	Inappropriate Color	Color attribute is contrary to nature.
Cp	Project Color	Incorrect color attributed to blot.
C$'_b$	Achromatic	Black, gray, or white are used as colors.
C$'_g$	Color (black,	
C$'_w$	gray, white)	
F	Form	Shape or spatial configuration used to explain response.
Sh	Shading	The light-dark dimension used to explain a response to an achromatic or chromatic area.
f	Failure to Justify	None of the above.

Scoring Complexities

1. Scoring blends of particular clinical significance are those which combine color and shading. These include any of the four color scorings combined with any of the achromatic or the shading scores.
2. Blends are scored in alphabetical order. Any justifications can be blended with the exception of failure to justify.
3. Imaginal Aspects scores are completely independent of justification scorings so that failure to justify may be combined with any of the Imaginal Aspect scorings.

Complex Examples

CD VIII, <u>W</u>	"Looks like a lion looking into his reflection in the water." I—"This is the lion and here's the water and there's his reflection. (lion?) well, it's got eyes, a mouth, ears, and the legs. (water?) well, it's blue and as it gets further away from the sun it starts to get a little grey. (sun?) yeah, here—it's the reflection of the sun. It's real bright."	C·C$'_g$·F·Sh
CD X, Dd2	"Two yellow objects—looks like an etching of a skull without the jawbone." I—"Two eyes, more, where the teeth would be there's a yellow background. The skull's a light orange."	C·Ci·F·Sh
CD II, D3 + 2	"flowers" I—"the red color" (AE?) "No."	C
CD II, W	"a schematic drawing of a cross-section of a flower." I—"The black is a 'pen and ink' of the petals, these red shapes represents the pistol, and stamen and stems."	Ca·C$'_b$·F
CD II, D2	"Two red sheep baaing at each other." I—"Yeah, here's the legs, the body, the faces. They're wooly looking. (wooly?) the way the fur is darker and lighter—like in rolls."	Ci·F·Sh

IMAGINAL ASPECTS: AM, HE, HM, OM, T, V

Many comments about the response are not efforts to justify the response but to communicate some aspect of the subject's inner experience as elicited by the blot. For example, subjects frequently give a response implying movement, not to suggest that movement is a physical characteristic of the blot, but to say they are reminded of something in motion. The major imaginal aspects are animal movement (AM), Human emotion (HE), human movement (HM), object movement (OM), tactile qualities (T), and perspective or depth (V).

When a reported percept is elaborated as having any of the following qualities, the appropriate symbol is recorded following the justifications column. Not all percepts will receive scores in the Imaginal Aspects column in this category. More than one Imaginal Aspect may be scored in a given response. Any of these imaginal aspects may be scored together in the same response. When more than one score is given, they are arranged in alphabetical order. Each symbol is separated by a dot.

Meaning	Symbol	Scoring Criteria
Animal Movement	**AM**	1. Animal percept is given.
		2. Animal is reported as engaging or having engaged in some postural stance, tension producing pose, or movement characteristic of its species.
		3. Responses of animals engaged in human-like action or affects are scored HM or HE, respectively.
		4. A response for which an animal is engaged in an activity uncharacteristic of its species is scored HM.

	Scoring Examples	
CD VIII, D1	"Ll 2 animals of some sort on the side, others, IDK, climbing," I— "Four legs, general, large animal shape, head."	AM
CD II, W	"Kind of looks to me a little bit like a cat's mouth, right in here." I— "Like these could be like ears and these are the eyes and this is the mouth and here's the nose. (eyes?) way they're oval (mouth?) a cat usually has his mouth open when he's playing (open?) Yeah, I've seen cats ll this when they're playing."	AM

Meaning	Symbol	Scoring Criteria (*Continued*)

Scoring Examples

CD II, D6   "Two bears dancing." I—"They're   *Not AM**
black bears—here's the head, paws
are touching the legs."

*Scored human movement because dancing is a characteristically human activity.

CD X, D1   "Two spiders just finished singing."   *Not AM**
I—"They have so many legs."

*Scored human movement because singing is a characteristically human activity.

Other AM: standing, looking, eating, drinking, running, leaping, climbing, sitting, snarling, trying to escape, flying, sleeping, resting, panting,* howling,* singing.

*These are species dependent. If inappropriate for the species, score HM.

Meaning	Symbol	Scoring Criteria
Human Emotion and Motivational States	**HE**	1. Human, humanoid, or animal percepts reported as experiencing characteristically human *emotional* states. 2. Human or animal percepts reported as experiencing characteristically human *motivational* states. 3. The presence of affective states in mammals is clearly discernible to some of us. However, by convention affect in animals will be scored human emotion.

Scoring Examples

CD I, W   "A happy jack-o-lantern." I—"He's   HE
happy because it's Halloween."
"Here are his eyes, his mouth, he's
round."

CD II, D6   "Two bears having a party" I—   HE·HM
"They look like they're dancing
and very happy."

CD IV, W   "A hungry man." I—"He looks like   HE·HM
he's tired and hungry—his head is
hanging down."

CD I, W   "A smiling face." I—"Here's the   Not HE
mouth, the nose, the eyes."

Scored human movement

Other HE: sad, happy, joy, tired, hungry, scared, angry, vicious, mean, kind, sweet, content, worried.

Meaning	Symbol	Scoring Criteria
Human Movement	**HM**	1. Human percepts reported as being or having been in: a. motion; b. postural tension; c. or interaction.

Meaning	Symbol	Scoring Criteria (*Continued*)
		2. Animal percepts reported as engaging in: a. movements; b. postural stances; c. or interactions which are characteristically human rather than characteristic of the animal reported. 3. Implicit fantasies of past human action.

Scoring Examples

CD I, W	"Two caped women on horseback galloping down a road at night." I—"Here are the women, their capes, the horses, the road" (night?) "It's dark."	HM
CD I, W	"A crying* face." I—"here are the eyes, the while ll tears, the nose is here, mouth here."	HM*

*Crying usually implies sadness but is basically an action. Crying can occur due to happiness or anger. If sadness were also mentioned, a double scoring (HE·HM) would occur.

CD III, D1	"A waiter bent over a table." "He's leaning over—here's his face, legs, arms."	HM
CD II, W	"A man with his tongue stuck out." I—"here his tongue, it's red, here's his mouth, eyes, cheeks."	HM
CD VI, W	"A dissected cat." I—"here's its head, it's paws, it looks flat, cut open like in a lab."	HM
CD VI, W	"A smashed* cat lying in the road." I—"Here are its paws, its tail, its head is missing."	HM*

*Less explicit than some, this is a fantasy of a cat hit by a car.

CD III, D1	"Two deformed* people." I—"The way they're shaped. They look strange—heads are here, backs are crooked, legs bowed."	Not HM*

*Deformed is used more as adjective descriptor than a verb.

Meaning	Symbol	Scoring Criteria
Object Movement	**OM**	1. An inanimate object or substance is reported as in or having been in: a. motion; b. a state of physical tension; c. precarious balance; 2. When objects or substances are, in and of themselves, movements.

Meaning	Symbol	Scoring Criteria (*Continued*)

Scoring Examples

	CD X, W	"Fireworks." I—"It's so bright and colorful—like the Fourth of July fireworks demonstration."	OM
	CD IX, W	"An erupting volcano." I—"The orange is the lava, this is smoke here, it's coming out here."	OM
	CD VI, D8	"An ancient totem pole." I—"It's tall, shaped like one." (ancient?) "It looks like it's about to topple over this cliff here."	OM
	CD IX, Dd5	"A river*." I—"Well, it's light blue and straight—just looks like it."	Not OM*

*Although rivers imply motion, the movement is not as central a feature of the percept as in explosion.

Texture or Tactile Fantasy	**T**	1. Percepts reported "as if" they have qualities which could be perceived through the sense of touch.
		2. Light/dark variations are sometimes alluded to in addition in describing the tactile characteristics and should be scored under justification.
		3. The tactile quality must be explicitly stated: soft, hard, hot, cold, sharp, jagged, rough, furry, fluffy, smooth.
		4. Tactile attributes are relatively rare; score conservatively.

Scoring Examples			J	IA
	CD IX, D6	"Fluffy pink clouds." I—"The variations in color, from light to dark, give it a fluffy look."	(C·Sh)	T
		Same response. I—"They just look soft."	(C)	T
		Same response. I—"The rounded edges make me think of fluffy clouds."	(C·F)	T
	CD IX, D6	"ice cream." I—"The round pink balls made me think of something frosty-cold ice cream."	(C·F)	T
	CD VIII, W	"sharp, jagged mountain terrain." I—"The straight edges, square shapes."	(F)	T

Meaning	Symbol	Scoring Criteria (*Continued*)		
		Scoring Examples (*Continued*)	J	IA
	CD VII, D4	"Reminds me of a saw" I—"here are the teeth along the edge here, the way they go in and out."	Not T	
Vista	V	1. The essential element of vista is the sense of distance between the subject and a focal point of the percept. 2. The distance between subject and percept may be experienced through: a. linear depth perspective; b. objects to which visual access is obscured to some degree by transparent or opaque substance. c. objects reported as covered up by being behind other objects. 3. Reflections are not scored V unless they are seen in the absence of the percept reflected, i.e. the reflection alone is seen or unless the reflection meets the above scoring criteria in some way. 4. A three dimensional object does not receive a V scoring unless it meets the above criteria; three dimensionality brings the percept close to the subject rather than farther away. 5. Shading or form are often accompanying justifications and are scored independently.		

Scoring Examples

CD IV, W	"A huge giant with his head in the clouds." I—"He has huge feet, legs, you can hardly see his head—it's like you're looking up at him."	V	
CD VI, D1	"an aerial photograph of a canyon" I—"There's the river down the center (river?) It's shaped like one—light with dark and narrow—like it's a canyon or valley with the river at the bottom."	V	
CD I, (W)	"a woman dressing behind an oriental screen" I—"You can't really see her upper body—here are her legs—here's the screen—you see the legs through the screen."	V	

	Scoring Examples	
CD IX, D8	"a huge bubble" I—"It's pale blue and shiny and its round in appearance—almost ll it could float up from the card here."	Not V

Scoring Overview—Imaginal Aspects

AM	Animal	An animal is seen experiencing behavior characteristic of animals.
HE	Human Emotion	A human or animal is seen experiencing human emotion or motivational state.
HM	Human Movement	A human or animal is seen engaged in a human activity.
OM	Object Movement	An inanimate object is seen as moving or in a precarious state.
T	Texture	Any of a number of tactile qualities are attributed to the percept.
V	Vista	Distance is perceived through a sense of perspective, transparency, or cover.

RESPONSE APPROPRIATENESS

Response appropriateness refers to the social appropriateness of the response given the conventions of the diagnostic situation. It is distinct from issues of originality, clarity, or congruence of contour as judged by the examiner, a point obscured by the labeling of this dimension as good or bad form in several earlier systems. Response appropriateness is defined in terms of the ability of the occurrence of a particular response to distinguish between psychotic and non-psychotic groups. Beck's tables are based on such a determination and have recently been amended in the light of comments made by a large number of Rorschach clinicians. Accordingly, response appropriateness is to be determined by the use of tables from the 1961 edition of *Rorschach's Test* by Samuel Beck. With permission of the publisher and authors, these tables, in modified form are reproduced on page 82 ff. The W location or whole blot area list is presented first followed by smaller areas in order of frequency of use. Beck presents schematic drawings of the blot area with attached D or Dd designation and number, E.g. D_1 or Dd_{21}. Unlike our system, frequency of use determines D or Dd score rather than size in Beck's system. Despite this difference, location number stays the same. Once the area has been located on the array and its number determined, the list of pluses and minuses can be entered and a determination made. The list can then be located. Be sure to check the general plus and minus categories which often precede the listing of individual responses and scores.

Scoring Problems

1. Response not listed for area:

  a. Look down the list for the closest percept conceptually similar to the one given and use that scoring.
  b. Look through the whole list to be sure there's no closer percept listed than the one you thought of.
  c. If there's really no close percept, you must judge whether the location is the problem, and you should look up a slightly different area, or . . .
  d. Whether you should go to a higher conceptual level, i.e. broader category and use that scoring for the location . . .
  e. If there is absolutely no response listed close to the one given for the area or approximate area, then score minus.

2. Precise area/location not listed:

  a. Find the closest approximation to the area given by:
     i. Choosing a slightly larger area that encompasses the area chosen and use that list, or
     ii. Use a slightly smaller area that encompasses most of the area chosen and use that list.
  b. The decision whether to reduce or enlarge the area for response appropriateness scoring purposes will depend upon the examiner's judgment as to which listed area comes closer to representing the subject's location.
  c. If the subject combines two listed areas the same principle holds.
  d. If there is absolutely no reasonable approximation to the area chosen by the subject and, therefore, no response list available, score minus.

Scoring Examples

CD I, D4 −
Dd31

"a penis"

1. D4-Dd31 is not listed so the obvious choice of area is D4 and its list.
2. D4 does not list "penis" but does list bone, vagina, and pelvis. Vagina is the closest percept in that it is sexual anatomy as is the penis.
3. Vagina is scored minus so penis is scored minus.

CD I, D2 +
D4

"a donkey kicking a sack of oats."

1. Look up donkey in its area (D2) listed minus.
2. Look up sack of oats in its area (D4). Sack of flour is listed as minus. Good enough!
3. The response is scored minus.

Scoring Examples (*Continued*)

| CD X, D9+D11 | "an evil face—the devil" | 1. The closest area listed to the one chosen is W.
2. There are few percepts listed in the position.
3. The closest percept listed is "oriental face" for the position, scored minus.
4. Therefore, "the devil's face" is scored minus. |

3. Plus (+) and Minus (−) Percepts.

a. If there is an attempt to integrate the response, each component percept must be a plus percept in order for the overall integrated percept to be scored plus. Otherwise score minus.

b. An exception is made when the minus percept is a minor aspect of the percept, either because of its size in relation to the other components of the percept or because of the nature of the response itself.

c. Plural response, e.g. "birds," to various blot areas in which there is no attempt to integrate should be scored + or − according to which type of percept predominates. If there are a greater number of plus responses and greater portion of the blot dedicated to plus responses, then score + and vice versa.

d. Plural responses in which there is an even ratio of plus to minus percepts and no attempt to integrate should be scored plus. The most common occurrences of these are listed in Beck's tables with +/− scores.

Scoring Examples

| CD X, W | "birds" (plural type R) | 1. Some locations for birds are plus and minus. On this "plural" response to Card X, the subject is given the benefit of the doubt. Beck lists +/−, score +. |
| CD X, D11 | "two tiny elves (Dd8) lifting an arrow." (D14) | 1. Be careful—if you look only in the list, you won't see "lifting an elf" listed. You must also read the general plus and minus listings at the head of the table.
2. While D11 is a D response overall in our system, Dd8 and Dd14 are each small areas. Elves are a plus scoring for Dd8 and arrow is a minus for Dd14. D11 lists a general plus category as two figures in human-like action involving a pole or tree. |

Scoring Examples (*Continued*)

		3. The overall response is scored minus because the minus component percept plays a significant role in the overall percept.
CD II, D1	"a cartoon-two bears (D1) ringing a bell" (Dd4)	1. Two bears are scored plus for the D1 areas. (Bear is plus for D1).
		2. Bell is scored minus for a small sized area, and Dd in our system.
		3. The overall percept is scored plus because bell is a relatively minor percept and, therefore, a minor aspect of the response.

CONCEPTUAL CONTENT

One characteristic of Rorschach behavior thought to reflect the quality and range of object cathexes is the range and type of content of the associations. The following list represents our conventions for scoring manifest conceptual content:

Meaning	Symbol	Scoring Criteria
Human	H	Percept is a whole human form.
Special Case of Human	(H)	Human is mythological, distorted, or a cartoon character, e.g., Darth Vader, ghost, giant, Mr. Magoo. Monster is always scored here unless animal characteristics are elaborated as in Godzilla, a dinosaur.
Human Detail	Hd	Percept is a part or parts of human other than face or head.
Special Case of Human Detail	(Hd)	Same as (H) but using some body part other than the face or head.
Human Face	H_f	Percept is face or head of human where some part of the face is perceptible. If face is mentioned as part of a whole human percept, score only H.
Special Case of Human Face	(H_f)	Same as (H) but using only the face or head. Mask is scored here if a mask of a human.
Animal	A	Percept is a whole animal form.
Special Case of Animal	(A)	Animal is mythological, distorted, or a cartoon character, e.g., dragon, Donald Duck. Monster may be scored here only if the subject elaborates animal characteristics.
Animal Detail	Ad	Percept is part or parts of an animal other than face or head.
Special Case of Animal Detail	(Ad)	Animal is mythological, distorted, or a cartoon character, e.g., dragon, Donald Duck.

Meaning	Symbol	Scoring Criteria (*Continued*)
Animal Face	A_f	Percept is a face or head of an animal where some part of the face is perceptible. If face is mentioned as part of a whole animal percept, score only A.
Special Case of Animal Face	(A_f)	Same as (A) but using only the face or head. Mask is scored here if a mask of an animal.
Abstraction	Abs	Content that is not associated with visual form, e.g. joy, fear, seasons.
Anatomy, Bony	An_b	Any part of skeletal structure.
Anatomy, Soft	An_s	All internal organs except bony structures and anything scored An_{sx}.
Anatomy, Sex	An_{sx}	Sex organs, e.g., breasts, vagina, uterus, penis, testicles.
Anatomy, X-ray	An_x	Percepts of X-rays of human or animal form.
Art	Art	Paintings, statues, etc.
Blood	Bl	Included all percepts of blood, either human or animal.
Botany	Bt	Plant life, e.g., trees, flowers, bushes.
Clothing	Clg	Articles of clothing or personal adornment.
Cloud, smoke, vapor	Cld	Percepts of a visible mass of particles of matter.
Death	Dth	Any mention of death, decay, or the process of dying in humans, animals, or plants, e.g., "a rotted tree trunk," "a dead moth."
Emblems	Emb	References to flags, insignias, coats of arms, etc.
Food	Fd	Food.
Fire	Fi	Actual fire and products of combustion, e.g., burning candles, flames from a torch.
Geography	Geo	References, not to maps, but to actual islands or continents.
Household	Hh	References to common domestic objects: lamps, furniture, kitchenware, etc.
Implements	Imp	References to tools.
Landscape	Ls	A view of natural scenery, e.g., fields, seascapes, harbors and mountains including singular geographical entities, e.g. volcano.
Music	Mu	Musical instruments.
Religion	Rel	Names of persons of religious significance and percepts involving religious associations, e.g., Jesus, Chalice, altar, church.
Schemata	Sch	Percepts that involve a sketch, plan, diagram, or map that are representations of the actual entity.
Scientific	Sci	All references to scientific tools, utensils, or instruments or scientific endeavors, e.g. microscope, telescope, test tubes, and forceps or references to science, e.g., chemistry, biology.
Toy	Ty	References to toys or sporting implements.
Travel	Tr	References to means of transportation: cars, ships, airplanes, etc., but *not* maps, which are *Sch*.
Weapons	Wp	All objects and means used for attack or defense in combat, e.g., guns, knives, bombs, guided missiles, battleships.

INTERPERSONAL EXPECTATIONS

One of the most potentially valuable resources of information from Rorschach performance is the quality of interpersonal relationships that can be inferred from the fantasies implicit in the patient's responses. Responses with manifest human content reflect relatively conscious expectations; less conscious expectations are sometimes discernable as well. What follows is a framework for evaluating such responses.

Human Articulation: HA1–HA4

[Scored only when any *human content* is scored, i.e. H, (H), Hf, (Hf), Hd, (Hd).]

Category	Symbol	Criteria
Level 1	**HA1**	1. Any human content is present: H, (H), Hf, (Hf), Hd, (Hd).
		2. Content is vague or very general.
		Scoring Examples: people, someone, they, somebody's
Level 2	**HA2**	1. Any human content is present.
		2. One clearly identified attribute is given. Attributes are: age, sex, a body part, mode of dress, etc.
		Scoring Examples: two youngsters, two women, a man—here's his mouth, a foot—here's the heel, a monster (scary person), a puppet, a doll, a giant, a midget, a doll's eyes, women's hand, robot, ghost.
Level 3	**HA3**	1. Any human content named.
		2. More than one attribute given, whether on one dimension or more than one.
		Scoring Examples: a face with ears and eyes—a little mouth, a doll with a dress on, big hands with long fingernails, a monster—very tall.
Level 4	**HA4**	1. Any human content named.
		2. Attribution of a specific identity or implies a full social role and function.
		Scoring Examples: a policeman, a bride, two circus clowns, two ballerinas, Napoleon Bonapart, Winston Churchill, my mother, Mrs. Johnson—my teacher, Frankenstein, a vampire's teeth, a vampire.

Motivational Articulation: MA1–MA4

[Scored only when HE or HM are scored.]

Category	Symbol	Criteria
Level 1	**MA1**	1. Vague, unspecified allusion to human activity.
		2. Postural movement or tension.
		Scoring Examples: two people bent over doing something, a man with his tongue stuck out, a woman standing.

Category	Symbol	Criteria (*Continued*)
Level 2	**MA2**	1. A clearly specified activity. 2. A human emotion or motivational state. *Scoring Examples:* a person running, two women looking at each other, a sad man, a vicious monster with ugly hands.
Level 3	**MA3**	1. Both HE and HM are combined into one, i.e. a clear activity which has motivational and/or affective components. 2. HE and HM or only HM may be scored. *Scoring Examples:* a crying face (HM), two people gossiping (HM), people fighting (HM), two penguins drinking tea (HM), an evil, smiling face (HE·HM), a haughty, laughing witch (HE·HM).
Level 4	**MA4**	1. Human or human-like interaction rooted in specific contexts of cause and/or outcome, i.e. more complex, story-like actions. *Scoring Examples:* two natives beating a drum to warn their village about the approach of a hostile tribe, a witch casting a spell at a sabbath with her underlings to control them, a man yelling because he was bitten by a dog.

Explicit Motivational Valuation: B, N, M.

Explicit Motivational Valuation is a measure of the quality of the more conscious and preconscious interpersonally-oriented fantasies. It is scored whenever HE or HM are present and based upon the motivation, affect, or action rather than on the nature of the actors.

Category	Symbol	Criteria
Explicitly Be- nevolent	**B**	1. The motive affect or action is positive, constructive. 2. In general, fantasies associated with life-promotion, construction of positive structures, shelter, pain avoiding or eliminating activities are positive; fantasies involving the exploitation or hope of reward, pleasurable contact or activation. *Scoring Examples:* a happy lady, two dancers doing a tango, waiters preparing some food, someone praying.
Explicitly Neutral	**N**	1. Not to be confused with the term neutralized, score neutral when the motive, affect, or action is neutral, mixed, or indeterminate. *Scoring Examples:* a man running, two men sleeping on their sides, two people talking across a fence, someone laughing and crying at the same time.

Category	Symbol	Criteria (*Continued*)
Explicitly Malevolent	**M**	1. The motive, affect, or action is negative or destructive.
		2. Fantasies of pain-producing activities, painful states or tension, destructive acts, death related activities, dangerous activities.

Scoring Examples: a witch casting a spell, two people yelling at each other, somebody shot in a duel, two angels destroying a city, a sad face, people gossiping, a hungry baby, somebody just died.

Implicit Motivational Valuation: (B), (N), (M)

Scored for all responses which contain no HE or HM, implicit motivational valuation captures the quality of the non-interpersonal environment.

Category	Symbol	Criteria
Implicitly Benevolent	**(B)**	1. The positive, constructive, life-promoting or gratifying, attractive percepts are scored (B).

Categories tending to be benevolent (B) are: Art, Bt, Fd, Mu, Rel.
Scoring Examples: fried shrimp, a beautiful butterfly, a baby, a rainbow, a heap of gold, candy, a flower, an angel, a church, water, bunnies, a guitar.

Implicitly Neutral	**(N)**	1. Neutral, mixed, or indeterminate percepts are scored (N).

Categories tending to be neutral (N) are: An_x, Cld, Emb, Hh, Imp, Ls, Sch, Sci, Tr.
Scoring Examples: a pole, a spaceship, a bird, a fish, somebody, a horse, mountain, rocks, a table, a dress, hands.

Implicitly Malevolent	**(M)**	1. Negative, destructive, dangerous, predatory, pain-promoting, depriving, ugly or distorted percepts are scored (M).
		2. (M) includes negative animal or object movement.

Categories tending to be malevolent (M) are: An_b, An_s, Bl, Dth, Wp.
Scoring Examples: a witch, a coyote, a volcano, a snake, a gun, worms, a monster, a rotten tree stump, a bat, a moth, a butterfly with holes in its wings, a funeral pyre, a bear, a jack-o-lantern, a ghost, a broken guitar, an apple with a worm in it, two coyotes chasing two foxes.

Judgments of implicit motivational valuation are unavoidably subjective. Friedlander (1984) has done a study to determine the degree to which consensus might exist with regard to such valuations of Rorschach content. Two hundred college and technical school students were selected to indicate like or dislike for 200 items derived from Beck's content categories. For example, highest like score (82%) was for "water," and the highest dislike score (73%) was for "cockroach." Friedlander also computed a difference score (Like-Dislike) for each item. To provide some guidance for judgments of implicit motivational valuation we include a table with these data.

Like Versus Dislike Scores for 200 Beck Content Categories

Case	Category	Diff	/	Case	Category	Diff	/	Case	Category	Diff
1	Water	81.		43	Eye	53.		85	Cave	38.
2	Apple	79.		44	Unicorn	52.		86	Statue	37.
3	Angel	78.		45	Lion	51.		87	Breast	37.
4	Flower	77.		46	Hot-dog	51.		88	Jack-o-lantern	36.
5	Ice-cream	77.		47	Jello	51.		89	Cow	36.
6	Steak	76.		48	Muscle	51.		90	Whale	36.
7	Mountain	76.		49	Owl	50.		91	Anatomy	35.
8	Lake	74.		50	Giraffe	50.		92	Rooster	33.
9	Island	73.		51	Plant	50.		93	Turtle	33.
10	Church	72.		52	Pumpkin	50.		94	Whisker	32.
11	Butter	72.		53	Puppet	50.		95	Wing	32.
12	Food	72.		54	Chick	50.		96	Ears	32.
13	Banana	70.		55	Leaf	50.		97	Buffalo	32.
14	Orange	69.		56	Carrot	49.		98	Goose	29.
15	Deer	69.		57	Bear	48.		99	Walrus	28.
16	Dove	69.		58	Fish	48.		100	Seed	28.
17	River	68.		59	Shell	47.		101	Neck	28.
18	Pond	67.		60	Canyon	47.		102	Lungs	27.
19	Clown	66.		61	Sheep	46.		103	Nose	26.
20	Swan	66.		62	Hill	45.		104	Tongue	25.
21	Dough	66.		63	Telescope	45.		105	Antler	25.
22	Heart	66.		64	Monkey	45.		106	Plume	25.
23	Animal	66.		65	Woodpecker	45.		107	Paw	24.
24	Forest	66.		66	Leg	45.		108	Cliff	24.
25	Feather	65.		67	Cocoanut	45.		109	Caterpillar	23.
26	Eagle	63.		68	Lobster	44.		110	Throat	22.
27	Seagull	63.		69	Meat	44.		111	Scarecrow	22.
28	Dog	62.		70	Teeth	44.		112	Mane	22.
29	Sea-coast	62.		71	Rocks	42.		113	Roots	19.
30	Kangaroo	61.		72	Glacier	42.		114	Ghost	18.
31	Tree	61.		73	Turkey	41.		115	Ram	18.
32	Tiger	61.		74	Evergreen	41.		116	Bull	16.
33	Ham	59.		75	Mouth	41.		117	Bone	16.
34	Bread	59.		76	Eggs	41.		118	Donkey	16.
35	Landscape	58.		77	Elf	40.		119	Goat	15.
36	Cat	56.		78	Harbor	40.		120	Flask	15.
37	Marshmallow	56.		79	Brain	39.		121	Gorilla	15.
38	Potato	56.		80	Camel	39.		122	Vagina	15.
39	Parrot	56.		81	Elephant	39.		123	Stomach	14.
40	Shrimp	55.		82	Mushroom	39.		124	Cricket	13.
41	Goldfish	54.		83	Elk	38.		125	Frog	12.
42	Peacock	54.		84	Arm	38.		126	Ox	11.

Case	Category	Diff	/	Case	Category	Diff	/	Case	Category	Diff
127	Tail	11.		152	Gun	0.		177	Possum	−20.
128	Wolf	11.		153	Seaweed	−1.		178	Spider	−23.
129	Knife	10.		154	Beetle	−1.		179	Snail	−23.
130	Volcano	10.		155	Bigfoot	−1.		180	Bomb	−23.
131	Horns	10.		156	Fire	−1.		181	Scorpion	−27.
132	Rhinoceros	9.		157	Crab	−3.		182	Teat	−30.
133	Kidney	7.		158	Monster	−3.		183	Gargoyle	−32.
134	Abdomen	7.		159	Spear	−4.		184	Intestine	−32.
135	Dinosaur	6.		160	Veins	−4.		185	Lizard	−35.
136	Weapon	6.		161	Skeleton	−4.		186	Pincer	−35.
137	Implement	5.		162	Crater	−5.		187	Snake	−35.
138	Hippopotamus	4.		163	Shark	−6.		188	Snout	−36.
139	Mask	3.		164	Christ	−7.		189	Eel	−36.
140	Pelvis	3.		165	Armadillo	−7.		190	Mosquito	−38.
141	Porcupine	3.		166	Crow	−7.		191	Sting	−39.
142	Badger	3.		167	Mummy	−7.		192	Termite	−39.
143	Beak	3.		168	Ant	−7.		193	Worm	−40.
144	Bee	3.		169	Bat	−11.		194	Devil	−42.
145	Nerve	2.		170	Witch	−11.		195	Tentacle	−44.
146	Goblin	2.		171	Skull	−12.		196	Rat	−48.
147	Pig	2.		172	Swamp	−12.		197	Carcass	−52.
148	Idol	2.		173	Penis	−12.		198	Anus	−52.
149	Tusks	2.		174	Animal	−13.		199	Tick	−58.
150	Hoof	2.		175	Octopus	−15.		200	Cockroach	−68.
151	Button	1.		176	Werewolf	−18.				

We also include a table summarizing Friedlander's findings with regard to both the consistency and the direction of the judgments.

Beck Content Categories
Grouped by Variations in Implicit Motivational Valuation and Intragroup Consistency

	Weak	Intermediate	Strong
Benevolent (B)	bone, cliff, flask, go-rilla, neck, roots, seed, wing, rhi-noceros, throat	tiger, owl, monkey, par-rot, pig, bear, hill, leaf, plant, rocks, canyon, tongue, arm, brain, mouth, vagina, puppet, statue, ghost, meat	banana, apple, hot dog, cocoa, orange, ice cream, jello, marshmal-low, steak, lake, water, mountain, pond, river, island, angel, unicorn, swan, flower, seagull, shrimp, cat, dog
Neutral (N)	beak, hoof, imple-ment, mask, nerve	armadillo, crab, porcu-pine, badge, fire, Christ, buttocks	
Malevolent (M)	ant, crow	mosquito, stinger, ter-mite, eel, lizard, bomb, penis	anus, carcass, tentacle

INFERRED PSYCHOSEXUAL DRIVE AND DEFENSE EFFECTIVENESS: Oo, Oc, Ao, Ac, Po, Pc, AND G, I, P

All behaviors can be regarded as motivated by basic psychosexual drives or their derivatives. Where the motivating drive for a response can reasonably be inferred, it is scored on the basis of the criteria below, as is the effectiveness of the defense deployed against the drive or in the modulation of it.

Inferred Drive

The type of drive discernable in a response is to be scored in two dimensions. The first relates the drive to oral, anal, or phallic origins. The second deals with the direct or indirect expression of the drive. Oral, anal, and phallic drives are scored "O", "A", and "P" respectively. Responses making direct biological reference are scored "o" for overt, while those making symbolic reference to the drive object are scored "c" for covert. Detailed rules for each scoring are given below.

When more than one drive is discerned in a response, score each drive separately and also score each drive for defense effectiveness.

Category	Symbol	Criteria
Oral, overt	**Oo**	References to food, food resources, or food objects, teeth, dentures, milk, breasts, baby bottles, sucking lips, nursery, womb, *emphasis* on lips, mouth, or beak, tongue; oral activities such as eating, biting, chewing, food, sucking, vomiting, kissing, tasting, spitting out food, salivating.
Oral, covert	**Oc**	References to mothers, babies, cooking, waiters, table setting, lipstick, fatness, skinny people or animals, nurturers, beggars, gifts, food providers or receivers, e.g., farmers, farms, cornfields, vampire, vulture, tapeworm, pig, hunger, stomach, esophagus, choking, arguing, yelling, spitting, touching or tactile gratification and having close nongenital physical contact.
		Scoring Examples
CD I, D4		"a woman standing at a <u>stove</u>. I—"hourglass figure in center (stove?) raising her hand, maybe she burned herself."	Oc
CD II, D2		"If you turn it, the right side that ll Christmas stockings or little socks." I—	Oc

Category	Symbol	Criteria (*Continued*)
		Scoring Examples
		"Shaped like them—Christmas presents and stuff—fluffed out—fattened up."
Anal, overt	**Ao**	References to anus, rectum, buttocks, feces, toilet, rear ends of creatures.
Anal, covert	**Ac**	References to bombs, explosions, flaming tail of rocket or spaceships, odors, gas or gas mask, pollution, dirt, smear, stain, splatter, spill, mess, erupting lava; references to neatness, time and schedules, money, controls, authority, external compulsion.

Scoring Examples

	CD III, D2	"These two remind me of blood spots." I—Just because I couldn't think of—somebody just stabbed somebody and wiped the knife right here—blood goes all over the place.	Ac
	CD VII, Dd11	"Right here ll a science drawing of a volcanic mountain—here's the big long hole where lava shoots out and drips down.	Ac

Category	Symbol	Criteria
Phallic, overt	**Po**	References to genitals: penis, vagina, labia, scrotum, menses, sperm, and other references to sexual intercourse.
Phallic, covert	**Pc**	1. References to pelvic girdle, sexual identity activities, references to competition, exhibitionism, gender-related attractiveness or ugliness, to dyadic rhythmic activities. *Emphasis* on elongated shapes or protruding anatomical members, dancing.
		2. Breasts are also scored here unless they are clearly in connection with oral activities.
		3. Note: There must be an emphasis on protrusion of an anatomical member, simply mentioning that something sticks out during inquiry is not sufficient.
		4. Guidelines for what constitutes an emphasis are as follows:
		a. the content is given during the free association.
		b. the content is separated or somewhat redundant.
		c. the content is the sole descriptor, central, or one of only two in the justification.

Category	Symbol	Criteria (*Continued*)
		d. the content is emphasized by use of adverbs or adjectives, e.g. this leg is <u>really</u> long or <u>really</u> sticking out.

	Scoring Examples		

	CD VI, W	"Two women <u>jumping up and down</u> on a pogo stick."	Pc
	CD IX, D3	"Two <u>ugly</u>, old <u>hags</u>—real witches."	Pc
	CD III, D1	"A <u>man</u> looking in the mirror, <u>shaving</u>."	Pc

	Double Scoring Examples		

	CD II, D3	"Also, that sort of reminds me of a bottom." I—"Edges and here's the <u>trash</u> (?) Cuz it's a bottom . . . only reason we use the bottom is to let the junk <u>food</u> out."	Oo Ao
	CD II, <u>D</u>	"If you look right here ll two hippos with their heads together—going like that. It's weird. I—"you know—how its <u>big mouth</u> is shaped. Really ll <u>dancing hippos</u>—<u>feet</u> are <u>stretched out</u> like ballerina hippos in a good mood.	Oo+c Pc
	CD IX, D8	"Bottom ll a church <u>steeple</u> that <u>extends way up</u> into haze—could be <u>pollution</u>." I—(steeple?) the form (haze?) probably pollutants—used to be red—lost the color and—the form is not rigid.	Pc Ac

Defense Effectiveness: P, I, G

The effectiveness of a defense in modulating and disguising libidinal and aggressive instincts or drives is measured by the presence of three critical variables: cultural or literary context, social appropriateness, shift or flexibility. Defense effectiveness is scored for each and every drive score.

1. *Cultural or Literary Context* The recognizable drive derivative is expressed in a context which makes it socially acceptable; a context is an abbreviated explanation by way of description of a situation which makes the drive derivation more socially sanctioned or appropriate.

Examples	No Context	Context
	"a mess—a bunch of running dirt"	"lava that has spilled out of a volcano"
	"an explosion"	"a rocket blasting off"
	"two men shooting each other"	"two men dueling"
	"a rectum—here's the feces"	"a medical illustration of a rectal exam—here's the rectum, feces"
	"two hippos dancing"	"a cartoon of two hippos dancing"
	"two breasts"	"an artist's sketch of a nude—the breasts, evident."
	"two people cooking"	"a mother fixing dinner"
	"a bottom"	"a baby's bottom"
	"a long pole sticking up into the clouds"	"a skyscraper—very tall—sticking up into the clouds"
	"a steeple surrounded by gas"	"a church steeple—tall—in a big city—surrounded it's by industrial pollution"
	"an open mouth with teeth"	"somebody at the dentist'—mouth open here—teeth here"

2. *Social Appropriateness* The response in which the drive derivative is given is socially appropriate, a *plus* response, indicating that the drive press is not so great nor the ego defenses so weak that the derivative has occurred in the context of poor reality testing.
3. *Shift*
   a. Flexibility is an index of drive modulation. Therefore, after a drive derivative has expressed itself, the next scorable response should:
      i. Shift to another psychosexual drive, or
      ii. Shift to no scorable drive (neutralized).
   b. Note: A shift from overt to covert or vice versa is not a sufficient shift.
   c. The next response is scored plus in the response appropriateness category.
   d. The last response in a record is scored as though a shift has occurred, i.e. the subject is given the benefit of the doubt.

Category	Scoring	Scoring Criteria
Poor	P	None of the criteria apply. Context, Social Appropriateness, Shift.
Intermediate	I	One or two criteria are met.
Good	G	All three criteria are met.

PERCEPTUAL-COGNITIVE CHARACTERISTICS

It is not enough to know that an individual evidences poor reality testing or social inappropriateness; a thorough assessment must include an understanding of the ways in which cognitive-perceptual functioning falters. Thus, in assessing psychological functioning, it is important to evaluate both elements of an individual's style of processing the incoming test stimuli and the success of the individual tested in responding in an appropriate and balanced way to the stimuli. Part of this evaluation may best include measures of perceptual-cognitive style which are non-pathological and adaptive and measures of various types of problems in thinking and perceiving stably, logically, and realistically.

Category	Symbol	Scoring Criteria
Affective Toning	**AT**	1. The subject invests more in the response, i.e., is more involved and more expressive through: a. vividness of language b. affective language and attributes posited c. degree and amount of elaboration 2. Percepts scored HE for Imaginal Aspects are usually scored AT.
		Scoring Examples: a monster, a blazing furnace, a beautiful sunset, a wretched wolf, a bullet coursing through the spinal column of someone who's just been shot, two cute little bunnies with cute little fluffy tails, a vampire, a two-headed, fire-breathing dragon. *Not* AT: two bunnies looking at each other, a lady with her arms in the air, two waiters, a bat with big wings.
Bizarre Content	**BC**	1. Responses in which the percepts reported have a bizarre quality, or in which the associational process has a quality of eerie symbolic elaboration. 2. Bizarre responses can be highly socially inappropriate, if not disgusting.

Scoring Examples		
CD IX, W	"A bullet coursing through someone's spinal column" I—"Here (D5) you can see the path of the bullet' this is the blood leaking out of the spinal column (D6), this is the cerebrospinal fluid (D8)—the rest are internal organs.	BC
CD IX, W	"Some kind of malignant condition." I—"The pink is like inflammation and it has a gangrenous green quality."	BC
CD X, Dd2	"Urine stain."	BC
CD X, W	"Blue blood, green blood, yellow blood—a mixture of bloods."	BC
CD X, D10	"two green worms—ll they're coming out of the eyes of a rabbit" I—	BC

Category	Symbol	Scoring Criteria (*Continued*)

Scoring Examples

		(worm?) "Large and comes down to a point (rabbit?) ears and mouth—two prominent teeth. Poor Bugs Bunny imitation."

Card Description	**CD**	1. The essence of CD is that it is a means by which the subject *distances* him or herself from the inkblot and the task at hand.
		2. CD's are usually delaying tactics, often presented before a real percept is offered to the examiner.
		3. CD's are usually given matter-of-factly, dispassionately or with only mild emotional tone.
		4. CD's must be distinguished from "loss of distance" from the blot. See LD, this section.
		5. Scored CD when the subject:
		   a. Gives an *evaluative* comment as to the aesthetics, level of difficulty of the card, or any other evaluative statement.
		   b. Comments on the *design* of the card or geometric shapes, or colors.
		   c. Comments on the *symmetry* of the card.
		Scoring Examples: "This is a hard one," "Oh, the colors are so pretty," "There's a line down the middle here and here are some triangles," It's the same here and here—here's a crab and here's one," "Here's some pink, and some green, and some orange."
		Not CD: "Oh my gosh—take it away—it's so ugly!"

Concrete Perservation	**CP**	1. Score on the third occurrence of exactly the same response. 2. Do not count populars. 3. Score only one CP for the same percept in any one record. 4. Indicate the percept at the side of the CP designation.

Scoring Examples		
CD I, W	"A dog."	
CD II, W	"A dog."	
CD IV, W	"A dog."	CP-dog
CD VI, W	"A dog."	*Not* scored again for CP

Category	Symbol	Scoring Criteria (*Continued*)
Contradiction of Reality	CR	1. *Combines odd parts*—Parts from different percepts are combined to create a *new organism* which does not exist in cultural reality. Essential criterion is that percepts are of unknown or impossible in reality and responses violate physical and/or logical reality in one of the following ways:

Scoring Examples

CD VIII, D8	"A rock-tree creature—this is its spine (Dd 21).	CR
CD V, W	"A rabbit with bat's wings."	CR

2. *Adds or distorts parts.* Creates a realistic percept with extra or distorted parts with parts organized in an unrealistic way, e.g. "A woman with three legs," or "a face with the nose where the mouth should be."

Scoring Examples

CD IV, W	"A man with three legs."	CR
CD II, W	"A face with a nose with one nostril."	CR
CD I, W	"A monster with two heads." Note: A monster may, by definition, have additional or distorted parts.	Not CR

CR   3. *Violates logical spatial organization.* Parts of percept are organized in such a way as would not occur in nature; this may occur with or without the subject's acknowledgment.

Scoring Examples

CD I, W	"A face with the nose where the mouth should be."	CR
CD IX, D9 + 3 + 8	"A tree in the Fall." I—"Here's the tree's base (D9) and the leaves (D3 + 8) and here's it's shadow (D11) on the ground.	CR

4. *Violates size/proportion found in nature.* Subject associates percepts or posits relationships between them which do not or cannot occur due to size.

Category	Symbol	Scoring Criteria (*Continued*)

<table>
<tr><td colspan="3" align="center">Scoring Examples</td></tr>
<tr><td></td><td>CD II, D6 + 3</td><td>"Two dogs climbing onto a BF."   CR</td></tr>
<tr><td></td><td>CD X, D10</td><td>"A rabbit with worms coming out his eyes."   CR</td></tr>
</table>

5. *Mixes percepts inappropriately.* Combines or associates responses which do not or cannot occur in nature.

<table>
<tr><td colspan="3" align="center">Scoring Examples</td></tr>
<tr><td></td><td>CD IX, D12</td><td>"Two Indian chiefs on motorcycle chasing two women."   CR</td></tr>
</table>

6. *Internal Conceptual Contradiction.* The response itself contains logical impossibilities in terms of motivation, action, or general concept.

<table>
<tr><td colspan="3" align="center">Scoring Examples</td></tr>
<tr><td></td><td>CD IV, W</td><td>"A man leaning against a tree, asleep—he's arguing with his wife."   CR</td></tr>
<tr><td></td><td>CD V, <u>D4</u></td><td>"A mangy bear—he has a beautiful coat."   CR</td></tr>
</table>

7. *Inappropriate Color* (Ci). The color given the percept does not occur in nature or known or expectable cultural contexts.

<table>
<tr><td colspan="3" align="center">Scoring Examples</td></tr>
<tr><td></td><td>CD X, D4</td><td>"Green sheep."   CR</td></tr>
<tr><td></td><td>CD II, D2</td><td>"Red seahorses."   CR</td></tr>
</table>

Category	Symbol	Scoring Criteria
Cluster Thinking	**CT**	Responses in which ideas, concepts or themes are so interpenetrated or indiscriminately combined that there are not recognizable causal or logical connections.

<table>
<tr><td colspan="3" align="center">Scoring Examples</td></tr>
<tr><td></td><td>CD X, W</td><td>"Could be a pretty garden. Blue like my sister's coat. She's a nice woman and her husband flows pleasantly into a column of green meadow."   CT</td></tr>
</table>

Category	Symbol	Scoring Criteria
Deterioration Color	**DC**	1. The subject uses color to justify content having to do with death, illness, weakness, decay, etc. 2. The colors most often used in this way are yellows, oranges, and browns.

Category	Symbol	Scoring Criteria (*Continued*)

		Scoring Examples
CD IX, <u>Dd7</u>		"Withered grass" I—"it's brown and old."	DC
CD X, Dd7		"A torn leaf" I—"Shape, autumn leaf, fallen." (Autumn?) It's orange."	DC

Cut-off Detail	**Dx**	1. The subject sees only *part* of a percept when the whole, larger percept would normally have been seen. 2. If the larger percept *has* been or is seen, do not score. 3. Note: To learn what is normally seen, note populars and most common areas and their percept lists in Beck's Tables.

		Scoring Examples
CD I, D2		"A bat's wing" (Bat is usually seen W)	Dx
CD II, <u>Dd4</u>		"a pair of hands, praying" (W is often seen as two people touching hands.)	Dx
CD III, D5		"Somebody's leg." (D1 is usually 2 people).	Dx
CD IV, <u>D2</u>		"A gorilla's foot" (The whole gorilla is usually seen.)	Dx

Egocentric Justi-fication	**EJ**	1. Verbalizations suggesting that the subject views his or her personal experience as adequate to fully define the reality of others (see Sullivan's parataxic thought). For example, "That's a bat . . . because I went to a Halloween party last week." It includes overemphasis of personal perspective or idiosyncracies. For example, (II, D_1) "That's my dog," (II, D3) "Menstruation . . . I revolt against being a woman and not a man," (II, W) "The mouth of something . . . I am inside looking out," "A face . . . I keep seeing faces everywhere." 2. Distinguish from SR where the reference to personal experience supplements the justification.

		Scoring Examples
CD V, W		"A bat" I—"I just thought of it because I went to a Halloween party recently."	EJ

Category	Symbol	Scoring Criteria (*Continued*)

		Scoring Examples
	CD IX, D6	"Cotton candy" I—"I don't know—I guess I'm just hungry." EJ
	CD IX, D6	"Cotton candy" I—"I guess I'm just so hungry and it looked so pink and fluffy." *Not* EJ
Fixed Concept Perseveration	**FCP**	1. Score FCP for the third occurrence, and on only the third, of a theme; the theme is written next to the FCP.
		2. Do not count populars.
		3. The same theme cannot be scored more than once per record.
		4. A theme is a concept or specific category represented by the percepts given.
		5. Do not score Humans or Animals in general as FCP; <u>predatory</u> animals or infants would be so scored.
		6. Note: it is usually best to score FCPs by going through the responses with solely this purpose in mind.

		Scoring Examples
	spaceship	Pile of sand church
	Martian	Dirt praying hands
	laser gun	Compost heap angel
	FCP-space or sci	FCP-dirt FCP-religion
Loss of Distance	**LD**	The subject becomes overly involved in the percept, overemphasizing personal perspective, personal idiosyncracies, or over-personalizing.

		Scoring Examples
	CD II, D1	"That's <u>my</u> dog." LD
	CD II, W	"The mouth of something—I am inside looking out." LD
	CD X, W	"Oh, my gosh! Insects coming at me." LD
	CD IV, W	"A giant—looking down at me—leering." LD
Lost Response	**LR**	1. A response in the free-association is forgotten or can not be found by the subject in the inquiry.

Category	Symbol	Scoring Criteria (*Continued*)
		2. Score in Perceptual-Cognitive Characteristic column of previous response.
Popular	**P**	1. Percept is reported on the average, in at least one-third of protocols from non-schizophrenic subjects. 2. The list of Populars are those reported by Beck (1961) and are listed by card, area, and response on p. 72.
Pantomime	**PM**	1. Action or gestures substitute for words, usually for adjectives.

Scoring Examples

You know it's shaped—you know—like this (subject circles with arms to illustrate roundness).

"It's a bat and he's got two of those things like this on top of his head" (subject perches 2 fingers atop front of head and wiggles in antenna fashion).

Category	Symbol	Scoring Criteria (*Continued*)
Perceptual Stabilization Defect	**PSD**	The cognitive-perceptual phenomenon scored is one in which the subject has difficulty stabilizing his or her perceptual experience of the blot. The more common manifestations are:
		1. *Figure-Ground Fusion.* Under normal circumstances, the white blot areas recede into the background or "ground" and the dark and/or colored areas project into the foreground, becoming the areas of interest, the "figure." If these areas are reversed, it is scored S or figure-ground reversal. PSD is scored when neither of these processes occur. Rather, the ground is also used to project forward with the figure or the ground is used to both project forward and recede, fusing the two.

Scoring Examples

CD II, W	"A man's face" I—Here are the eyes (Dd30), the nose, (D5) the cheeks (D6). (D5 should recede as does Dd30, rather than project as a nose would do).	PSD

Category	Symbol	Scoring Criteria (*Continued*)

Scoring Examples

	CD II, D5+D3	"a rocket blasting off" I—"here's the rocket (D5) and here's the exhaust (D3)."	*Not PSD*
	CD II, W	"A man's face" I—Here are the eyes (Dd30), the nose (D4) and the mouth—it's open (D5). (Mouth (D5) recedes).	*Not PSD*

2. *Perceptual Fluidity.* Reports the percept changing, as if the blot elements were actually changing shape, spatial configuration, or meaning.

Scoring Examples

	CD IV, W	"An Indian with a hide over him . . . now he's beginning to transform . . . as his hide droops down, it becomes two enormous feet."	PSD
	CD VIII, W	"Rats climbing a tree . . . now the whole thing has turned into a flower." (Q) "The whole center was the tree, but is quick-like turned into a flower."	PSD

3. *Condensation.* Sometimes known as contamination, a response is given which is a fusion or condensation of two different percepts seen in the same blot area. The fusion demonstrates an inability to keep the logically separate percepts apart.

Scoring Examples

	CD IX, D9	"Liver of a respectable statesman" (D9 = liver and D9 = Winston Churchill).	PSD
	CD I, D24	"A Southern Belle" I—"This is a bell and a clapper—it also looks like a woman."	PSD
	CD III, D2	"This bloody splotch here . . . bloody island where they had so many revolutions."	PSD

Predicate Thinking	**PT**	1. Autistic reasoning or idiosyncratic induction in which the subject relies *exclusively* on a *non-criterial* attribute(s) in justifying a percept (non-cri-

Category	Symbol	Scoring Criteria (*Continued*)
		terial means peripheral, incidental, or irrelevant characteristics of the blot).
		2. Types of predicate thinking are:
		a. *Confabulations.* The subject leaps from perceiving a part or parts to a large percept, based only on the perception of the part or parts.

Scoring Examples

CD VI, W	"A cat" I—"Because of the whiskers here (D26)."	PT
CD IX, D3	"a magician" I—"because this ll a wand" (Dd7) (person?) I don't know.	PT
CD X, D1	"a crab" I—"Because of its multiple legs."	PT

b. *Non-criterial color.* The subject bases the justification on color which is not a central or unique characteristic of the percept and not on any additional criterial attribute.

Scoring Examples

CD X, D4	"A worm" I—"Because it's green." (AE?) "No."	PT
CD II, D2+3	"Blood" I—"because it's red."	Not PT

c. *Position Responses.* The subject bases the justification on the relative location of the percept.

Scoring Examples

CD VII, Dd24	"The North Pole" I—"because it's at the top."	PT
CD VIII, D6	"A man's kidneys" I—"Because that's where a man's kidneys are—they're red."	PT

d. *Participation Thinking.* The subject inappropriately generalizes from one percept to another based upon a non-criterial attribute held in common between the percepts.

Scoring Examples

CD X, Dd6	"A crab." I—"Because it's just like this crab (D1) (Just like?) "Well, they're both blue." (AE?) "No."	PT

Category	Symbol	Scoring Criteria (*Continued*)
		Scoring Examples

	CD X, D1&D8	"Crabs" I—"Because of the legs and *Not PT* the shape (Legs?) "Well, these (D1) have several legs like crabs and so do these." (D8).
Card Rejection	**Rej**	1. The subject does not respond to the card. 2. Score next to card number.
Figure-Ground Reversal	**S**	1. White space becomes the area of interest, the figure, and the darker or colored area become the background or are ignored.

| | | **Scoring Examples** |

| | CD I,
D26
CD II, D5
CD IX,
D8 | "Ghosts"

"A rocket ship taking off"
"a violin" |
| Incorporated on
White Space | **(S)** | 1. Score when the subject uses a white space on the card as part of a response to a printed blot area, making the white space an integral part of the percept."
2. Score when the white space is used specifically as a background for a blot-area figure. |

| | | **Scoring Examples** |

| | CD I,
D4 + D26 | "An actress waving to her audience"   (S)
I—"Here are her arms held high, her
costume, these are the spotlights
shining behind her (Dd26)." |
| Self-Reference | **SR** | 1. The subject justifies the response in some way and . . .
2. Self-discloses as an associated elaboration to the initial percept or some part of the inquiry. |

| | | **Scoring Examples** |

| | CD VI, W | "A cat skin—that's like the one my   SR
dad brought back from Colorado."
I—"It's got paws here, and here are the
whiskers." |

Category	Symbol	Scoring Criteria (*Continued*)

Scoring Example

	CD II, W	"My mouth" I—"Here are my teeth, *not* SR my tonsils are here, my tongue." "My tongue is red like this."
Transposition Response	**TR**	The subject partially avoids seeing a response in its proper location by displacing it to another one through one of the following: 1. *Transposition.* Transposes from an area of the blot where the percept is usually seen to another area of the blot etc.

Scoring Example

	CD VII, D3	"a rabbit" TR 2. *Shifting.* Shifts to a smaller area of the blot a percept that is usually seen in a larger area of the blot.

Scoring Example

	(I, top half)	"A bat" (instead of whole blot as bat.) TR 3. *Inversion.* Inverts the blot area to see a response usually seen in that location in the inverse position. Scored TR only if a plus response is now minus.

Scoring Example

	CD II, D7	"Poodle." TR
Extreme Verbal Peculiarity	**VP**	In verbalizing a response, the subject's use of language noticeably violates common norms of syntax or semantics. These deviations of word-choice or language usage serve to reduce the accuracy of verbal interpersonal communication. The more serious forms to be scored here include: 1. *Neologisms.* New words or phrases are coined with idiosyncratic meanings. Careful investigation is sometimes warranted when testing individuals of highly technical educational and vocational backgrounds.

Category	Symbol	Scoring Criteria (*Continued*)

Scoring Example

"That is a study of the growth of   VP
plants, a sort of hydraulic <u>hydro-
cyanic</u> method."
"A wi<u>tch</u> holding a sabbath." I—"She's   VP
conjuring up a <u>grebolication</u> to de-
stroy her enemies."

2. *Homonymic or clang association.* One word re-
calls another word because of their similarity in
sound rather than meanings (including words
spelled and pronounced alike, but having different meanings).

Scoring Example

"A bell <u>jar</u> . . . that should <u>jar</u> them out of their scientific complacency; it <u>sort</u> of half <u>fits</u> everything
. . . it isn't sort of <u>fish, flesh</u>,—what <u>is</u> that game?
. . . Not animal, vegetable, or mineral."

3. *Metonymic distortions.* Distortions in the denotative use of language in which the word or phrase
used by the subject is an imprecise approximation (metonym) of a more common denotative
term.

Scoring Examples

CD X, D1	"A crab that has captured his first <u>menu</u> of the day."	VP
CD II, D6	"A dark cloud that is <u>intervening</u> the sunlight."	VP
CD III, D1	"Two native men . . . men because of the <u>male sense</u> here."	VP

Mild Verbal Peculiarity	**(VP)**	1. The subject uses a word, phrase, or more in a slightly idiosyncratic manner which deviates mildly from everyday verbal convention. 2. There is no clear violation of common semantic or syntactic form. 3. This type of language might pass as appropriate outside the test situation, but close scrutiny will reveal idiosyncratic use of words subjectively rather than socially determined.

Table of Beck's Populars

Cd I	Cd VI
W: Bat, Butterfly, Moth	W/D1: animal hide, skin or rug
D3/4: Human	Cd VII
Cd II	D1: human heads or faces
W: Two humans	D2: whole person
D1: dog or bear	Cd VIII
D3: butterfly, moth	D1: Animal (not cats or dogs)
Cd III	Dd3: rib portion of skeleton
D1: two humans	D4: tree or bush
D3: bowtie, ribbon, butterfly	Cd IX
Cd IV	D3: human
W: animal skin or coat; massive animal	D4: head or face
D2: human foot, shoe	Cd X
D6: boot, human leg	D1: crab, lobster or spider
Cd V	Dd2: dog
W: bat, butterfly, moth	Dd5: rabbit head
Dd1: human or animal leg	

USING THE BURSTEIN-LOUCKS SUMMARY SHEET

After the scores have been transferred from the last column of the response sheets to the scoring sheet, the scores are tallied and recorded on the summary sheet.

Responses (R)

R is figured by counting all the responses in the free-association. Each response should have been thoroughly inquired into, but without biasing the inquiry (see pages 18 ff). It is important to establish R carefully in the scoring phase because R is used to arrive at most of the percentages.

Do not count into R "additional responses," "precision alternatives," or "lost responses" (see page 27), but note the number of each, if any, on the summary sheet (see sample). Lost responses (LR) are also scored in the Perceptual-Cognitive Characteristics category (see page 66). In addition, if there are any "card rejections," note which card or cards were rejected in the appropriate space. A card is considered rejected if no percept is reported during the free-association.

Location

Count separately the number of W through Dd on the scoring sheet and place each sum by the corresponding symbol on the summary sheet. When all location scores are added together, they will equal R (see example).

Responses (R): _____ 31 _____

Additional Responses: _____ 1 _____

Lost Responses: _____ 0 _____

Precision alternatives: _____ 2 _____

Card Rejections: _____ 0 _____

W%, D%, and Dd% are figured by adding together the appropriate scores shown on the summary sheet and dividing each sum by R.

LOCATION

W	=	9			
W	=	1	= 11/31	W%	= 36%
(W)	=	1			
(W)	=	___	= 11/31		
D	=	14	= 14/31	D%	= 45%
D	=	___			
Dd	=	5			
Dd	=	1	= 6/31	Dd%	= 19%
Total	=	31	= R		
		Rare	= 2/31	r%	= 6%

The r% is figured by adding together the number of W (W), D, and Dd and dividing by R.

Cognitive Complexity

Since each response receives only one designation for cognitive complexity, the total will equal R.

Justifications/Imaginal Aspects

To facilitate consistency, each component of an J/IA should be alphabetized within itself according to the following convention.

Justification(s) first
f or C Ca Ci Cp C′ F Sh

Followed by Imaginal Aspect(s), if used
AM HE HM OM T V

Each J/IA should then be listed alphabetically on the summary sheet according to the above convention (see sample).

A mark for each score is placed in either the + or − column depending on the response appropriateness (see page 82 ff).

Identical scores are listed only once and given the appropriate number of marks. One might wish to arrange the scores of a lengthy protocol on a piece of scratch paper before transferring to the summary sheet. Since each response should have one mark, the marks in the plus column, when added with the marks in the minus column, will equal R. It is especially important to be sure the scores are tallied correctly because they are used to figure several percentages.

When using the subscripts for black, white, and gray with C', alphabetize them as well, e.g.:

$$C'b \quad C'bg \quad C'g \quad C'gw$$

List Justifications in alphabetical order (f or C, Ca, Ci, Cp, $C'_{b,g}$, w, F &/or Sh) followed by Imaginal Aspects in alphabetical order (AM, HE, HM, OM, T, &/or V).

	Response Appropriateness	
	+	−
f	1	
C	1	1
C·F	2	
C·F·Sh·T		1
C·F·AM		1
C·HE	1	
Ca	1	
C'b·F	1	
C'bw·F	1	
C'w·F·V	1	
F	8	4
F·Sh	1	
F·AM	1	
F·HM	3	1
Sh·HE·HM	1	
Total =	23 +	8 = R

Using the Normative Values Tables

Most of the normative tables are fairly straightforward.

The tables for the Imaginal Aspects and Justifications may require some explanation before use, however, it has been previously mentioned that originally Imaginal Aspects were alphabetized before Justifications. The organization is the same for both adults and children. To simplify coding the 1216 adult responses and 4,121 child responses, the response appropriateness was disregarded. In other words, AM·C·F + and AM·C·F − for example, were considered identical.

The first table, "Common Imaginal Aspects/Justifications", lists the mean number of responses for scores that were either frequently given, such as HM, F, or are commonly attended to by clinicians, such as pure C. The following two tables, "Imaginal Aspects" and "Justifications", gives the mean number of times subjects used one of the imaginal aspects or justifications alone or in a blend. For example, "All C" includes HM·C, C·F, C·Sh·T, etc., *and* pure C. It does not include the use of Ca, Ci, or Cp, which have their own means.

To use the "All AM through All T" norms, count the number of times an Imaginal Aspect or Justification is used and compare it to the mean. In the sample on the previous page, HM is used a total of five times:

$$
\begin{array}{lcc}
 & + & - \\
\text{Sh·HE·HM} & 1 & \\
\text{F·HM} & 3 & 1 \\
\hline
 & 4 + & 1 = 5 \\
\end{array}
$$

The expectancy for a "normal" adult is 3.5 (Healthy Adults, page 185 ff).

To further simplify the coding, the subscripts for C' were disregarded. To use the norms, count all C' regardless of subscript and compare to "All C'". In the sample, C' is used three times:

$$
\begin{array}{lcc}
 & + & - \\
\text{C'b·F} & 1 & \\
\text{C'bw·F} & 1 & \\
\text{C'w·F·V} & 1 & \\
\hline
 & 3 + & 0 = 3 \\
\end{array}
$$

Page 186 of the Normative Values Manual shows an adult mean of 1.5 for "All C'".

Content

Each response must have one score for content and may occasionally have more than one. Any content categories that do not fit into a specific category should be counted as "other" with the total. They may also be listed below.

To figure the A%, add all animal responses shown on the summary sheet and divide by R. To figure the H%, add the human responses and divide by R as indicated in the summary sheet.

The norms for the A% and H% for children and adults were computed by utilizing all categories of animal content and all categories of human content.

Psychosexual Drives and Defense Effectiveness

Only a few of the responses will receive a score in this dimension, as a rule. Once the finest distinctions are scored, the different categories may be added together, e.g. all Oral Overt (Oo). Then both oral categories may be added together (Oo + Oc), etc. Finally, all psychosexual drives are added together and noted next to "total". This sum is divided by R to obtain the Psychosexual Drive percent (PD%). Norms for both children and adults are available in the Normative Values table for each individual category.

Interpersonal Expectations

Articulation of human percepts

HA will be scored with *any* Human content, i.e., H, (H), Hf, (Hf), Hd, and Hdx.

Motivational articulation

MA will be scored only when HM or HE is scored. It would be possible to have a *content* scoring of A if an animal were engaging in human movement or emotion.

Implicit motivational valuation

Explicit Motivational Valuation will be scored for every response scored HM or HE. Implicit Motivational Valuation will be scored for all other responses.

Perceptual-Cognitive Characteristics

Some responses will have no perceptual-cognitive characteristic score, and others may have more than one. Therefore, no consistent total is expected in this category.

Percentages

When the scores have been correctly recorded on the summary sheet, the totals are used to form different ratios. Never include additional responses, lost responses, or precision alternatives when figuring totals. Some ratios are new in the Burstein-Loucks system, some use traditional names but different components, and some are figured identically to other systems.

The figures in the sample will be taken from the sample summary sheet shown on page 74.

Afr (Affective ratio)

This ratio indicates how the colored cards (VIII, IX, and X) influenced the subject's previous level or responsiveness. It is figured by dividing the total number of responses to the colored cards by the total number of responses given to the first seven cards.

$$\text{Afr} = \frac{\# \text{ of R for VIII} + \text{IX} + \text{X}}{\# \text{ of R for I} - \text{VII}} = \underline{\quad}$$

$$\text{Afr} = 14/17 = .82$$

As a check, add together the numerator and denominator of the ratio. The sum equal R.

F%

This ratio indicates the percentage of pure form used without an intervening expression of fantasy or emotion. Count only those responses scored pure F (both plus and minus). Do not count F used with any imaginal aspect, e.g., F·AM or F·HM. Do not count f. Divide by R.

$$\text{F\%} = \frac{\text{Pure F}}{\text{R}} = \underline{\quad}$$

$$\text{F\%} = 12/31 = \underline{39\%}$$

F + %

This ratio suggests how socially appropriate an individual perceives the environment when expressing him or herself objectively (pure F) rather than with fantasy or emotion. It is figured by dividing just the pure F + responses by all pure F (above).

$$\text{F} + \% = \frac{\text{Pure F} +}{\text{Pure F (both} + \text{ and } -)} = \underline{\quad}\%$$

$$\text{F} + \% = 8/12 = \underline{67\%}$$

Notice that the numerator of the F% and the denominator of the F+% are the same.

B+%

This ratio is a measure of social appropriateness when emotion or fantasy is being expressed. Count all the plus responses except those scored pure F or pure f. Count, for example, f·AM or f·HM; they are not considered pure F. Divide by all plus and minus responses together except those scored pure F and pure f. In other words, it is the same idea as F+% except using the remainder of the scores. Note, however, that pure f is not used in either ratio.

$$B+\% = \frac{\text{Non-pure F scores* } +}{\text{Non-pure F scores* } + \text{ or } -} = \underline{\quad}\%$$

*Except pure f.

$$B+\% = 14/18 = \underline{78\%}$$

As a check, the denominator of the F+ ratio and the denominator of the B+ ratio plus pure f should equal R.

$$12 + 18 + 1 = 31$$

It is especially important to write in the ratios of the above four percentages on the summary sheet so others using the summary sheet will know what figures were used to arrive at the percentages.

f%

Add together pure f *and* f used with imaginal aspects, e.g., f·AM and f·HM. divide by R.

$$f\% = \frac{\text{All pure f } + \text{ f.AM thru V}}{R} = \underline{\quad}\%$$

$$f\% = 1/31 = \underline{3\%}$$

PD%, H%, A%

Figuring the PD% was discussed in the section on Psychosexual Drives and Defense Effectiveness, and the H% and A% were discussed under Content. Transfer the information to the Percentages section.

Add together the means for HE and HM as well as for Ca, Ci, and C and divide by the mean number of R. This will determine the percentages expected for HE + HM and Ca + Ci + Cp.

W% (Whole %)

This percentage indicates the proportion of responses which encompassed the whole or nearly whole area of the inkblot. The formula is as follows:

$$\frac{[W + \underline{W} + (W) + \underline{(W)}]}{R} = W\%$$

D% (Large detail%)

This percentage indicates the proportion of large detail responses given by the subject. The formula is:

$$\frac{D + \underline{D}}{R} = D\%$$

Dd% (Minor detail%)

This percentage indicates the proportion of responses which utilize minor blot areas. The formula is:

$$\frac{Dd + \underline{Dd}}{R} = Dd\%$$

r% (Rare%)

This percentage indicates the proportion of responses which are given to rarely utilized areas. The formula is as follows:

$$\frac{\underline{W} + \underline{(W)} + \underline{D} + \underline{Dd}}{R} = r\%$$

4
LOCATION AND RESPONSE APPROPRIATENESS TABLES

For each card, first will be found a listing of the commonly and rarely chosen Beck areas. Next will appear an array of the numbered areas for each card graded from largest to smallest, with the demarcation between large areas (D) and small areas (Dd) indicated. Finally, in numerical order, for each area are listed the common appropriate (+) responses and inappropriate (−) responses.

CARD I
Commonly and Rarely Chosen Beck Locations

Commonly chosen	Rarely chosen
Whole	Dd1
D2	D3
D4	Dd5
	Dd6
	D7
	D8
	D9
	Dd22
	Dd23
	D24
	Dd25
	D26
	Dd27
	Dd29
	Dd30
	Dd31
	D32

Adapted, with permission, from Beck (1961).

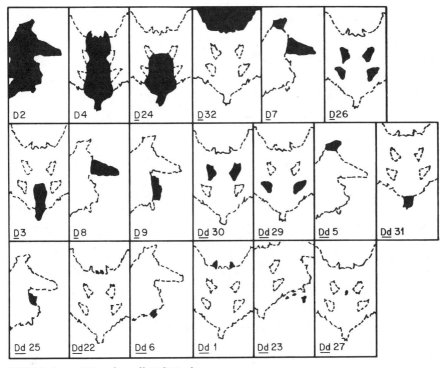

CARD I. Large (D) and small (Dd) Beck areas

W
See also D2

General Plus Categories:

face (animal, human or inanimate); and winged objects (animate or in-
    animate, except a few insects)

+ angel
+ animal, marine
+ animal, prehistoric
+ beetle
+ bench ∨
+ biologic cross-section
+ bond, skeletal
+ brain, cross-section
+ bronze (Chinese), cross-
    section ∨
+ cap, auto radiator

+ carving, stone ∨
+ castle ∨
+ cave
+ children
+ Chinese art
+ Christmas tree decoration
+ clouds
+ coat of arms
+ coral formation
+ crab
+ crawfish

+ crown ∧∨
+ crustacean
+ dancer
+ design
+ dragon
+ figurehead
+ flying squirrel
+ forest
+ fossil in stone
+ fountain with angels
+ girls
+ hat ∨∧
+ helmet ∧∨
+ insect
+ insignia, medical
+ island
+ jack-o-lantern ∨∧
+ kite
+ landscape and reflection <
+ leaf
+ lion, winged, in fountain ∨
+ lobster
+ map, topographic ∨∧
+ mask (Ws) ∨∧
+ monster, fairy tale, four-eyed
+ monument
+ moth
+ mountains
+ mythologic characters
+ nightmare figure
+ ornament, including personal
+ pagoda, Japanese
+ pattern, lace
+ pelvis
+ photograph
+ pumpkin, Halloween
+ rock formation
+ scarab
+ sea animal
+ sedan chair
+ skeleton, bird
+ sketch, charcoal

+ skull (W or Ws) ∨
+ sky, clouded
+ spinal cord, cross-section
+ stencil
+ top, spinning
+ totem pole form
+ tunnel
+ turban
+ urn, Japanese
+ vertebra, outline of
+ witches, two
+ woman, winged
+ x-ray plate (nonspecific)

− abdomen
− amoeba
− animal, split open
− bats, two
− bear
− blood, spilled
− blouse
− body, human
− butterflies, two (divided horizontally)
− canoe, outrigger
− cat
− chest ∨ (An.)
− Chinese letter
− clown
− cocoon
− dancer ∨
− dinosaur
− dirt on floor
− dish, fancy
− dragonfly
− explosion, atom bomb
− fireplace
− fish
− flower
− fly
− football player ∨
− frog

- governor on motor
  head: (no facial features)
    - animal
    - bull
    - moose
    - rabbit
    - ram
- hill
- lake
- man with legs apart V
- marine growth
- orange peel
- picture
- planet
- rocketship
- rug, fur
- saddle
- sea shell
- sheep
- ship
- shrimp
- skeleton, outline of
- skin, animal
- snowflake
- spider
- sponge
- swamp
- train, front
- tree
- tree bark
- turtle
- United States
- wasp
- x-ray plate (scored + when the specific anatomy detail named would be +, e.g., pelvis)

W without D7

+ animal, microscopic
+ beetle
+ butterfly
+ jack-o-lantern ∧V
+ pumpkin, Halloween
+ sting-ray

W without D8

+ pelvis
- man, hands on hips V

Upper half of blot

+ airplane
+ bat
+ bird
+ butterfly
+ emblem
+ head, fox
+ insignia
+ mountains

Lower half of blot

+ bat ∧V
+ butterfly ∧V
+ crown, with jewels V
- collar, shirt
- pelvis
- prow, ship's

Dd 1

General Plus Category:

animal extensors (horns, feelers, claws)

+ antennae	− boulders
+ coral	− cactus plant
+ crab	− collar, woman's dress
+ crustacean	− fish
+ feelers	− fork and spoon
+ fingers	− heads, animal
+ hands	− human figures
+ heads, bird	− rocks
+ heads, duck	− roots, tree ∨
+ heads, snake	− sticks
+ mandibles	− teeth
+ mittens	− tongues
+ pincers	

D1 with Dd22

+ crab	+ lobster
+ head, deer's	+ nest, bird, with birds
+ insect	
	− genitalia, female

D2
See also W

General Plus Category:

human figure (including winged)

+ angel	+ island
+ animal	+ map
+ bird	+ mountain, or part of
+ brontosaurus	+ Pegasus
+ cliff	+ profile, witch
+ cloud(s)	+ rock
+ dove	+ sky
+ elephant (D8 is ear)	+ stork
+ face (outer edge of D2 as pro- file, D8 long nose)	+ trees
	+ wings
+ gargoyle	
+ Gibraltar	− bat
+ griffon	− bear
+ head, Pinnocchio	− butterfly

- carcass, hanging
- chicken
- country
- dog
- donkey
- dragon
- Great Britain
- head, swordfish
- lungs

- pig
- profile, dog
- rack, newspaper
- sea horse
- skin, bear
- stones, prehistoric
- water, bodies of
- wolf, dancing

D3

General Plus Category:

human figure

+ aqueduct of Sylvius
+ bell
+ body, baby
+ bowling pin ∨
+ chalice
+ legs
+ medulla
+ midbrain
+ scarab
+ spinal cord

+ statue of human
+ vase

- body, human ∨
- penis
- skeleton, human, lower half
- snake
- submarine
- x-ray machine

D4

General Plus Category:

human figure or figures

General Minus Category:

infraprimate mammals

+ beetle
+ body (unspecified)
+ body, bird
+ body, insect
+ brain stem
+ Buddha
+ cello
+ centipede
+ crab
+ flower pot
+ gorilla
+ gymnastic apparatus

+ humans, two
+ insect
+ lantern ∨
+ lobster
+ medulla
+ monument
+ scarab
+ scorpion
+ shield
+ Sphinx
+ spider
+ suit

+ urn ∨∧
+ vase ∧∨
+ violin

− alligator
− ant
− bat, wings folded
− bee
− bone
− caterpillar
− fish
− fly (with Dds 26)
− frog
− head, clown

− lizard
− log
− mountain
− owl
− pelvis
− rocket ∨
− sack of flour
− ship, front view
− skeleton
− tower
− tree
− turtle ∨
− vagina
− vampire

D4 without Dd24

+ armor, suit of
+ crab
+ insect
+ lobster
+ people kissing
+ spider

− clip

− crater
− face, deer
− face, monkey
− head, owl's
− manta ray
− pelvis
− toad

Dd5

General Plus Category:

human head

+ comb, rooster
+ face, man's
+ face, wolf's
+ hat
   head:
      + bear
      + bird
      + dog
      + fox
+ mountains
+ profile

− bird, sitting
− chicken
   − parrot
− horn
− horse
− house
− jaw, bear's
− rabbit
− shoe

Dd6

General Plus Category:

human head

+ bust, of man   + tree (usually ∨)
+ celery
+ crown   − bell clapper
+ hay, bunch of   − head, dog
+ mushroom   − human, whole
+ shocks, of wheat   − leg
                                  − tail, poodle

D7
See also D8

+ birds   + mountains <
+ dog   + Sphinx
+ eagle   + wing
+ flying horse
  head: − Africa
    + bear   − animal (when accent is on D8
    + coyote   as tail)
    + dog   head:
    + fox   − duck
                                  − leaf
                                  − South America <

D8
See also D7

General Plus Category:

wing (animate or inanimate)

+ cliff   − bird with beak
+ fin, shark   − blade, knife
+ gargoyle   − cloud
+ head, dog or wolf   − dog
+ mountain   − face, human <
+ mountain peak   − face, animal
+ nose, fox's   − flint
+ rock   − funnel <
+ seal (animal)   − ghost <
                                  − head, alligator
− anvil   − head, Indian <
− arrow   − horn

− insect
− isle, coral
− thigh

− tree
− tree, fir <
− umbrella

D9

+ cliffs, rock
+ clouds
+ dog <
+ face, dog
+ face, human
+ cat
+ dog

+ human
+ lion
+ monkey

    head:
      − animal
      − buffalo <

Dd22

+ boulders
+ head, bumps on
+ head, split open
+ heads
+ hills
+ labia
+ mountains

− breasts
− eggs
− humps, camel
− mosquito bites
− rectum
− testicles
− trees

Dd23

+ islands
+ notes, musical

− dots

− flies
− insect
− mosquitoes

D24

+ bell
+ cello
+ crest (on shield)
+ insignia ∨
+ lantern, Japanese ∨

− alligator
− beetle

− bellows
− chipmunk
− hourglass
− human figure ∨
− people, two
− spinal column

Dd25

+ animal
+ bushes
+ face
+ gnome

+ head, old man's

− cliff
− pig

D26
See also Dds29 and Dds30

+ carvings
+ eyes, four
+ glaciers
+ puzzles, cutout
+ ventricles

wings:
+ airplane
+ butterfly

− fly

Dd27

+ buckle, belt
+ central canal

− heart, human
− moon

Dd29

+ pumpkin, Halloween, mouth of
+ windows
+ wings, butterfly

− eyes ∨∧

− heads, human ∨∧
− mittens
− sails
− triangles

Dd30

+ eyes ∧∨
+ windows

− arms, doubled up
− brides
− faces, animal

− ghosts
− gloves
− heads, rooster
− pelvis (with intervening dark
    area)
− rectangles

Dd31

+ feet
+ fiddle, bass, top
+ head, dog ∨
+ head, eagle, as emblem

− bird ∨
− exhaust, jet plane
− face ∨

− hawk ∨
− nose, goose <
− phallus
− rectum
− root, tree
− stick
− tail, animal
− vagina

D32

+ canyon
+ road overpass ∨

− dish

CARD II
Commonly and Rarely Chosen Beck Locations

Commonly chosen	Rarely chosen
Whole	Dd4
D1	D7
D2	Dd22
D3	Dd23
D5	Dd24
D6	Dd25
	Dd26
	Dd27
	Dd28
	Dd29
	Dd30
	Dd31

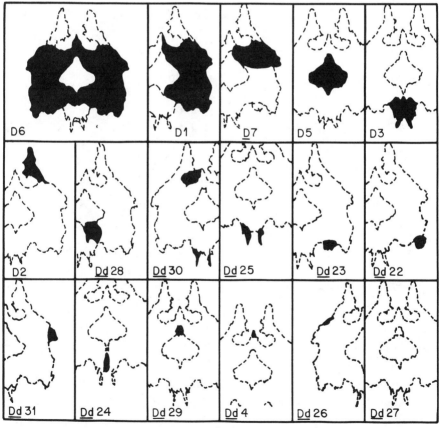

CARD II. Large (D) and small (Dd) Beck areas

W
See also D1 with D2

General Plus Category:

human figures, two (∧ only)

General Minus Categories:

face, inframammalian animal (except butterfly and moth)

+ airplane, any (e.g., jet, with Ds5 as plane, D3 as exhaust, D6 as smoke)
+ anatomy, general
+ bears (in any movement)
+ brain, cross-section
+ butterfly ∧∨
+ cave
+ Christmas tree ornament
+ designs
+ devils
+ explosion
+ flame and smoke
+ insignia
+ lava
+ moth, fire
+ nervous system, central
+ organism, primitive
+ painting
+ ribs, x-ray of
+ rocket ship
+ spinal cord, section
+ statues
+ toys
+ volcano

− anemone, sea
− bacteria

− bat
− biologic, something
− cat
− creature
− duelers ∨
− egg, fried
− firefly
− football player kneeling (rear view)
− head, human, bloody with hole (top view)
− heart
− house
− map
− mask
− meat, piece of
− men ∨
− orchid
− pelvic girdle
− pot, flower
− rectum
− sun in eclipse
− throat
− tooth
− vagina
− vocal cords
− woman wearing fur coat

D1
See also D6

General Plus Category:

human figure (with or without D2, but only)

+ animal ∧>
+ ape ∧

+ bear
+ bison <

+ body, animal
+ calf (D31 as muzzle)
+ coat
+ cow
+ cub
+ dog <
+ elephant
+ lamb (Dd31 as muzzle)
+ monkey
+ mountain
+ pelt
+ pig
+ rabbit
+ rhinoceros <
+ ribs, showing through skin
+ rock, as mountain
+ skin, animal
+ wing

− animal ∨
− ape ∨
− Australia
− bird
− boat

− body, camel
− calf (D4 as muzzle)
− cat
− chest, human
− clouds
− clown ∨
− dog ∨
− embryo
− fish
− goose
− gorilla ∨
− grass
− guinea pig
− heart
− hippopotamus
− human, fighting, dancing ∨
− lamb ∨
− lamb (D4 as muzzle)
− lion
− map
− skeleton
− tree trunk
− turtle

D1 with D2
See also W

+ carcass hanging by leg
+ gorilla

− anteater <
− boar, wild
− camel <

− chicken
− duck
− head, human (profile)
− rabbit
− rooster
− sheep

Outer edge D1

+ face, weird

+ map contour

D2
General Plus Categories:
headgear of any type; human figure (only); human head or face

General Minus Categories:

animal head; anatomy

+ animal
+ bird
+ blood
+ boot
+ butterfly
+ cat
+ centaur
+ creature, animated
+ devil
+ dog (and specific breeds)
+ dragon
+ fire
+ foot, human V
+ fox
+ hare
+ hippopotamus
+ Italy
+ lantern, Japanese
+ lava
+ leg
+ mask
+ monster, ancient
+ proboscis, shellfish
+ rabbit
+ seal ∧V
+ slide, microscope
+ snail
+ South America V
+ Sphinx
+ stocking, any kind V><
+ torch

− andiron
− anteater
− automobile
− bison
− bonfire
− bug
− bugle
− bull >

− candle, lighted
− cells, body
− chicken
− chipmunk
− dove
− duck
− ear, human
− England
− face, camel <>
− face, horse <>
− finger <
− fingerprint
− fish
− flag
− flower
− flying horse
− foot, human
− glove, boxing
− goat
− hand
− holster, gun
− hoof V
− human form V
− kidney
− knight, chess V
− leg V
− lion
− mitten
− oxen (in yoke)
− penis
− piano, grand
− pillar
− rat
− shell, clam
− squirrel
− tissue, body
− tongue
− tooth roots ∧V
− turkey
− worm

Dd projections of D2

+ beak
+ cigarette
+ claw
+ finger
+ nose

+ tongue sticking out

− bird
− dove
− turtle

D3

+ beetle
+ blood
+ bug
+ butterfly
+ buttocks
+ darning needle (insect) V
+ explosion
+ fire V∧
+ genital organ, female, any
  head
    + snail
+ insect
+ menstrual flow
+ metal, molten
+ moth
+ rectum
+ snow crystal
+ sun, rising or setting V
+ torches with wicks
+ unicorn

− anemone, sea
− bagpipes V
− bird
− bush
− chairs, two
− coral formation
− crab
− cradle, end view
− crawfish

− daddy longlegs
− devil
− easel
− fish V
− flower
− girl with arms V
− hand, human
  head:
    − crab
    − devil
    − lobster
− heart
− jellyfish
− lobster
− lungs
− marine creature
− mask
− meat, piece of
− minarets V
− mouse
− pot, paint, with brushes V
− Sacred Heart
− sherbet
− stand, artist's
− stoves, two
− udder, cow's
− uterus
− water from faucet
− wine

Dd4
Starred responses may include adjacent dark areas

+ arrow
+ building

+ can opener
+ castle

+ clippers
+ cornucopias
+ dagger
+ delta, river ∨
+ dome, building
+ drill
+ forceps
+ hands
+ gargoyle head
+ instrument, surgical
+ monument
+ pen, point
+ pipe reamer
+ pliers
+ pyramid
+ scissors
+ spearhead
+ temple
+ tower
+ tree
+ tree, pine

− beak, eagle
− bell
− bone
− bottle
− Buddha
− bud, flower
− candle
− claw*
− clitoris
− clothespin
− Crucifixion
− curtain
− drawbridge
− face, lizard
− fetus
− figures, human
− flashlight

− flowers*
− glasses (vessel)
− gorillas, two
− hat
head:
    − bird
    − human
− headdress
− heart
− helmet, knight's
− hoof, horse's
− house
− jaw
− kidney
− knife*
− man
− mountain
− mouse
− nose, goose
− package*
− penis
− rabbit*
− rocket*
− seashell ∨
− shell, oyster
− shoe trees*
− shuttlecock*
− slippers
− snake, coiled
− snout, pig's
− sword
− tail
− Tibetan
− tree, palm
− unicorn
− uterus
− vagina
− veil
− wishbone

Dd4 with D5

+ castle and gate
+ channel

+ church
+ lamp

+ tornado funnel

− boat
− violin

D5

General Plus Category:

building of any type

+ airplane, jet (may include D3 and D4)
+ basket, hanging
+ bellows
+ bottle
+ bowl, for lamp
+ castle
+ cave, entrance ∨
+ chandelier
+ cover, pottery
+ fissure, in rock
+ fountain ∨
+ gate
+ goblet ∨
+ guided missile (may include D3 and D4)
+ hole
+ inkwell
+ lake
+ lamp
+ lantern, Japanese
+ light bulb, electric
+ pond
+ promenade
+ rocket
+ steeple, church
+ top (toy)
+ tunnel, entrance
+ water, body of

− bat
− beet
− bell
− boat ∨∧
− body, girl's, any part
− butterfly
− cat
− Christmas tree
− cocoon
− crown
− dancer, ballet
− dress, flared, old-fashioned
− ghost
− hat
− heart ∨
− island
− kite
− manta ray
− mask
− motor or engine
− mouth, open
− sting-ray
− stomach
− throat
− turnip ∨
− umbrella
− uterus
− vagina (may include D6)

D6
See also D1

+ airplane, wings
+ brain stem, cross-section
+ butterfly
+ cave, entrance

+ clouds
+ fireplace
+ forest
+ moth

+ mountains
+ pelvis
+ ribs, x-ray of

− animal, track of
− bat
− bear rug
− bird
− body, human, interior of
− collar, coat
− flying squirrel

− heart
− house
− inner tube
− insect, winged
− island
− lungs
− New York State
− rug
− soot
− United States

D6 with D5

+ cave opening
+ land, with pond
+ pelvic girdle
+ well platform

− crab shell
− doughnut

D7

+ dog
  head:
    + animal
    + ape (muzzle at Dd31)
    + dog
    + Dracula (face at Dd31)
    + horse (muzzle at Dd31)
    + Indian (face at Dd31)
    + monkey
    + sheep (muzzle at Dd31)

− Africa <
− bird
  head
    − poodle ∨
    − turtle
    − whale
− hips (both D7) ∨
− leg, human
− South America <

Dd22

+ chicken ∨∧
+ bush ∨
+ face ∨
+ feet, bear's
+ foot, kangaroo

+ head, boy ∨
+ man, old ∨
+ profile, whistling ∨

− head, dog

Dd23

+ head, old man
+ mountain ∨

− bush ∨
− frog ∨

Dd24

+ anus
+ beacon on building ∨
+ discharge system (An)
+ genitalia, female
+ "sexual"
+ totem pole
+ vagina

− bowling pin

− candle
− dumbbell
− face
− head, goat
− penis symbol <
− person with scarf
− waterfall
− woman

Dd25

+ antlers
+ candle sticks
+ crystals
+ feelers, insect
+ horns, unicorn
+ icicles
+ legs, insect
+ sticks, candy

− clubs

− pens, fountain
− spears
− stalagmites
− sticks
− swords
− table legs
− tail, lobster
− tusks, elephant
− veins
− whiskers

Dd26

+ caterpillar
+ sunset

− seal
− tail ∧>
− walrus

Dd27

+ bridge
+ canal locks

− bones
− cigarettes
− claws

Dd28
See D3

Dd29

+ dome [Ar]
+ flask
+ lake

+ pot

− nose

Dd30

– chicken	– eyes
– embryo	– sea shell

Dd31

+ beak, bird	– ears, donkey
+ crag, mountain	– ears, rabbit
head:	head:
+ turtle	– fish
+ man, old, ∧∨	– rabbit
+ profile, animal	– mouth, camel
+ profile, human	– mouth, fish
	– saddle seat
– claw, lobster	

CARD III
Commonly and Rarely Chosen Beck Locations

Commonly chosen	Rarely chosen
D1	Whole
D2	D4
D3	Dd6
D5	D8
D7	Dd10
D9	D12
D11	Dd21
	D22
	D23
	D24
	Dd25
	Dd26
	Dd27
	Dd28
	Dd29
	D30

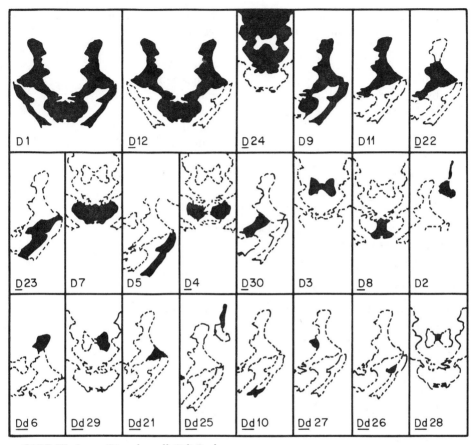

CARD III. Large (D) and small (Dd) Beck areas

W
See also D1 and D9

General Minus Categories:

face; anatomy

+ arch ∨
+ design
+ figure, human ∨
+ fireplace with ornaments
+ fly ∨ (magnified)
+ frog ∨

+ fruit, bowl of
+ heraldry symbol
+ insect, magnified ∨
+ leader, orchestra ∨
+ pelvis
+ praying mantis ∨

+ puzzle, picture
+ sketch, done in shadows
+ vase

− ant ∨
− bug
− butterfly
− cat
− crab

− flower, blossom and leaves
− gorilla
− human
− insect ∧∨
− knight (chess)
− map
− owl ∨
− skeleton, human ∨
− spider

D1
See also D9 and D12

General Plus Category:

human figures, two

General Minus Categories:

face; animals, two (except fowl and anthropoids)

+ birds, large, resembling humans
+ bones (in x-ray)
+ chickens
+ cocks, fighting
+ dolls
+ Donald Duck, two
+ figure, human, arms up ∨
+ gorillas, two
+ hips
+ ostriches
+ pelvis
+ sketch
+ toy
+ vase

− ant
− animal
− bacteria
− bug
− crown ∨
− dragon

− figure, human, from waist
   down, squatting
− frog
− gorilla ∨
− insect ∧∨
− jawbone
− lobster
− map
− monkeys
− monster
− roots, tree
− skeleton
− skull ∧∨
− smoke
− spider ∧∨
− toad
− torso ∧∨
− tree
− turtle
− water, falling

D2

General Plus Category:

human figure, including mythological, such as elf, gremlin, etc.

+ ameba
+ anemone, sea
+ animal ∧∨>< (in any move-
     ment)
+ bagpipe
+ bird >∧
+ blood splotch
+ branch and leaves
+ cat
+ chicken <∧
+ cocoon
+ dejection ∨ (Ab)
+ devil
+ dipper, water
+ dog >∨∧
+ embryo, human
+ esophagus and stomach
+ figure, human ∨
+ fire
+ firecracker
+ flying creature
+ germ under microscope
+ gourd
+ hat with string
+ head, horse
+ horse
+ kidney, with ureter
+ microscopic life
+ monkey ∨∧<
+ nerve process
+ paramecium
+ parrot on pole ∧∨
+ pipe, smoking
+ plant bent by wind ∨
+ portiere
+ puppet
+ rooster

+ sea horse
+ seaweed
+ stage decoration
+ stomach
+ tadpole
+ trapeze performer
+ tree ∨
+ turkey
+ umbilical cord
+ witch, on broomstick ∨

− ape
− artery and lung
− bananas
− butterfly
− centipede
− club
− crab
− dandelion
− dragon
− eagle <
− fish
− flesh
− flower
− fork
− guitar
− heart (Dd25 artery)
− hook
− insect
− instrument, musical (or any
     specific one)
− intestines
− island
− lightning flash
− lion
− lobster
− lung(s)

- meat, cut of
- microphone, hanging
- note, musical
- ostrich
- ovary
- pork chop
- question mark
- rabbit
- rat
- river and pond

- seed in garden
- shoe, hanging by lace
- snail
- snake rising from basket
- spider
- stick
- tree limb
- udder on cow
- vase
- venison hanging from hook

D3

+ backbone, section of
+ blood
+ bone
+ bowknot
+ butterfly ∧∨
+ drapery
+ fire
+ gray matter of spinal cord
+ hip bones
+ kidney
+ lung(s)
+ moth
+ necktie
+ pelvic bones
+ ribbon, any
+ spinal cord, piece of
+ water wings
+ wings, butterfly

- antlers
- apples
- bird
- bivalve
- brassiere
- breastbone
- chair, back of
- coccyx
- dam

- dancers, ballet
- dumbbell
- ear warmer(s)
- eye glasses
- figure(s), human
- fly
- gum of mouth
- heart(s)
- hourglass <
- insect
- intestine
- lamb(s)
- mask
- mustache
- nose, human
- nosepiece, spectacles
- notes, musical ∧∨
- oranges
- pants
- protector, athletic
- roof of mouth
- skeleton, parts of
- sky, red
- stagecoaches
- testicles
- thorax
- werewolf
- wishbone

D4
See also D7

+ bags
+ baskets
+ bear cubs V∧
+ boxing gloves
+ child(ren)
+ embryos
+ faces, human
+ fans
+ gourds, water
+ hats
   heads:
      + cannibal V
      + human V
      + skeleton
+ kettledrums
+ lamp, Chinese
+ mittens
+ muffs
+ porcupines
+ possums
+ pots
+ purses
+ rocks
+ sacks, any
+ shrubbery V
+ skulls, any ∧V
+ stomachs, x-rays of

+ stones, round
+ trees V

− balls, bowling
− boots
− buffalo(es)
− bust, woman's
− chickens
− cups
− dogs
− ear muffs
− eyes, any
− feet, human
− frogs
− hands
   heads:
      − animal V
      − elephant
− hens
− kidneys
− lungs
− mountains
− rats
− slippers, bedroom
− sunglasses
− testicles
− turtles

D5
See also D9

General Plus Category:

leg of large, hoofed, animal

+ arm V
+ claw, crustacean
+ club <
+ firewood V
+ fish
   foot:
      + human
      + ostrich

+ hand V
+ Italy V
   leg:
      + human
+ log
+ shark <
+ skeleton, human, part of
+ sleeve V

+ stick
+ tree limb ∧∨
+ wood, broken

− arm
− bird
− frog
− gun
− hand ∧
− island

leg:
  − grasshopper
− Madagascar
− peninsula
− reef ∨
− river
− seaweed
− sleeve ∧
− torpedo
− tree

Dd6
See also D9

General Plus Category:

head of bird or fowl

head:
  + dog
  + skeleton
  + mask
+ rock

− acorn
− animal
− coconut

− eye
− football
head:
  − animal
  − ant
  − bug
  − monkey
− nostril
− shell, clam

D7
See also D4

General Plus Category:

circular container, such as pail, pot, bowl

+ bivalve
+ body, lower part
+ butterfly
+ cauldron, witch's
+ drum
+ entrance to park ∧∨
+ fireplace
+ gate
+ mask, modernistic
+ mushroom, atomic blast ∧∨
+ nest
+ painting, Japanese
+ pelvis

+ sacroiliac
+ shadows
+ shrubbery
+ stage property
+ stove

− brain section
− bulldog
− crab
− eyeglasses
− face, human
− globe
− head, fly

- insect
- kidney(s)
- lung(s)
- motor, outboard
- record player
- rectum
- spider

- spinal cord
- torso, human
- turtles
- uterus
- vagina
- vertebra

D8

+ bones
+ brook
+ chest, human
+ crab ∧∨
+ doors, swinging
+ fireplace
+ firewood
+ gate ∨∧
+ goblet ∨ (with or without Dds)
+ jack-o-lantern
+ lamp
+ landscape with inlets
+ pelvis
+ precipice
+ reflection, land in water >
+ ribs
+ river, section of
+ shell, crab, frayed

+ skeleton
+ vase ∨ (with or without Dds)
+ water (shore and creeks)
+ wood, splintered

- boat
- brainstem, section of
- breastbone
- cloud(s)
- Crucifixion
- face
- fountain
- genitalia, female
- hourglass
- lungs
- pubis
- pumpkin (with or without Dds)
- vagina (with or without Dds)

D9
See also W and D1

General Plus Category:

human figure

General Minus Category:

animal, any (except fowl and anthropoids)

+ bird (large varieties)
+ cartoon character
+ chicken
+ design
+ doll
+ dummy
+ monster

+ mountain with snow (with
    Dds23)<
+ ostrich
+ scarecrow
+ swampland >

- cloud(s)

– monkey
– parrot
– root(s), tree

– tree
– turtle
– woodpecker ∨

Dd10

+ finger ∨
+ hand ∨
+ hoof, any
+ shoe, high-heeled

– finger ∧
– foot, frog
– hand ∧
– paw
– woman

D11

+ bird ∨
+ chicken
+ cliff(s), rocky ∨
+ Donald Duck
+ figure, human, legless
+ man ∧
+ rooster
+ seal ∧
+ torso, human

– animal

– arms
– bird ∧
– bomb, atomic
– bulb (plant)
– dog ∧∨
– face, human
– hair, woman's ∨
– insect
– kangaroo
– skeleton
– thigh, human

D12
See also D1

+ archway ∨
+ frog
+ landscape ∨
+ park
+ pelvic cavity

+ snow scene

– crab ∨
– figure, human

Dd21

+ beak, bird ∨
+ bird ∨ (any type)

– dog ∨
– head, any animal's ∨∧

Dd22

+ airplane ∨
+ eagle ∨>∧
+ mountain

+ rat
+ rodent
+ turkey ∨

- chipmunk
- dancer, ballet
  head:
  - animal ∧∨

- deer
- human ∧∨
- North America
- saddle

Dd23

+ Adriatic Sea
+ design
+ eagle <
+ water

- ears
- dress, woman's
- head, dog
- machine part

D24

+ bowl
+ chalice
+ Christmas tree
+ flower, conventionalized ∧∨
+ lamp, with glass chimney
+ mushroom ∨
+ road ∨

+ shirt front ∨
+ snow
+ stencil

- face, cat
- face, human ∨
- lake

Dd25
See also D2

+ esophagus
+ pole
+ queue (Chinese)
+ root, plant
+ rope
+ stick

+ string
+ ureter

- bird ∨
- tail, lion

Dd26

+ penis
+ skirt

- leg, human

Dd27

+ breast
+ head, rodent ∨

- cap, auto radiator
- nose, dog

Dd28

- bone
- door
- face

- tooth
- vagina

Dd29
See also D3

+ tail, bird   − peanut
                                               − plate, dental
− bean   − tooth
− breast   − "U" <
− chicken   − Valentine
− fetus   − vase
− figure, human

D30

+ hand   − foot
                                               − penis
− cloud(s)

Projections from D30

+ fingers   − icicles
                                               − knives
− head, bird ∨

CARD IV
Commonly and Rarely Chosen Beck Locations

Commonly chosen	Rarely chosen
Whole	D2
D1	D3
Dd4	D5
D6	D7
	D8
	Dd21
	D22
	Dd23
	D24
	Dd25
	Dd26
	Dd27
	Dd28
	Dd29
	Dd30

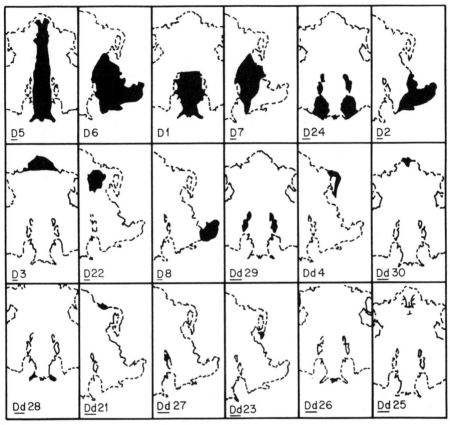

CARD IV. Large (D) and small (Dd) Beck areas

W
See also W minus D1
General Plus Categories:

large, furry animal; human figure

+ airplane
+ anchor ∨
+ animal, four-legged (rear view)
+ animal, sea
+ baby
+ bat ∧∨ (may be hanging)
+ battlements, castle
+ bell

+ block, design of ∨
+ body, human, x-rayed
+ boots on a pole
+ burner, incense ∨
+ butterfly ∧∨
+ cactus
+ carcass, animal
+ carpet

+ cave (Ws)
+ chandelier
+ clouds
+ clown
+ coat
+ column with winged figures
+ creature, mythological
+ crest ∧∨ (official seal)
+ design
+ developmental form
+ dragon, winged ∨∧
+ elephants, back to back
+ embryo
+ escutcheon ∨
+ fern
+ flower
+ flying squirrel
+ forest, reflected in lake <
+ fossil, of animal
+ fungus
+ giant
+ gorilla
+ hide
  head:
    + buffalo
    + ram
+ impression, sinister (Ab)
+ insignia ∨
+ integration [Ab]
+ iris (flower)
+ jellyfish
+ kite, Japanese ∨
+ landscape, reflected <>
+ leaf, torn
+ lily
+ lyre ∨
+ man (D2) on sleigh (D7), ice re-
    flected below >
+ man, headless
+ map
+ mashed object
+ mollusk
+ monkey

+ moth
+ mountain
+ Niagara Falls (D6 as mountains,
    D5 as water)
+ orchid ∨∧
+ parachute uniform
+ pattern, art
+ phantom
+ plant
+ pond in woods, landscape re-
    flected <
+ robe, fur
+ rock formation
+ rug (fur)
+ sacrum
+ scarecrow, on post
+ seaweed
  skin ∨∧:
    + furry animal
    + lion
    + tiger
+ sloth
+ smoke (clouds of)
+ sponge, plant
+ squid
+ statue
+ sting ray ∨
+ structure, Oriental
+ swamp ∨
+ temple, Chinese ∨
+ thistle
+ tree ∧∨
+ troll
+ urn
+ wineskin
+ x-ray plate

− alligator
− ameba
− auto
− bird ∧∨
− brain section
− bull ∨

- candle and candlestick
- coral, broken
- core ∨
- crab
- dog
- eagle
- elephant
- face
- fish
- frog
- giraffe
- governor on engine
  head:
    - ant
    - fish
    - dog ∨
    - rocket
- horse
- insect, any ∨∧
- intestines
- island

- lizard
- lobster
- lung
- man, standing on head (D1
    head)
- octopus
- pelvis
- pig
- 'possom ∨
- root, tree
  skin ∨∧:
    - frog
- snail
- snowflake ∨
- spider
- squab, plucked
- starfish
- tick (insect)
- turtle
- walnut kernel
- worm, squashed

W minus D1
See also W

+ baby
+ bat
+ coat sleeves ∨
+ gorilla
+ pants, pair

+ scarecrow

- frog
- mouth, open <
- pendant

Lower half of blot

+ bat with wings ∨
+ castle between two crags ∨
+ fountain with seals on side ∨
+ tail and two feet of animal

- animal ∨
- fly, big ∨
- pelvic bone
- pendant

Upper half of blot

+ animal
+ butterfly
+ cow with horns
+ embryo design
+ flower ∨∧
+ fountain

head:
  + animal
  + antelope
  + ram
  + reindeer
+ skull, steer

+ x-ray   − fox ∨
                                 − man
− bird   − spinal cord, section, with
  head: nerves

D1

General Plus Categories:

small, horned animal; head of large, horned animal

+ animal   + smoke
+ bug   + snail
+ cactus plant ∨   + spine, section of
+ candle ∨∧   + squid
+ castle ∨   + stone
+ caterpillar   + stool
+ coccyx   + stump
+ cow   + tail
+ crab, hermit ∨   + throne
+ crown, king ∨   + totem pole
+ figure, Hindu ∨   + tower ∨
+ fountain   + tree ∨
+ fur, piece of   + tree trunk
+ ghost ∨   + urn with legs
+ goat   + vase
  head: + vertebra
      + caterpillar
      + dragon   − arms, hanging
      + fly (magnified)   − cart
      + human ∨   − cat
      + insect   − chair
      + snail   − crawfish
+ helmet with radar device   − figure, human
+ hydra   − fish, without tail
+ hydrant, fire   head:
+ idol   − alligator
+ insect   − catfish
+ lamp   − centipede
+ lighthouse ∨   − crocodile
+ medulla   − dog
+ owl ∨∧   − fish
+ pelt   − horse
+ shrubbery   − rat
+ skin, animal   − wolf

- intestines, hanging   - seashell
- lobster   - skirt
- motorcycle   - snake
- neck, chicken   - stove, old
- penis   - worm
- sea horse

D2

General Plus Categories:

human figure; human head, face, or profile (usually >)

+ bear   - boat
+ branch ∨   - bone(s)
+ Cape Cod   - cow
+ cloud(s)   - deer ∨
+ dog ><∧   - elk ∨
+ emblem   - grass
+ foot, human   head:
+ leg, animal   - camel <
+ map   - horse <
+ peninsula   - lamb <
+ shoe   - sea serpent <
+ smoke   - seal <
+ Sphinx >   - turkey <
+ totem pole >   - jaw, moose
+ wing, bat   - Norway ∨
                                 - pig
- bird   - profile, moose

D3

+ bud, flower   + helmet, ancient or oriental
+ butterfly ∧∨><   + insignia, air corps
+ cabbage   + leaf(s)
+ collar, lace   + lichen
+ crown   + secretion, squid's
+ delta   + toupee
+ fan   + vagina
+ flower, any   + wings, insect
  head:
     + animal, mythical   - anus
     + bat   - bird, wings out
     + cat   - buttocks
     + human   - candle
     + owl   - clam

- face, bird
- flying saucer
  head:
  - fox
  - rocket
  - walrus
- larynx

- mollusk
- octopus
- rectum
- seashell
- skin, animal
- tail, fish
- whiskers, cat

Dd4

+ aorta
+ arm, human
+ branch, tree
+ cap, stocking
+ claw, crab or lobster V
+ eel
+ figure, human (bending over)
+ handle, pot ∧V
+ hand
+ harpoon
+ head, birth (any with prominent neck)
+ hook
+ horn, animal
+ icicle
+ lizard
+ log
+ neck, long, of bird or animal
+ peninsula
+ root, tree V
+ snake
+ tree
+ trunk, elephant
+ tusk, elephant
+ vine

- alligator
- animal
- belt
- bird
- boy(s)
- cat
- crutch
- dripping (of liquid)
- ear, dog
- ear, elephant
- finger
- fish
- flipper, seal
- horse
- knife
- leg, human
- lock, oar
- penis
- sickle
- strap
- tail, animal
- tears, flowing
- tentacle (octopus)
- tongue, shoe
- tube, fallopian
- wing

D5

+ column
+ crater, volcano
+ devil, little V
+ figure, human
+ fountain

+ neutral groove
+ penis, dissection of
+ pole
+ post
+ river

+ rocket ∧∨
+ spinal column
+ stand, flower
+ statue
+ totem pole
+ tree, fir
+ tree trunk
+ vertebrae
+ x-ray

− boar ∨
− crawfish
− fish
− husk, corn
− insect
− sex organs, female
− shrimp

D6
See also D8

+ boot
+ face, bearded >
+ foot, big
+ figure, human ∨>
+ Italy
+ leg
+ shoe
+ sky, stormy

+ smoke, from volcano
+ trouser leg
+ wing, bat

− fort
− ram
− sea horse ∨

Heel of (D6) "boot"

+ handle
+ heel
+ horn, animal ∨
+ lever
+ stick ∨

− bone
− hat ∨
− mountain

D7

General Plus Category:

human figure (∨ only)

+ Africa
+ animal, formalized
+ arch of trees (both D7)
+ crag
+ foot
+ rock(s)
+ root
+ seal
+ sea lion ∧∨
+ South America
+ statue

+ tapir

− bird
− chicken ∨
− elephant ∨
− figure, human ∧><
− handle of jar
− lion
− mouse >
− tree
− wolf

D8
See also D6

General Plus Categories:

human head (usually <>); animal head (usually <>)

+ camel   + poodle
+ man, old

                                               − Florida ∨

Dd21

+ building, on hill   + landscape, distant
+ face, human <>∨∧
+ figures, human, far off   head:
+ gnome   − pig
   head: − squirrel
      + grotesque
      + human

   face or head: − breast(s)
      + dog   face or head:
      + human   − horse
+ profile, human   − teeth, animal

D22

Dd23
See also D4

+ beak, bird   + head, bird

D24

   heads: − ladies with bustles
      + bird   − tadpoles
      + dog
      + duck

Dd25

+ face, human or any animal   − stomach, x-ray of
+ head, human or any animal

Dd26

+ feet, human   − clitoris
+ heads, human ∨   − ears
+ legs, human   − hands
+ toes   − hooves
                                               − mountains ∨

− claw

− mouth
− pedals, piano

− penises
− udder, cow

Dd27

+ foot, animal
+ hoof, horse

− foot, human

Dd28
See also D1

− feet, human
− legs, animal

− penises
− tusks

Dd30

+ flower
+ iris (flower)
+ lips, vagina
+ thalamus

− core, apple
− heart
− penis
− pin
− womb

− anus

CARD V
Commonly and Rarely Chosen Beck Locations

Commonly chosen	Rarely chosen
Whole	Dd1
D10	Dd2
	Dd3
	D4
	Dd5
	D6
	D7
	Dd8
	D9
	D11
	Dd22
	D23
	Dd24
	Dd25
	Dd26
	Dd27
	Dd28
	Dd29
	Dd30

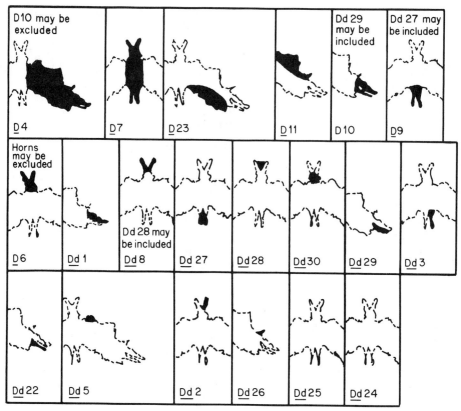

CARD V. Large (D) and small (Dd) Beck areas

W

General Minus Category:

anatomy

+ airplane
+ angel
+ animals, run into each other
+ animal, squashed
+ bat ∧∨><
+ beetle
+ bird(s) ∧∨><
+ bookends
+ bridge
+ bug

+ butterfly ∧∨><
+ cape, fur
+ child in costume
+ cloth, black
+ clouds
+ crow
+ dancer
+ deer, split
+ devil, flying
+ duck, taking off

+ eagle
+ felt
+ figures, human, lying back to
    back ∧∨
+ figure, human, winged
+ flying squirrel
+ hill with trees at shore line
+ insect, winged, spread out or
    flattened
+ land in water
+ landscape (aerial)
+ moth ∧∨><
+ mountain
+ ostrich, with plumage
+ owl
+ peacock(s) ∨
+ rabbit, with blanket, or flying
+ rams butting heads
+ ridge, mountain
+ robe, black ∨∧
+ standard, Roman
+ stole, mink
+ tightrope performers ∨
+ wings, airplane
+ woman, dancing ∧

− bee
− building(s)
− cockroach
− dragon
− fly
− flower ∨

− fowl
− fungus
− germ
− grasshopper
− hands, skeleton ∨
− head, cow ∨
− head, bird
− lake
− leaf(s)
− map
− meat
− monster, two-headed
− mops >
− mosquito
− phallic symbol <
− raccoon
− ray (fish)
− roller coaster
− sail
− skin(s), animal
− smoke reflected in water <
− spider
− steak
− tend
− United States
− vagina
− vase
− wig (with or without exten-
    sions)
− windshield, fogged
− woman, dancing ∨>

Dd1
See also D10

General Plus Category:

leg, animal or human

+ bone
+ exhaust from airplane
+ foot, animal
+ Italy

+ muscle ∨
+ nose, alligator

− figure, human

- fish
- Florida
- head, horned, skeletal

- head, horse
- spear
- stream (mountain)

Dd2
See also Dd8

General Plus Category:

human figure

+ bone
+ ear, donkey
+ ear, rabbit
+ elf
+ feeler, butterfly
+ foot, human $\vee$
+ handle(s), sword
+ hat
+ head, human
+ horn
  leg $\wedge\vee$:
    + human
    + table
+ spout, water fountain
+ stocking, Christmas

- bird
- bottle
- chair
- chicken, fried
- comb, rooster
- foot, human $\wedge$
- finger
- head, animal
  leg $\wedge\vee$:
    - animal
- mustache
- paw, cat
- penis
- tree, part of
- worm

Dd3
See also D9

General Plus Categories:

leg, any type; head of bird

+ antenna
+ beak, eagle
+ bone, animal
+ club
+ cone of rocket
+ feet
+ flower, petals $\vee$
+ match stick(s)
+ snake $\vee$
+ stick, hockey
+ swan $\vee$

- bell $\vee$
- carrot $\vee$
- face, ostrich
- finger
- hand
- root, tooth
- ski
- stinger, bee
- teat, on dog
- worm

D4
See also W

+ blanket, stretched out
+ bush(es)
+ carcass, animal
+ cloud(s)
+ curtain
+ drapery
+ driftwood
+ face, man, bearded
+ faces, two
+ figure, human (reclining)
+ goat (head at D7)
+ hill
+ landscape with clouds
+ man with wooden leg
+ peacock ∨
+ plumes
+ profile, man, bearded
+ smoke billows
+ train of costume
+ wing

− animal, on its back
− banana
− brush
− cat
− caterpillar
− circle, half
− dandelion, just burst <
− face, pig
− horse
− kangeroo
− leg, animal
− lion
− skin, rabbit
− snails
− snowflake
− stump, tree
− swordfish
− table (D3 supporting legs)
− tree, part

Dd5

+ face, human
+ head, Satan's
+ hill
+ stone

− bison
− breast
− lamb

D6

+ devil
+ elves
+ face
+ figure, hooded ∨
+ figure, human ∨
   head:
      + deer, with horns ∨
      + donkey
      + human
      + rabbit

+ mouth, fish, open ∧<
+ scissors
+ sling shot
+ snail
+ wishbone

− chair ∨
   head:
      − cow ∨
      − dog

− insect   head:
− mouse   − rat
− praying mantis   − mountain top

D7

General Plus Category:

human figure

+ animal, on hind legs   − chicken
+ devil   − dog
+ donkey (front or rear view)   − fish ∨>
+ figure(s), human (two)   − goat
+ rabbit ∧><   − insects, two
                                                  − skate (fish)
− bug

Dd8
See also Dd2

General Plus Category:

open mouth, any animal (usually >)

+ antennae, insect   + slingshot
+ bone(s)   + vase
+ figure(s), human
+ horns   − chair ∨
  legs: − hoof, cloven ∨
    + human ∨   legs:
+ plant, open   − animal
+ scissors   − frog
+ seed, tree   − tree with two trunks

D9
See also Dd3

General Plus Category:

bifurcated tools or instruments

+ beak, bird's, open (with or   + tweezers
    without Dd27)   + wishbone
+ chopsticks
+ feet, animal   − bells ∨
+ legs, animal   − dress, v-neck of
+ legs, human   − root, tooth
+ mechanical device   − tail, scorpion
+ swans, two ∨   − vagina
                                                  − vase

D10
See also Dd1 and Dd22

head:
+ alligator
+ bird
+ crocodile
+ legs, human
+ mouth, alligator or crocodile
+ nutcracker

− clouds
− coral
− fork
head:
  − hog
− plants, sea
− snake, mouth open (with or without Dd29)

D11
Starred responses may include D5

+ crags*
+ face, monkey
+ hills*
+ Indian chief
+ mask*
+ mountains*
+ nose
+ profile, human* <
+ stone
+ wing

− animal, horned
− breast, woman's
− fingers
− head, animal
− hump, buffalo*
− lion
− mouth, camel, open
− stethoscope

Dd22
See also D10

+ arrow
+ bayonet ∨
+ bone
+ cane
+ gun barrel
  leg:
    + animal
    + wooden
+ serpent
+ spear

+ tail, animal
+ tail, horse

− finger
− fish
− head, crane
− head, ostrich
− limb, dead tree >
  leg:
    − horse

D23
General Plus Category:

human face, head, or profile (either ∧ or ∨)

Dd24

+ figure, human   − breast
                                       − nipple

Dd25

+ cannon ∨   − snout, pig

Dd26

+ branch   − snake
+ twig   − tongue

Dd27

+ harbor   − morning glory, closed
                                       − vagina

− ear lobe

Dd29

+ bay   − leg
+ inlet   − worm

Dd30

+ dome (Ar)   + head, human
+ face, owl
+ hat, derby   − human, sitting
                                       − penis

CARD VI
Commonly and Rarely Chosen Beck Locations

Commonly chosen	Rarely chosen
Whole	Dd2
D1	D6
D3	Dd7
D4	Dd9
D5	Dd10
D8	Dd11
Dd21	D12
	Dd25
	Dd26
	Dd27
	Dd28
	D29
	Dd30
	Dd31

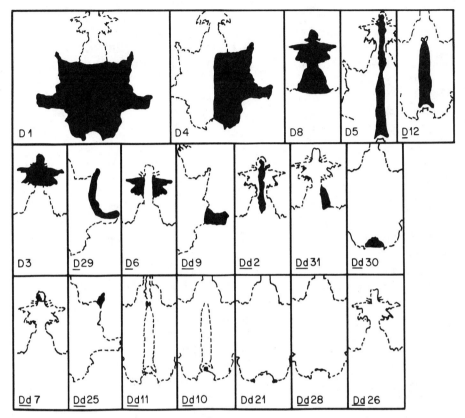

CARD VI. Large (D) and small (Dd) Beck areas

W
See also D1

Note: Starred responses may exclude Dd9 and/or D6

General Plus Categories:

animal pelt or rug; stringed musical instrument

+ airplane >
   animal:
      + being skinned
      + grotesque
+ badge
+ bears, two V
+ bell with handle*
+ blanket

+ blossom V
+ bottle*
+ bug ∧V
+ building with beacon top
+ candle, dripping wax
+ cat (cut open or flattened)
+ cathedral
+ cement, wet

+ chicken, opened up
+ Chinese decoration, hanging
+ church
+ cliff and water, with reflec-
    tion >
+ club*
+ coat rack
+ Christmas tree ornament
+ cross, covered
+ crumb plate V
+ desert
+ design
+ doll, rag
+ door
+ dust brush ∧V
+ duster V
+ dust pan* V
+ eruption, volcano
+ explosion, any
+ fan*
+ figures, human, leaning against
    post V
+ fountain
+ goose, flying >
+ gorge in mountain
+ hinge
+ ice sheet, melted
+ insect (squashed)
+ instrument, twirling
+ lamp, table
+ landscape, reflected >
+ lantern, Japanese
+ leaf, maple ∧V
+ leather
+ map, topographic
+ mask, jester's
+ mirror, hand* V
+ Oriental structure
+ painting, finger
+ pan, frying*
+ penis and pubic hair V
+ picture, from airplane <

+ piston
+ plant, cactus
+ rattle, baby or Indian* V
+ river between mountains
+ rug
+ sedan, Louis XIV style
+ shield V
+ snowman
+ statue
+ sweater coat
+ tiger
+ totem pole
+ tree* V
+ turtle
+ wastebasket, with handle*
+ weathervane
+ woods > <
+ worm, squashed
+ x-ray

− ameba
  animal:
    − sea
− Australia
− bat
− bear
− bee
− bird
− body, human
− bow and arrow <
− brain section
− butterfly
− catfish
− crayfish V
− crown
− duck
− face, dog >
− figure, human ∧V
− fish <>
− flower
− fly
− flying squirrel

- fox
- fowl, hung up
- frog
- germ
- hat
- head, dog
- Indian
- insides, human
- island continent
- jellyfish
- lion
- moth
- octopus

- pelt, bird's
- ray, manta ∨
- scorpion
- shrimp
- skin, fish
- skunk
- snowflake
- spider
- star, Jewish
- tent
- toupee
- windpipe and lungs

D1
See also W and D4

General Plus Categories:

animal skin or pelt; rug

+ animal, cut open
+ apes, back to back (on hook) ∨
+ book, open
+ candleholder
+ cloud(s)
+ coat, spread out ∨∧
+ container
+ door(s) (swinging) ∧∨
+ field
+ grass patch
+ lake, with landscape >
+ land, piece of
+ landscape, and reflection > <
+ leaf, maple or oak
+ map, topographic
+ mat
+ melon, inside of (excludes D9)
+ mountains and river, aerial
    view
+ photograph, microscopic
+ picture, rural

+ rock
+ sack
+ scoop of shovel
+ stone
+ twins, Siamese ∨

- ameba
- chest, x-ray of
- cocoon
- creature, winged
- ear muffs
- face, dog
- fish (opened up)
- flesh, piece of
- lungs
- moth
- rectum
- seashell
- star
- tail, animal
- vagina

Lower half of D1

+ buttocks   − face, bug
+ heads, human ∨

Midline

Note: Starred responses may include adjacent dark areas

+ crack in ground   + track, railroad
+ highway   + zipper
+ pipeline
+ shaft, mine   − caterpillar*
+ smoke left by rocket   − incision
+ spinal cord*   − worm*

Dd2
See also D5

+ beacon, traffic   + rod, ebony
+ candle   + shaft, rotating
+ candlestick   + snake
+ eel, electric   + thermometer
+ embryo   + wood, turned ∨∧
+ figure, human
+ esophagus (x-ray of)   − arms
+ god   − dancers, two
+ head, reptile   − fish
+ head and neck, insect   − fly
+ lamp, street   − grasshopper
+ leg, furniture   − knife
+ mast   − neck, ostrich
+ passage [An]   − needle, darning
+ penis (erect)   − rodent
+ phallic symbol   − spear
+ piston   − submarine
+ pole, iron   − termite

D3
See also D6 and D8

General Plus Category:

winged insect

+ airplane   + animal, winged

+ banner
+ beetle
+ bird
+ design
+ eagle
+ flower
  head:
    + cat
    + fox
    + wolf
+ insect
+ insignia
+ motif, military
+ owl
+ penis, winged
+ pigeon
+ rocket
+ seaweed
+ tadpole, winged
+ totem pole

+ tree
+ wings

− animal
− bat
− cat
− flying fish
− fish
  head:
    − insect
− lizard
− nervous system, embryonic
− shawl
− spider
− snail
− snake
− throne
− tiger
− witch doctor

D4
See also D1

General Plus Category:

human head or face ∨

+ ape ∨
+ Buddha
+ cloud(s)
+ dragon <
+ gorilla
  head:
    + dog, with pug nose ∨
    + lion ∨
    + wolf ∨
+ jungle
+ king, wearing crown ∨
+ landscape >
+ mask ∨
+ mountains ∧∨><

+ rock ∨∧
+ steamboat (with funnel) ><
+ tank, army <>
+ tombstone >

− animal
− bull, bucking >
− camera ∧∨
− lamb
− legs
− pants, pair of
− pig ∨
− United States <
− whale <

D5
See also Dd2 and D12

+ backbone
+ base, lamp
+ bone
+ canal
+ canal (An)
+ caterpillar
+ fissure in earth
+ gorge
+ knife
+ knife, handle of
+ lathe
+ lava stream
+ leg, furniture
+ mountain range
+ paddle, canoe
+ pen, fountain
+ penis
+ pipe
+ pole
+ projectile, path of

+ rack hat
+ river
+ road
+ shaft, coal mine
+ snake
+ spine
+ stick
+ thermometer
+ totem pole
+ trees <>
+ vagina
+ water, shooting up
+ wood, turned
+ worm
+ x-ray

− gate
− lady
− rabbit
− tree ∧∨

D6
See also D3

General Plus Category:

wings, any type

+ bird, any
+ branches
+ butterfly
+ cactus <∧
+ corona, sun
+ duck
+ feathers
+ flames or fire
+ flowers
+ geese, flock of
+ gulls, flying
+ headdress, Indiana
+ leaf(s)

+ light, rays of (sun)
+ mane, flowing
+ moth
+ pelts, bunch of
+ trees <>
+ weathervane

− antlers
− arms
− membrane
− stalactites
− vagina
− whiskers, human

Projections from D6

+ asparagus tips
+ beaks, birds, any
+ heads, turtles
+ turtles

− icicles
− opener, can
− pin, rolling
− wolfhounds

Dd7
See also D3

+ animal, microscopic
+ bug
+ creature, with whiskers
+ eyes, animal
+ fist
+ hands, clasped
+ handle, cane
head or face:
   + bird
   + bug
   + cat
   + cobra
   + human

head or face:
   + insect
   + owl
   + snake
   + turtle
+ mouth, animal

− figure(s), human
− heads, bugs, two
− nose, animal, any

D8
See also D3

+ bird, on tree stump
+ bug, crawling from cocoon
+ Crucifix
+ dragonfly
figure, human
   + on pedestal
   + on hilltop
+ flames and smoke
+ flower
+ fountain
+ gravestone
+ insect
+ light, with rays emanating
+ lighthouse, on rock
+ oil well
+ pedestal

+ scarecrow
+ seaweed
+ spire, church
+ statuette
+ totem pole(s)
+ tree

− animal
− bell
− bottle
− caterpillar
head:
   − cat
   − catfish
   − wolf
− mountains

− potato masher   − turtle
− spinal cord

Dd9

+ castle >   + smokestack >
+ figure, human >   + tower >
+ foot, animal
   head: − boot >
     + dog ∧∨   − glass, drinking >
     + fox ∧∨   head:
     + wolf ∧∨   − bird >
+ leg, animal >   − camel ∧∨
+ peninsula   − nose, animal ∧∨
+ rock formation   − pole
+ sleeve   − stalactite <
+ smoke >   − stick, candy

Dd10

Note: Starred responses may include adjacent dark area

+ eggs   + sacks
+ eyes, insect   + testicles
+ heads, human*
+ heads, insect*   − claws*
+ insect(s)*   − flap, in throat
+ jewels   − spinal cord* section
+ rear end, animal*   − vagina

Dd11

+ brain, ape or monkey   − bridge
+ eggs   − butterfly
+ jewels   − embryos
+ lights, street   − flames
+ molecule, splitting   − flowers
+ shell, clam, open   − kidneys
                                           − lungs
− ants   − mice
− beans   − nuts
− birds   − testicles
− boats   − tonsils

- vagina
- "W"

- woodpeckers
- worms

D12
See also D5

+ candlestick
+ cocoon
+ guided missile
+ passageway
+ pole
+ river
+ road
+ rocketship
+ shaft, mine
+ spinal column

+ trunk, tree
+ umbrella stand

- boat
- figure(s), human
- hot dog, in bun
- needle, hypodermic
- penis
- rectum
- spear
- vagina, opening of

Dd21

+ claw
+ feet, insect
+ hair, tufts V
+ heads, snake
+ heads, turkey
+ hooks
+ horns, cow

+ pincers, crab
+ talons, eagle
+ tongs, ice

- hands
- teeth

Dd25

+ beads, strung
+ figure, human
+ Florida V
+ foot, human
+ head, woman
+ mountain
+ paw, animal
+ prow, ship
+ shoe
+ toe

- cigarette lighter and flame
- chicken
- foot, pig
- hand
- head, dog
- penis
- stalactite
- wing(s)

Dd26

+ antennae   + whiskers, any
+ rays of light
                              − horns, animal

Dd28

+ claws, crab   − breakwater
+ fangs   − feelers, fish
+ heads, birds ∨   − knives
+ jaws, snake   − labia minora
+ talons   − x-rays

D29

+ head, human, with arms up   + shore line
+ profile, human

Dd30

+ gulf   mouth: (may include Dd21)
+ insect pit   − animal
+ lamp   − bird
                                − snake

CARD VII
Commonly and Rarely Chosen Beck Locations

Commonly chosen	Rarely chosen
Whole	Dd5
D1	Dd6
D2	Dd8
D3	D9
D4	D10
D7	Dd11
	Dd21
	Dd24
	Dd25
	Dd26
	Dd27

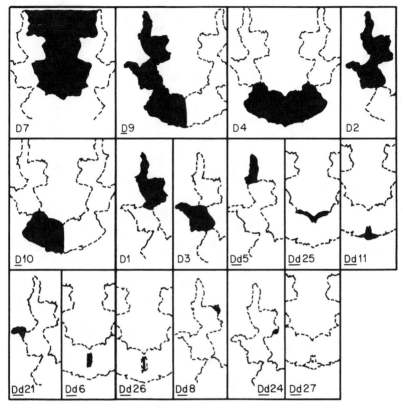

CARD VII. Large (D) and small (Dd) Beck areas

W
See also D9

General Plus Categories:

two human figures ∧∨; natural, topographic entities based on a central
    space, such as canyon, harbor, lake

+ apes, two   + carving
+ archway ∨   + cave mouth ∨
+ bowl   + clouds
+ bread, piece of, broken   + coat of arms
+ bridge ∨   + coast line
+ busts, two   + collar, for woman's dress ∨
+ canal and lock   + crown ∨
+ candy, cotton   + design, symmetrical

+ dogs, two (dressed as women)
+ dolls, two
+ driftwood
+ food, fried, pieces of
+ fountain
+ furpiece
+ gate (fancy) V
+ ghosts, two
+ horseshoe
+ house, Japanese V
+ islands, map of
+ lamp, kerosene
+ map, pieces of
+ marine life
+ monument
+ mountains, above cloud
+ necklace
+ paper, torn
+ peel, orange
+ peninsula(s)
+ piecrust, out of shape
+ pile or pieces of (metal, candy,
     ice, etc.)
+ puddle (mud)
+ puzzle, piece of
+ rabbits
+ reef, coral
+ rock(s)
+ scarf (fur) V
+ sculpture work
+ seacoast
+ smoke
+ snow, melting
+ spittoon
+ stadium
+ stone(s)
+ stool V
+ twins, Siamese
+ vase
+ wreath

− animal, cut apart
− bed, end view V

− beefsteak
− bird
− blueprint
− body, human
− bone
− bracelet
− bug
− cap, fur V
− chain
− chair V
− chops, pork
− cover, bed
− crab
− figure, human V
− fly
− footprint
− fungus
− frog
− grass plot with shrubs
− hairdo, long V
− insect V
− legs, frog
− mask
− moth
− mouth, insect ∧>
− nutcracker
− pincers
− plants
− ponies, two
− potatoes, fried
− rag
− sheep, two
− shrubs
− skin, animal
− sleeves, kimono
− stove, old fashioned
− table ∧V
− trap
− tweezers
− vise
− wig V
− womb, open

D1
See also D2 and D9

General Plus Category:

human head or face (may be deformed)

+ ape
+ cameo
+ cloud(s)
+ doll, crude
+ dwarf
+ goblin
+ gorgon
+ gnome
  head:
    + animal
    + dog
    + elephant, with trunk V
    + monkey
    + rabbit
+ Indian
+ mask
+ rabbit V
+ sculpture, modernistic
+ statue

− breeches, riding, and boots
− camel V
− cat ∧V
− Central America V<
− chair

− chicken
− coffee grinder, with lid
− duck
− England
− excreta, human
− face, snarling (Dd8 nose, Dd below Dd8 mouth)
− fish
− Florida V
− France
− goose
− hand, thumb up
  head:
    − alligator
    − donkey
− horse V
− leg, table V
− mountain
− pipe, smoker's <
− porcupine V
− skunk
− squirrel
− stomach
− tiger
− turkey

D2
See also W and D9

Note: most quadrupeds are seen <

General Plus Category:

human figure

+ ape
+ angel
+ animal <
+ cloud(s)
+ cracker(s), animal
+ dog (any) >∧

+ dwarf
+ elephant, head and trunk
+ face, clown
+ hemisphere, Western V
+ island(s)
+ lamb <

+ map
+ mountain(s)
+ North and South America ∨
+ rabbit
+ sculpture
+ seaweed
+ Spain and France
+ stone(s)

− ameba
− arm
− calf
− cat ∨∧<
− chair
− chicken
− cow ∧<
− donkey

− England
− fish
− fox >
− hair, long ∧∨
− horse, reared up
− kangaroo
− lion <
− pot, coffee
− sheep <
− shrimp, fried ∧∨
− shrub
− thumb and fingers <
− tiger <
− tree, part of
− turkey
− United States
− "W" >

D3
See also D2

General Plus Categories:

human head or face (may be deformed); animal head or face (except
    horned animals)

+ animal head
+ bear >∧
+ candy, cotton
+ creature
+ dwarf
+ figure, comic ∨
+ gargoyle
+ gnome
+ goblin
+ island
+ mask
+ Rock of Gibraltar
+ rock(s)
+ South America >
+ Spain

− Alaska
− beard
− beehive <
− brooch
− buffalo
− Central America
− cleaver, meat (Dd21 as handle)
− cornucopia <
− dinosaur
− ham
− head, buffalo
− head, goat
− horse
− mug, shaving
− pig
− sheep
− shirt on line

D4
See also D10

General Minus Category:

infrahuman mammal

+ apron, short
+ arch(way) ∨
+ background for painting
+ bat
+ bird ∧∨
+ book, open
+ bowl
+ bridge
+ butterfly
+ cloud(s)
+ collar
+ hill
+ hinge, open
+ hips
+ insect, winged ∧∨
+ land with canal
+ mountain(s)
+ neckpiece
+ paper, torn
+ pelvis
+ ribbon
+ rock(s)
+ shell, open
+ stone(s)

+ water color wash
+ wings

− arms and shoulders
− boat
− bow
− buttocks
− caterpillar
− chair
− couch
− crab
− cradle
− crown ∧∨
− fan
− fly
− horse, rocking
− map
− pants (short)
− shoes, big
− spinal cord
− teeter-totter
− tub
− x-ray

Dd5

General Plus Category:

animal tail

+ caterpillar
+ coiffure
+ comb
+ feather
+ hair, sticking up
+ headdress
+ leg ∨
+ plume
+ smoke

+ tassel (hat)
+ trunk, elephant
+ worm

− arrow
− castle
− claw, lobster
− colon (An)
− dog

- horn, animal
- intestine(s)
- knife
- leg, any
- mantilla
- mountain
- phallic symbol
- pistol
- plant

- potato, sweet
- reptile
- saw <
- snake
- stalactite
- sword
- volcano
- wig
- wing, bird

Dd6
See also Dd26

General Plus Categories:

human figure ∧∨; flowing body of water between land areas

+ anus
+ bridge
+ dam
+ doll
+ gateway
+ guided missile(s)
+ hinge
+ holder, cigarette
+ post(s)
+ projectile(s)
+ river
+ twig(s)
+ vagina
+ water
+ zipper

- blood vessel (drawing up)
- cannon(s)
- cap
- casket
- couch
- fence
- fly
- hat
- house ∧∨<
- insect(s)
- mustache
- penis, diagram of
- roots (in ground)
- spine
- tree(s)
- worm(s)

D7

General Plus Category:

natural, topograph entities based on a central space, such as lake, bay, canyon

+ arrow (head) ∨
+ bottle, perfume
+ cave entrance
+ cloud, mushroom
+ fan
+ head, human ∨

+ helmet
+ lamp ∨
+ mushroom ∨
+ ocean
+ pagoda ∨
+ pool (swimming)

+ pot
+ shield
+ Sphinx
+ tent V
+ urn
+ vase

− airplane
− bell
− body, human V
− dress, girl's
− face, cat
− grass plot

− heart
− keyhole
− mountain V
− mouth, animal or human ∧>
− path
− river
− shovel
− stomach
− trap, fish
− tree V
− uterus
− window

Dd8

+ cliffs
+ cock's comb
+ figures, human
+ forehead
+ head, bird
+ horns
+ icicles
+ snail, horned
+ snout, seal
+ stalagmite(s)
+ splash of water
+ village on cliff

− beak
− devil, with spear
− face, human ∧<
− hair
− head, squirrel
− monster
− seashell
− teeth
− turtle

D9
See also W

General Plus Category:

human figure (∧ or V)

+ animal, with human head
+ art, primitive
+ cloud(s)
+ dogs, two, kissing >
+ elephant >V
+ mountain
+ rocks, piled or balanced
+ stones

− horse
− key
− lake
− pillows
− sheep >
− sideburn
− tree

D10
See also D4

+ clouds ∨∧
+ crag
+ dog ∧∨>
  head:
    + dog
+ hill(s)
+ land
+ pillow
+ support(s)

− animal, crouching
− building
− blood vessels, enlarged
− cat
− chair, rocking
− child (sleeping)
− coccyx

− fan
− football player
− hat, woman's
  head:
    − horse ∨
    − human
    − lion ><
    − monkey
    − whale >
− knight (chess)
− lake
− lion ><
− mouse
− rabbit
− South America
− squirrel
− tree trunk

Dd11

General Plus Category:

building

+ archway ∨
+ eagle
+ entrance
+ figures, human, two
+ insignia, winged ∨
+ wings

− boat

− head, goat (skeleton of) ∨
− ice cream, dish of, melting
− jello
− toadstool ∨
− stamen
− sun setting, with clouds ∨
− whipped cream

Dd21

+ arm
+ finger
+ garment, piece of
+ hand
+ head, snake

+ horn
+ paw
+ tail, dog
+ thumb
+ trunk, elephant

- appendix
- child >
- dragon
- face, witch >
- feather
- head, animal

- island
- leg, animal or human
- peninsula
- receiver, telephone
- teat, cow
- worm

Dd26
See also D6

+ Christ on cross
+ figure, human
+ lamp post

+ vagina

- body, human, cut in half

Dd27

+ anus
+ post(s)
+ windows

- bullets
- teeth
- whiskers

CARD VIII
Commonly and Rarely Chosen Beck Locations

Commonly chosen	Rarely chosen
Whole	Dd3
D1	D6
D2	D7
D4	Dd21
D5	Dd22
D8	Dd23
	Dd24
	Dd25
	Dd26
	Dd27
	D28
	Dd29
	D31
	Dd32

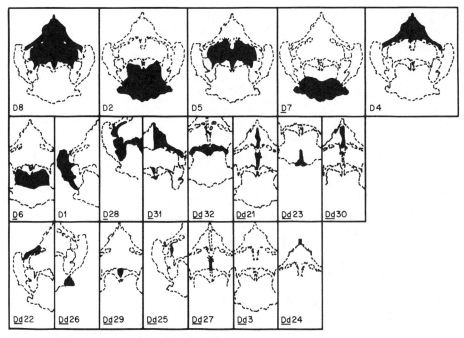

CARD VIII. Large (D) and small (Dd) Beck areas

W

Note: Starred responses may exclude both D1 without change in form
quality scoring, though they should not then be scored as W. The
general response categories also apply to these responses

General Plus Categories:

ornaments, such as emblem, badge, jewelry; gross human anatomy,
such as "insides" or medical illustrations

General Minus Categories:

face, animal or human; insect

+ art, modern   + color print
+ astrological symbol   + crown
+ boat (end view)*   + design
+ bowl   + doorknocker ∧∨
+ bubble, iridescent   + drawing, scientific
+ carousel   + float, parade
+ chandelier   + flower (with leaf)* ∨
+ Christmas tree (with presents)   + foliage*
+ coat of arms   + headdress (ornate)

+ hill*
+ ice cream (brick of)
+ iris ∨ (flower)
+ kaleidoscope
+ landscape, mountainous* ∧>
+ lantern, Japanese*
+ monument
+ moss, sea
+ mountain (scene)* ∧>
+ pagoda
+ Painted Desert
+ pyramid
+ quartz
+ reefs, coral
+ rocket*
+ rocketship*
+ rocks*
+ seal (crest)
+ seashell(s)
+ shield
+ ship (with sails) (end view)*
+ sign, electric
+ skeleton, drawing of
+ stain [biology]
+ tropical scene
+ underwater scene
+ vase ∧∨
+ volcano (erupting) ∨*
+ x-ray (chest)*

− bat
− basket
− bed
− biological illustration*

− bird
− bivalve*
− butterfly* ∨∧
− cabbage
− cage*
− cave*
− crab (opened)*
− egg, Easter
− figure, human
− fish*
− frog (dissected)*
− globe
− head, peacock
− heart
− intestines
− jellyfish*
− map
− mask
− moth* ∧∨
− paramecium
− pelvic cavity ∨
− rainbow*
− rubbish, pile of*
− scarf(s)
− shell, crab or lobster
− skull, animal*
− stalactites
− statue
− stomach*
− torch ∨
− tree*
− turtle
− uterus

D1

General Plus Categories:

canine; feline; rodent

General Minus Category:

insect

+ animal
+ armadillo

+ art figure
+ badger

+ bear
+ beaver
+ ferret
+ Gila monster
+ gopher
+ groundhog
+ handle, bowl
+ lizard
+ mink
+ mole
+ mongoose
+ otter
+ pig
+ possum
+ racoon
+ salamander
+ sloth
+ weasel
+ wolverine
+ woodchuck

− bird
− blood
− boar

− buffalo
− bull
− camel
− cloud(s)
− cow
− dinosaur
− dolphin
− dragon
− fallopian tube
− figure, human
− fish
− flower
− frog
− goat
− lamb
− lobster
− lung(s)
− porpoise
− ram
− reptile
− seal
− sheep
− shrimp
− tadpole

D2
See also D6

General Plus Category:

any species of flower ∧∨

General Minus Category:

internal organ (An)

+ atomic bomb blast
+ butterfly(s)
+ cliff(s)
+ cloak ∧∨
+ coral
+ explosion
+ fire
  head:
    + cows, two ∨
+ ice cream

+ jacket, gaudy
+ jello
+ landscape
+ moth
+ mountain(s)
+ petal, flower
+ quartz
+ rock(s) (colored)
+ sculpture, cubist
+ slide(s), biology

+ smoke, colored
+ stone(s) (precious)
+ suit, grotesque ∨
+ sunset(s)
+ tissue, body, stained
+ waistcoat ∨
+ wings, butterfly

− animal (sea)
− bat ∨
− buttocks
− chest (An)
− cloth, torn
− crown ∨
− dog ∨

− fur
head:
   − antelopes, two ∨
   − dog <
   − lamb
   − lion <
− insect
− leaf
− orange
− pelvis
− scarecrow
− spinal cord section, stained
− steak split in middle
− vagina
− waist and hip area

Dd3

General Plus Category:

bony anatomy

+ blouse, woman's
+ bones
+ corset
+ costume, white, ruffled
+ medical insignia
+ skeleton
+ skull, steer

− boat
− Buddha
− buoy
− cave
− ducks, flight of <
face:
   − goat
   − human
   − tiger

− flowers
− funnel
− god, statue of
− head, goat
− lobster
− mask
− netting
− pagoda ∨
− scarab
− shears
− teeth
− vines
− web

D4
See also D8

General Plus Category:

Arboreal botany responses

+ airplane
+ archway

+ butterfly
+ cap, fur

+ castle on hill
+ cliffs(s)
+ cover, bowl
+ crag
+ crown
+ foliage
+ forest
+ hat
+ house
+ ice
+ mountains(s)
+ rocket (nose of)
+ rock(s)
+ roof
+ roots, tree
+ stump, tree
+ support (Ab)
+ temple
+ water, streaming down

− abdomen
− animal (sea)
− antlers (deer) ∨
− arrow (head)
− bat ∧∨
− beard ∨

− boomerang
− breast <
− cell, microscopic
− cloud
− crab
− crawfish
− creature, prehistoric
− dinosaur(s)
− figure(s), human
− fish ∧>
− frog
− fur
− head, antlered animal ∨
− insect
− kite (fish)
− lobster(s)
− octopus
− polyp
− pubic (with hair) ∨
− ray (fish)
− sail, ship
− scorpion
− ship
− silk
− skull
− spider

D5

+ accordion
+ cliff(s)
+ cloth, (torn)
+ corset
+ flag(s)
+ ice, cakes of
+ jacket, laced ∨
+ ledge
+ paper, torn
+ pillow
+ rock(s)
+ sails, ship
+ sky
+ trees

+ water

− bat
− bird
− butterfly
− can, trash (cracked)
− crown ∨
− fish (mouth Ds3) <
− flowers(s)
− fur
− hay
− head, tropical fish <
− house ∧∨
− lake

− leaf(s)
− lungs
− map
− moth
− pelvis

− ribs
− seashell
− shoulders, human
− spider
− trousers ∨

D6
See also D2

General Plus Categories:

flower; human head or face

+ apes
+ buffaloes (water)
+ butterfly ∧∨
+ cow(s)
+ design
    head or face:
       + animal
       + ape
       + cattle
       + lamb(s)
+ ice cream
+ petals, flower
+ quartz
+ rock formation
+ sheep

− cats
− donkey

− frogs
  head or face:
    − bear
    − dog
    − frog
    − lion
    − pig(s)
    − rodent
    − tiger(s)
− larynx
− lungs
− moose
− potatoes
− rabbit(s)
− sea lions
− toads
− tower <
− web

D7
See also D2

+ bloodhounds
+ bloodstains
+ butterfly ∧∨
+ coat, fur
+ crystal
+ glass, cut
+ hips
+ ice, orange
+ mountain
+ rock(s)
+ seashell

+ stone(s)
+ sun
+ wings, butterfly

− bat
− bird
− bread, loaf
− buttocks
− cat(s)
− duck
− face, human

- hairdo
- head, penguin ∨
- head, sheep ∨
- leaves
- monster ∨

- sassafras
- tent
- thighs
- tree
- turban

D8
See also D4

+ bed, ornate, end view
+ church (inside of)
+ flower ∨
+ hill
+ rocket
+ sailboat
+ tree

- anatomy, unspecified
- butterfly
- fish
- head and body, gorilla
- insect (water)
- lakes with land between
- shell, crab

Dd21
See also Dd27 and 30

+ bones, two, any
+ rocket
+ spinal column
+ spinal cord, insect

- esophagus
- figure, human
- gearshift lever
- mud streak
- smoke, rising

Dd22

+ arm and hand
+ branch, tree
+ hand
+ horn(s)
+ roots(s), tree

+ wood, dead

- alligator
- Central America <
- figure, human
- paw, wolf

Dd23

+ club(s), golf
+ collar and ruffle
+ genitalia, female
+ mountain (snow-covered)
+ pathway

- arms
- bladder
- bone
- canoe
- hourglass

Dd24

+ feelers
+ figures, human, two
+ legs, human ∨
+ trees

- arrows
- birds
- pincers

Dd25

+ fish
+ island
+ rocket
+ stone

− dog, lying down

− figure, human
− lake
− otter
− submarine
− tadpole

Dd26

+ dog ∨
  head: (usually <)
    + animal ∧∨<
    + bison ∨
    + dog ∨
    + sheep ∧∨
+ rock (colored)
+ Sphinx <
+ turret <

− bird >
− bottle, perfume <
− cone, ice cream >

− elephant
− figure, human, in chair <
  head: (usually <)
    − duck
    − horse ∧∨
    − human
    − kangaroo
    − sea horse
    − turtle
− monkey <
− shell, conch
− turtle

Dd27
See also Dd21

+ pen [writing]
+ pole (May)
+ spear
+ stick

− alligator
− snake
− teardrop
− worm

D28

+ hen ∨
+ rooster ∨
+ water, bodies of ∧∨

− boy, wearing hat ∨
− clouds ∨

Dd29

+ bell ∨
+ bottle, milk ∨
+ pendant
+ stirrup ∨

− bridge

− crutch, upper part
− statue
− tower ∨
− vagina
− wishbone

Dd30
See also Dd21

+ caterpillar
+ club (knobbed)
+ eel
+ flute
+ rocket
+ snake

+ spinal column (piece of)
+ twig
+ worm

− swordfish

D31

− bird
− devil

− dog, mouth open
− figure, human, reclining

Dd32

+ bird
+ gull, sea

+ lamp (Aladdin's)

CARD IX
Commonly and Rarely Chosen Beck Locations

Commonly chosen	Rarely chosen
Whole	D2
D1	Dd7
D3	D10
D4	D21
Dd5	Dd22
D6	Dd23
D8	Dd24
D9	Dd25
D11	Dd26
D12	Dd27
	Dd28
	Dd29
	Dd30
	Dd31
	Dd32

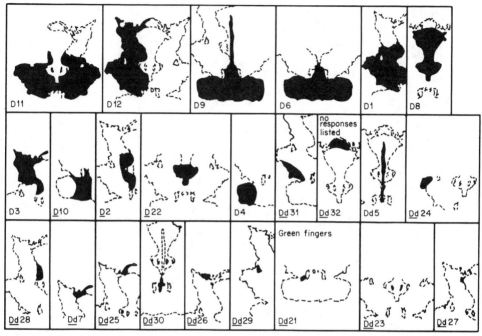

CARD IX. Large (D) and small (Dd) Beck areas

W

General Plus Category:

any species of flower

General Minus Categories:

face (animal or human); insect

+ art, modern
+ candle, dripping wax
+ cauldron, witch's
+ clothes, on a person (Ws) ∨
+ coat of arms
+ decorative piece
+ design
+ eruption
+ fan ∨
+ figure, human ∨
+ fireworks
+ flames

+ flower arrangement
+ fountain
+ garden, with fountain
+ hat, any ∧∨
+ Indian ∨
+ lady, with parasol ∨
+ lamp
+ landscape ∧<
+ map
+ mask, goblin
+ medical chart
+ movement (Ab)

+ ornament, glass
+ paint, smear of
+ painting, any ∧<>
+ palette, artist's
+ philosophy of life (Ab)
+ pigeons, sitting below
      draperies ∨
+ plant, exotic, with red
      blossoms ∨
+ rocks, colored
+ scenery ∧∨<>
+ Spring
+ tree ∨
+ vase
+ waterfall
+ whirling object with water
      shooting out
+ woman, gazing into mirror, and
      reflection
+ women

− anatomy
− bird
− bivalve, illustration of
− blood

− brain, cross-section of
− bug
− butterfly
− cathedral ∨
− clouds
− crab
− fungus
− head, cat's
− hill
− island(s)
− jellyfish ∨∧
− leaf
− lobster
− moth
− rocket ship
− sea life
− seashell ∨∧
− shears, garden <
− skull
− sunrise
− throat ∨
− tissue, under microscope
− tree ∧
− x-ray

W minus D6

+ seaweed

− crab
− face, human

D1
See also D11

General Plus Categories:

human figure; blunt-nosed animal, (muzzle at midline)

General Minus Category:

specific geography responses

+ animal
+ ape (Dd24 as head)
+ buffalo
+ busts, human
+ child on toy, riding <

+ cloud
+ coat, woman's ∨
+ face, Irish (outer edge as pro-
      file)
+ foliage

+ forest
+ grass patch
+ head, human (profile Dd24)
+ jacket
+ jade
+ land
+ lawn
+ leaves, mass of
+ map
+ monster
+ motorcycle rider >
+ nature scene
+ pig (muzzle at midline)
+ pottery, pieces of
+ profile
+ shrubbery
+ skirt(s)
+ smoke
+ trees, massed in woods
+ water, green

− animal life, undersea
− baboon
− bear
− beryl
− bird(s)
− bottle(s)
− butterfly
− cactus
− chipmunk
− circle
− dinosaur
− dog ∧>∨
− dragon ∧>
− elephant

− fan
− fish(es)
− flower sepals
− frog
− harp
− hat ∨
− head, hippopotamus (snout at Dd24)
− head, hog (snout at Dd24)
− heart
− intestines
− leaf
− lion ∨∧
− liver
− lungs ∨∧
− metal, rusted
− peacock ∨
− pitcher, water
− plant
− porcupine
− rabbit ∧>
− rock(s)
− sailboat
− seaweed
− State (Ge.)
− thistle
− toadstool(s) ∨
− tree
− tree stump <
− trenches
− turkey ∨
− valley
− willow ∨
− wing(s)

D2

+ alligator
+ crocodile
  face:
    + animal
    + dragon

+ goat
  head:
    + camel
    + cow
    + crocodile

+ deer
+ dog
+ elk <
+ moose
+ reindeer, with antlers
+ mountain(s)
+ rock(s), in landscape

− bacteriology slide
− beak, rooster's >
− castle
  face:
    − on moon <

− turtle
head:
  − bird
  − fish
head:
  − horse
  − monkey
− man, prehistoric
− monkey
− snake
− tree, broken <
− walrus

D3
See also D12

General Plus Category:

human figure (∧ only)

+ animal
+ bird ∧∨
+ blaze
+ blood smear
+ caricature
+ cliff
+ clown
+ crab
+ creature, mythical
+ deer
+ dragon
+ face, human
+ fire
+ flower cup (both D3)
+ ghost
+ gremlin
  head:
    + devil, with horns
    + human
    + moose
+ hill ∧<
+ land, arid
+ lava

+ lobster ∧∨
+ map, relief, with mountain and
    fords
+ mask
+ moose, running >
+ mountain(s)
+ owl, on twig ∨
+ parrot ∨
+ petal, flower
+ plant, insect-catching (both D3)
+ rock <
+ sand beach
+ Scandinavia
+ skirt, orange (both D3) ∨
+ smoke, trail of
+ unicorn
+ wing, any
+ witch

− ape
− bison
− body, butterfly
− carrot

- chicken
- clouds
- club, caveman's
- cow
- dirigible <
- dog
- fish
- foot, human
- gold, vein of
  head:
  - elephant
- horn
- insect
- island
- leg, chicken, cooked ∧∨
- lung(s)

- man ∨
- orchid
- praying mantis
- rat
- scorpion
- sea horse (with Dd)
- serpent, sea
- shrimp
- sun, going down <
- thistle, prickly part
- tiger
- tissue, body
- toadstool ∨
- whale
- woods

D4
See also D6

General Plus Category:

human face or head

General Minus Category:

animal face or head

+ bust <
+ caricature of man
+ flower
+ head (any position)
+ rock

- apple
- bird
- blood
- buffalo ∧∨

- chicken
- dog
- elephant
- eye, ant
- fence
- fish
- lungs
- meat
- pottery, clay
- vase

Dd5

General Minus Category:

animal, any genus

+ backbone, human
+ bat, baseball
+ bone
+ brook

+ candle (stick)
+ cane
+ cascade
+ cooking spit

+ dagger
+ Eternal Light
+ fountain
+ horizon, town, sky and shore >
+ hose, water
+ lake, edge of >
+ lamp, floor (with D8)
+ landscape >
+ nervous system, embryonic
+ obelisk
+ river
+ road
+ rocket
+ sceptre
+ smoke, rising
+ smokestack
+ stalactite
+ stem, flower
+ stem, mushroom (Dd22 as
    mushroom)

+ stem, tree
+ sword
+ tube
+ watercolors, running together
    water:
    + current of
    + shooting up

− arrow
− body, insect
− esophagus
− gun <
− horn, animal
− peninsula
− penis
− rainbow
− tree
− trunk, elephant

D6
See also D4

+ babies, newborn ∧>
+ ballerinas, four
+ balloons
+ blossom(s)
+ bomb, atomic, cloud ∨
+ bonnet ∨
+ candleholder
+ cloud(s)
+ fire
+ flowers ∨∧
+ fountain, base of
+ heads, human ∨∧
+ hoopskirts
+ man >
+ mushroom ∨
+ petals, flower
+ pillows
+ pots, flower
+ powder puffs
+ rock(s)

+ roses, pink
+ sherbet, raspberry
+ shoulder pads, football ∨
+ shoulders, human ∨
+ skirt
+ smoke
+ stain, berry
+ stone(s)
+ tornado
+ vase, base of

− animal(s)
− ant, bottom view
− apples
− bag, punching
− basket
− bird
− boat
− buffaloes
− buttocks

- caterpillar
- cocoanuts
- collar, woman's V
- eagle
- gums (mouth)
- heads, elephant, two ∧<∧
- island
- marshmallows
- ostrich V
- pigs

- radishes
- rectangles
- reservoir, water >
- section in microscope V
- shark, pink
- skin, burned
- toadstools, four
- vagina
- wings

D4 plus D10, i.e., half of D6
See also D4 and D6

+ baby ∧>
+ bust of human
+ fetus

+ figure, human, sitting or
    squatting <∧

- chipmunk <

Dd7
See also Dd25

+ antlers
+ arm of statue
+ bones, connected
+ branch(es), tree
+ claw, crab or lobster
+ fingernails
+ fire
+ gun(s)
+ hand(s)
+ horn(s), animal
+ horn (music)
+ leg, bird V∧
+ root(s) V

+ sword(s)
+ telescope
+ tree(s) ∧V>
+ vegetable growth

- dog
- eagle
- feeler(s), bug
- figure, human (in any move-
    ment)
- lightning
- map
- wing(s)

D8

General Plus Categories:

circular, glass object; body of water

+ bottle top
+ canyon
+ cave
+ chandelier
+ chasm V
+ design

+ dress
+ dummy, dressmaker's
+ fiddle
+ figure, human, female
+ garden vista ∧>
+ hole

+ hourglass
+ lamp
+ landscape, various types
+ picture, under water
+ shaker, salt ∨
+ sky
+ vase ∧∨
+ ventilator on ship
+ violin
+ water

− animal
− bell
− buttocks
− chest cavity
− church
− crab (with both Dd25's)

− elephant ∨
− face, animal
− globe, world
− head, creature ∨∧
− holder, screwdriver
− kettle, tea
− keyhold
− man, funny ∨
− masher, potato
− mask
− moon
− skull
− skyscraper
− Sphinx
− uterus
− veil ∨

D8 with both D3

+ canyon
+ flower
+ mountains and canyon

+ skirt, open
+ volcano

D9

+ atom bomb explosion
+ chandelier ∧∨
+ explosion ∨
+ fan
+ flower ∨
+ fountain
+ lampshade ∨
+ mushrooms ∨
+ roses, bunch of

+ spindle, office ∨
+ street light
+ tree ∨
+ umbrella

− barrel of wine
− figure, human
− hammer ∨
− island

D10

Note: human faces and heads are scored plus for this detail only when
the response includes both D10's and both D4's, i.e., D6. If D10 or
both D10 are singled out, these responses are scored minus.

+ bird
+ buttock
+ head, elephant's ∨ (with D5)
+ penguin
+ poppy

+ rock
+ roots, tree, in burlap
+ ruffle, dress
+ tulip ∧∨

- animal
- breast
- lung

- map
- pear
- vase

D11
See also D1

+ bat
+ butterfly
+ pelvic area

- beard
- cradle
- cup
- rock

D12
See also D3

+ creature
+ god, Chinese
+ landscape <
+ workmanship on vase

- chicken
- fungus
- toadstool
- tree V
- x-ray

D21

+ claws
+ fingers
+ hand(s)
+ toes

- guns, machine

- icicles
- keys, piano (with Dd)
- nerves of teeth
- spears
- teeth

Dd22

+ bridge
+ cavern
+ columns
+ doors, swinging
+ eyes, goblin, mask, or monster
   face: (may include adjacent
     dark areas)
     + Halloween
     + human
+ garden, terraced
+ jack-o-lantern
+ lace
+ lakes
+ mask (may include adjacent
   dark head: areas)
+ pillars

+ ponds
+ tunnel
+ wall, castle

- candles, four
- egg white, rotten
   face: (may include adjacent
     dark areas)
     - animal
- fish
   head:
     - flatfish
     - fly
     - octopus
- jellyfish
- mechanism, auto

– mushroom   – skull
– pelvis

Dd23
See also Dd22

+ doors   + slits in material
+ excavations   + windows
+ eyes
+ holes for animal's home   – island
+ holes shot through   – moon, quarter
+ hollows, two   – mouth
+ ponds   – nostrils, horse
                                        – shells, oyster

Dd24
See also D1

+ dog, Scotty   head:
+ face, animal   + camel
  head: + ram
    + bear
                                        – face, human

Dd25
See also Dd7

+ archway (both Dd25)   + stick(s)
+ bridge (both Dd25)   + tentacle(s)
+ claw(s), crab
+ dome, building (both Dd25)   – bone, fish
+ feeler(s)   – hook
+ finger(s)   – Italy, heel and foot of
+ lights, Northern   – nerves
+ liquid, squirted   – whisker(s)
+ smoke from gun

Dd26

+ bugle   – boat
+ figure, human ∧>   – dog
+ gun ∧>   – foot, human
+ horn (music)   – nose
                                        – saw

Dd27

+ figure, human ∧>

− angelfish
− animal

− bull
− head, dog
− penguin
− squirrel

Dd28

+ breast
+ stomach

− balloon
− blood splotch

− dog
− head, animal
− moss
− tank, fuel, airplane <

Dd29

+ Caspian Sea
+ lake
+ watershed

− Africa ∨
− bell

− cat
− face, lady
− figure, human
− North America ∨
− triangle

Dd30

+ blood, drops of
+ bone
+ tallow, dripping
+ tears, dripping

− alligator

− caterpillar
− intestine
− penis
− root, tree
− vagina

Dd31
See also D1

+ cover, kitchen utensil >
+ face, animal
+ face, human

− breast and nipple

Dd32

Note: Responses to this area often include the long extension of both
    Dd25's.

+ bridge, covered
+ ice cream cone

+ iris (of eye)

CARD X
Commonly and Rarely Chosen Beck Locations

Commonly chosen	Rarely chosen
Whole	Dd5
D1	Dd14
Dd2	Dd22
Dd3	Dd25
D4	Dd26
Dd6	D27
Dd7	Dd28
D8	D29
D9	D30
D10	Dd31
D11	Dd33
Dd12	Dd34
Dd13	
Dd15	

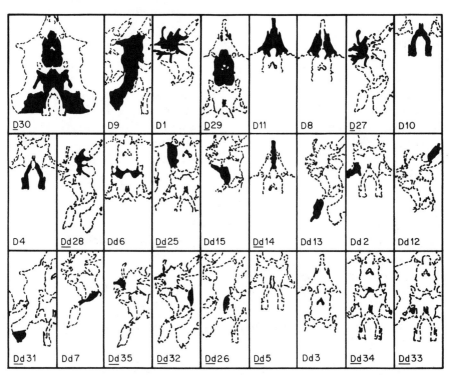

CARD X. Large (D) and small (Dd) Beck areas

W

Note: Certain plural responses, i.e., "animals," or "fishes," contain
   equally strong elements of good and poor form quality, and hence
   must be scored both plus and minus. Such responses are indicated
   in the table by the symbol ±. They should be distinguished from
   their parallel collective nouns, like "menagerie," and "aquarium,"
   which are usually scored plus only. If the response includes many
   D indiscriminately, but not all of them, the scorings are D F + and
   D F − .

General Plus Category:

figured design or object based on a figured design, such as painting,
   tapestry. (Position of card is usually immaterial.)

+ algae
+ anatomic design
+ aquarium
+ bandolier
+ biology slide
+ botanic exhibit
+ chandelier
+ coat of arms
+ dance of life (Ab)
+ dream jumble
+ emblem
+ fair, country
+ fan ∨
+ festival
+ figures, weird
+ fireworks ∧∨
+ flower(s) ∧∨
+ fungus growth, microscopic
+ garden
+ glass, colored
+ islands
+ kaleidoscope scene
+ menagerie
+ mobile
+ music (Ab)
+ ocean bottom
+ orchid ∨
+ painting, modern

+ paints, splashed
+ palette, artist's
+ party, gay
+ plants
+ postcard, picture
+ poster (illustrating Paris)
+ puzzle
+ rocks, colored
+ Spring [Ab]
+ stain, microscopic
+ temple, Oriental
+ tissue, under microscope
+ tropical scene
+ undersea life
+ Walt Disney cartoon or scene
+ zoo

± animals (marine)
± bacteria
± birds
± buds, flower
± clouds
± crabs
± figures, human
± fish (tropical)
± germs
± insects, any type
± seashells

± seaweed
± worms

− balloon, burst
− butterfly
− Chinese alphabet character
− Christmas tree ∧∨
− cobwebs
− elephants, fairy tale
− face, Oriental
− foods, different (on table)
− headdress, fantastic

− insides, human
− leaves
− lizards
− map
− mask, Halloween
− pagoda
− pliers
− salad
− spiders
− tool, mechanical
− trees

D1

General Plus Categories:

microscopic or tiny object seen as magnified (position of card is immaterial); two or more human or mythical human figures, such as elves, goblins (position of card is immaterial)

+ ameba
animal:
    + deep sea
    + grostesque
    + prehistoric
+ beetle
+ bouquet
+ branch
+ branches and stumps
+ bug, many-legged
+ cell, nerve
+ coral
+ crab(s)
+ crustacean(s)
+ fern, sea
+ flower
+ germ
+ ink, spilled
+ insect
+ landscape with trees
+ larkspur
+ leaf(s) (torn)
+ lobster (may include Dd12 as claw)

+ nerves
+ octopus
+ orchid
+ painting
+ pansy(s)
+ roots, mass of
+ scarab
+ scorpion
+ seaweed
+ snowflake
+ spider(s)
+ starfish
+ water
+ web, spider
+ weed
+ witches (one may be on broom)
+ wood, dead

− bird, long-legged <
− camel <
− Chinese alphabet character <
− cloth, piece of
− cockroach
− crow

- dragon(s)
- earring (with Dd12)
- endive
- figure, human
- fish
- flea(s)
- head, deer <
- island

- jackass, braying
- jellyfish
- lettuce
- map
- mask
- seashell
- string, bunch of
- teapot(s)

Dd2

General Plus Categories:

bird, any species; dog, any breed, flower

General Minus Category:

human figure

+ ameba
+ butterfly
+ cell with nucleus
+ design
+ egg, fried or scrambled
+ lion
+ petal, flower
+ pod, milkweed
+ poodle
+ seal
+ stain, microscopic
+ sun

- angel
- animal
- baby
- body, animal, baby inside
- chair, easy <

- chicken
- clown
- coat of arms
- cricket
- deer
- eye
- fish
- flesh
- frog
- goldfish
- head, rabbit
- jellyfish
- monkey
- pitcher
- sea horse
- shoe
- witch on broomstick

Dd3

+ airplane, jet
+ apricot
+ boomerang
+ bud(s)
+ cherries
+ design
+ diver, high ∨
+ figure, human ∨

+ flowers on stem
+ governor of engine
+ instrument to measure wind
    speed
+ knocker, door
+ lavaliere
+ lights, electric
+ marigold

+ parachutist
+ pawnbroker's symbol
+ pod, seed, maple
+ pollen, grains ∨
+ prunes, two
+ seaweed
+ seeds
+ stethoscope
+ tongs, ice
+ twig
+ weathervane
+ wishbone

− antennae, insect ∨
− antenna, T.V.
− bicycle
− bird
− boxer, holding hands out
− bug

− buzzard
− circlet
− crab
− ear muffs
− figure, human
− handle, to wind clock
− lobster
− mouth, human ∧∨
− necklace ∨
− notes, musical
− ovaries, with fallopian tubes
− rubber band
− scissors
− scissors, handle of
− spoons
− testicles
− "V" ∨
− "Y" ∨

D4
See also D10

Note: Singular responses refer to either lateral half of the detail; plural
    responses refer to the entire detail

General Minus Categories:

human figure ∧∨; infrahuman mammal ∧∨

+ animal, mythologic
+ caterpillar ∧∨
+ dragon
+ eel
+ head, dragon ∨
+ head, peacock ∨
+ horns
+ knight (chess)
+ peacock
+ plant life, feathery ∨
+ prawn
+ saxophone
+ sea horse ∧∨

+ seaweed
+ snake
+ stamen ∨
+ tail, lyrebird (whole detail)
+ tail, peacock
+ worm

− alligator
− animal
− Argentina ∧∨
− arms, human
− beard
− bug

- California ∧∨
- chicken
- Chile ∧∨
- corncob
- cucumber
- dinosaur ∨
- esophagus
- fan
- fish
- giraffe
- grass, blades of
- head, human, grotesque
- head and neck, swan or turkey
- hen, sitting
- horse, toy
- insect
- legs, human
- lobster
- porpoise
- snail
- stem, flower
- swan
- swordfish
- tree
- turkey
- wings

Dd5
See also D10

+ angel ∧∨
+ Christ on cross ∨
+ devil
  face:
    + animal
    + creature
+ figure, human, diving ∨
+ figure, human, with halo
+ gargoyle
  head:
    + animal
    + devil
    + figure, grotesque
    + rabbit
    + snail
+ mask
+ swing, with person ∨

- acorn
- calf, with long ears
- clippers (hedge)
- clothespin
- Crucifix ∨
- dog

face:
- dragonfly
- elk
- frog
- handle, nutcracker
head:
  - ant
  - donkey
  - giraffe
  - goat
  - grasshopper
  - human
  - Indian
  - insect
  - llama
- insect ∨
- key
- labia
- lobster
- pliers
- starfish
- vagina
- wrench

Projections of Dd5 ("ears")
See also Dd5

General Plus Category:

animal ears

+ legs V

− candles
− fingers

− icicles
− legs ∧
− teeth

Dd6

+ angel(s)
+ animals
+ bagpipes
+ bird(s) ∧V
+ bluebird(s) ∧V
+ bridge
+ chicken(s)
+ coral
+ dogs
+ dolls
+ dove(s)
+ duck(s)
+ figures, human:
   + shaking hands
   + performing on stage
+ ghosts
+ gods, Roman
  heads:
   + animal ∧V
   + dog ∧V
   + elephant
+ hips
+ pelvis
+ skeleton, human

− apes
− bat(s)
− brassiere
− breasts
− bulbs, light
− cartilage (An)

− cloud(s)
− eagle(s)
− ear, inner (bones)
− eyeglasses
− faces, hook-nosed
− fishes
− flowers
− flying squirrel
− girdle
− gorillas
− hands
− insects
− insides, human
− kidneys
− lakes
− lungs
− masks, gas
− moose
− mountain(s)
− ostriches
− ovaries
− pigs
− pipes, smoker's
− pitchers
− rocks
− seals
− storks
− turkeys
− United States, two
− vise
− water

Dd7

General Plus Category:

insect

General Minus Category:

birds and fowl

+ animal, leaping
+ cocoon, on branch ∨
+ crab
+ crayfish
+ deer (leaping)
+ kangaroo
+ mouse <∧>∨
+ moss, sea
+ nest in branches
+ pod, seed
+ rat
+ roots, bulbous (potato) ∧<
+ tree section, with roots and dirt

− alligator
− bat
− cat
− clam
− cobweb
− cow
− dog

− embryo
− figure, human <
− fish
− frog
− Gila monster
− goblin ∨
− horse
− kidney and ureter
− leaf
− lion
− lobster
− monster, little
− sea horse
− sea urchin >
− skull ∨
− spider
− squirrel
− stork
− turtle
− worm

D8
See also D11

Note: Responses refer to either lateral half of the detail

General Plus Category:

human figure, especially mythical (elf, dwarf) or unusual

+ animal (prehistoric)
+ beetle
+ bug
+ chipmunk
+ creature, weird
+ dragon
+ face, grotesque ∨

+ flea
+ god, Egyptian
+ griffin
+ head, human
+ insect
+ Martian
+ mask

+ mouse, field
+ mold, furry
+ plant
+ pollywog
+ rat
+ rodent
+ roots, tree
+ tadpole
+ unicorn
+ woodchuck

− ant
− bat, wings folded
− bee
− buffalo
− bull
− chicken
− crab
− deer
− dinosaur
− dog
− fish
− flower
− fly
− frog
− goat

− head, grasshopper
− hen
− horse
− kidney
− kitten
− leaf
− lion
− lizard
− lobster
− monkey
− moss
− octopus
− ovary
− parakeet
− parrot
− pheasant
− porcupine
− rabbit
− sea leopard
− shrimp
− skeleton, piece of
− smoke
− spider
− squirrel
− testicle
− turtle

D9

General Plus Category:

human figure (D8 may be seen as head or hat)

General Minus Category:

anatomy

+ animal, fairy tale
+ blood spot
+ California
+ caterpillar (magnified)
+ Christmas tree attachment
+ cliff
+ cloud(s)
+ coastline
+ coral, pink

+ curtains, stage, opened (both D9)
+ design on coat (both D9)
+ fire or flame
+ gateway (both D9)
+ island
+ Italy
+ map
+ monster, marine (prehistoric)

+ mountain(s)
+ mummy
+ petal, flower ∧∨
+ rock
+ sea horse
+ sea shore
+ snowsuit

− ameboid mass
− arch
− bacon
− bear
− bone structure
− bug
− Central America
− chicken
− dolphin
− Florida

− foot
− grub
− hair, red
− head, human (profile outer edge)
− insect, reared up
− jellyfish
− meat, cut of
− Netherlands
− ocean
− planet
− pliers (both D9)
− porpoise
− seashell
− tissue, human
− trunk, tree
− ulcerated region
− worm

Both D9 and Dd6

figures, human:
  + blowing bubbles
  + drinking from straw
  + holding hands

+ playing horn
+ smoking pipe

− butterfly
− skeleton

Both D9 plus D11 and D30

+ "A"
+ bell (D10 as clapper)
+ flower ∧∨
+ funnel ∨
+ vase

− butterfly
− face, any (may exclude D11 or include D10) ∧∨
− necklace
− pelvis (may include D6)

D10
See also D4 and Dd5

General Plus Category:

head of two-horned animal ∧∨

+ candleholder ∨
+ comb, old-fashioned ∨
+ design
+ devil (Dd5 face)
+ door knocker ∨

+ doorway
+ drapery
+ fountain
+ horns, animal ∨
+ lyre

+ man, with halo and wings V
+ music stand
+ parachutist V
+ seaweed
+ snake, with two bodies
+ worm, on fish hook
+ wreath

- amphibian, prehistoric
- animal, marine
- beard
- bird ∧V
- creature
- Cross
- devilfish
- dog
- flower ∧V
- funnel
- harness, horse's
- headdress

- horseshoe
- insect
- light, electric, hanging V
- marine scene
- monster, sea
- octopus
- pliers
- praying mantis
- rocketship
- saddle, with stirrups
- sea horse
- stamen V
- steeple
- tulip V
- tweezers
- "U" V
- "V" V
- vulture V
- wig
- wishbone

D11
See also D8 and D14
General Plus Category:

two figures in human-like action involving a pole or tree, such as supporting, leaning against, dancing around

+ animals, supporting tube or
    tree
+ art piece, Oriental
+ backbone and attached bones
+ bamboo stem, with roots
+ castle
+ chandelier
+ diving bell
+ Eiffel Tower
+ flower
+ funnel V
+ headgear, Oriental
+ insects, leaning against pole
+ lamp, hanging
+ marionettes, on string

+ mice, gnawing on stalk
+ mistletoe
+ plant
+ rats, strung up on post
+ rocketship
+ roots, with tree
+ scarecrow
+ spine and pelvis
+ statue
+ stem, flower V∧
+ stick, toy, with bells
+ stove, old-fashioned
+ trachea and lungs
+ transformers, on telephone pole
+ tree V

- airplane
- airplane, front end <∧
- anteater
- arteries
- beavers, gnawing at tree
- bells, two
- body, human, part of
- broom
- centipede
- dagger
- fireplace
- hammer

- implement, for tree pruning
- intestines
- map
- mirage
- nervous system
- pelvis
- pencil sharpener with pencil <
- shellfish ∨
- skull, steer
- tree
- universal, on automobile ∨

Dd12

+ bison
+ bull
+ cow
+ fish
+ lamb
+ leaf
+ plant (sea)
+ plume
+ scarab
+ sheep
+ unicorn
+ whale

- angel
- animal
- ax
- bean
- bird
- bomb
- broom
- bud
- bug

- cat
- caterpillar
- claw
- cloud
- cocoon ∧
- coral
- dog
- fan
- frog
- goat (mountain)
- grasshopper
- horseshoe
- island
- limb, tree
- mouse
- parrot
- rat
- rock
- seed
- snow bank
- tree

Dd13

General Plus Category:

dog, any breed ∧∨<

+ animal
+ bear

+ buffalo
+ cloud

+ face, dog
+ island
+ leaf
+ mold
+ New Zealand
+ paint, daub of
+ rock
+ slug (insect)

− beetle
− bird
− bug
− cat
− caterpillar
− chicken, roast
− chip, potato
− cocoon
− duck ∨
− figure, human
− fish
− flower

− honeycomb
− insect
− lemming
− lion, lying down
− pig
− porpoise
− potato
− rabbit
− rat
− reindeer
− seashell
− sheep
− shell, oyster
− skin, chicken, piece of
− snail
− sponge
− stomach
− tonsil(s)
− turkey, roast
− whale
− worm

Dd14
See also D11

+ baton
+ branch
+ candle
+ candleholder
+ cane
+ cannon >
+ chimney
+ face, African, ebony, carved
+ face, human, long and thin
   figure, human:
     + headless
     + tall and thin
     + wearing tall hat
+ flashlight
+ guided missile
+ gun (may include D8)
+ hammer
+ log

+ Maypole
+ pen
+ pencil
+ penis
+ pipe, piece of
+ post, lamp
+ rocket
+ spinal cord, piece
+ stalk
+ statue
+ stovepipe
+ test tube
+ thermometer
+ trunk, tree
+ vase

− arrow
− bone

- bullet
- cigar
- dissection, piece of
- finger
- key
- knife (in sheath)
- monkey
- necktie

- opener, bottle
- pistil, flower
- root
- snout
- stump, tree
- throat, interior of
- tree
- urethra

Dd15

+ ameba
+ bird
+ bud
+ cloud (across sunrise)
+ flower
+ rose

- animal
- bag
- bean
- canary
- drill, hand, power <
- fish
- Florida <
- hat, Santa Claus

- head, rabbit
- insect
- island
- jellyfish
- key
- popcorn, kernel of
- rabbit
- rat <
- rug
- seal
- seashell
- sheep
- South America <
- walrus <

Dd25
See also D9

Note: Responses may include all of upper half of D9

General Plus Category:

face or head of human or mythical human

- dog

Dd26

+ face, funny
+ man, old

+ profile, human

Dd27
See also D1

+ clown on trapeze
+ figures, human
+ goblin
+ horse

- head, wolf
- sea horse
- vulture (s)

Dd28
See also D1

+ cat, sitting (reaching out)
+ head, horse
+ knights (chess)
+ monkey

− head, fox
− sea horse(s)

D29

+ Buddha
+ chest protector (baseball)
+ face, human (front view)
+ faces, human (profiles outward)
+ fan (Dd14 handle) V∧
+ lantern (with Dd14)

+ papoose
+ tennis racket (D14 handle)
+ violin (Dd14 neck)

− bar, ice cream (Dd14 stick) V
− dog
− foliage

D30

+ canal and locks
+ canyon
+ pathway

− body, human, part of
− skeleton

Dd31

+ face, human <
+ face, monkey <

+ head, animal <

− cat

Dd33

+ acorn
+ head, baby
+ leaf, autumn
+ walnut

− diamond

− dog
− eye
− handkerchief
− head, dog
− orange
− tooth

Dd34

+ bone
+ connection, water-pipe
+ gate
+ rock

− ball

− bathing suit, top woman's
− boat
− candleholder
− horns, animal
− muff
− skull

5
NORMATIVE POPULATIONS

The issue of how to standardize test scores, what expectations to have about the performance of subjects, and how to interpret the performance observed is by no means straightforward. Central to the difficulty of the question is the viability of the assumption that a "typical" subject or group of subjects exists. The heart of the controversy is illustrated in the joke about the average family containing 2.7 children. What is the meaning of a fractional child?

It is our view that Rorschach's test is intended to illustrate individual differences, and that the concept of an average record has only very limited application. For that reason, rather than collecting a large standardized population, stratified by variables weighted by the probability of their occurrence with respect to some arbitrary standards, we have focused on the collection of carefully specified populations of clinical or theoretical interest. These populations currently include well educated, socially productive adults free of major psychiatric symptoms, children doing well in school and regarded as healthy by parents and teachers, foster children rated as healthy, talented college students without major symptoms, problem school children, acute hospitalized psychotics, paranoid schizophrenics, and individuals seeking sex change operations. Obviously, none of these populations is "typical," but each represents a group of interest.

Critical to the development of appropriate norms is not only the selection of suitable populations, but the collection of reliable data from those populations. Scoring generally is a basic data reduction technique. It involves reducing or eliminating some aspects of an event in order to focus more closely on other aspects. This is the case whether the "score" is the assignment of a number, assignment to a nominal category, a sociometric observation, or a clinical description. Rorschach scoring is basically a set of rules or conventions for recording some aspects of an event at the expense of other, quite possibly meaningful, aspects (e.g., tone of voice or other vocal gestures). The scores have no inherent meaning other than as the result of applying conventions which are, hopefully, clear and consistently applied.

Rorschach scoring has been much criticized for its lack of reliability. Some of that lack is the result of illogicality or ambiguity in the conventions, and we have made an effort to reduce such factors as much as we could. In addition, however, the judgments made in connection with some scores are inherently difficult, and sometimes arbitrary. For example, is "a man standing" human movement? Some systems say no, some say yes, if kinesthesia is involved (but determining *that* is not easy), some say position is *not* movement. Our system says position *is* movement, but articulates degrees of movement in the MA scores, permitting the recognition that all movement is not equal.

But if "a man standing" is human movement, is "a lamp standing" object movement. The answer to that question is "no," but on *conventional* not empirical or unassailably logical grounds.

To learn to make the inherently difficult judgments involved in Rorschach scoring consistently requires training, but even thorough training will not totally eliminate unreliability. For that reason, we have adopted a very stringent and demanding system of collecting normative data. All the scorers have been trained by us. That means a minimum of 12 hours of didactic instruction in addition to reading the manual and practice scoring of prescored records.

Further, with the exception of the data on children with school problems and the transsexuals, every record was *independently* scored by at least two individuals. Any discrepancies were then reviewed and resolved by one of the authors. For many of the healthy child records, the third scoring involved review, not just of discrepancies, but of each scored response. Finally, the scores for each response are entered into the computer, and the entries proofread for accuracy.

In terms of time, this means that administering, scoring, rescoring, reviewing, and entering a Rorschach record can easily involve eight hours or more. We are convinced that nothing less will provide suitable data.

Below you will find the norms for each of the indicated populations tested, measures of central tendency (mean, median, mode), measures of dispersion (standard deviation, quartile range and range), and measures of the distribution's shape (kurtosis and skew).

Healthy Adults (N = 50)

Variable	Mean(%)		Median	Mode	St.dev.	Skew	Kurt	Range	IQ Range
				Location					
W	6.0	(25.8)	6.0	5.0	1.6	0.6	0.1	7.0	2.0
W̲	0.7	(3.0)	0.0	0.0	1.0	2.2	6.0	5.0	1.0
(W)	0.0	(0.0)	0.0	0.0	0.0	.	.	0.0	0.0
(W̲)	0.0	(0.0)	0.0	0.0	0.0	.	.	0.0	0.0
TOTAL W	6.6	(28.8)	6.0	5.0	2.0	0.8	0.8	10.0	3.0
W%	28.8		28.6	26.2	11.1	1.1	1.0	51.8	12.1
D	13.3	(53.5)	13.0	9.0	5.0	0.5	0.6	24.0	8.0
D̲	0.5	(1.8)	0.0	0.0	0.9	1.8	2.3	3.0	1.0
D̲+D	13.8	(55.3)	14.0	17.0	5.4	0.6	1.2	27.0	8.3
D%	55.3		56.4	47.4	11.5	-0.4	0.4	55.6	15.7
Dd	3.5	(13.8)	3.0	4.0	2.5	1.9	7.5	15.0	2.3
Dd̲	0.5	(1.8)	0.0	0.0	1.1	2.2	3.8	4.0	0.0
Dd̲+Dd	4.0	(15.6)	4.0	4.0	3.1	2.4	10.1	19.0	3.0
Dd%	15.6		14.3	0.0	8.8	0.1	-0.8	33.3	14.1
W+(W)+D̲+Dd̲	3.5	(13.1)	3.0	1.0	3.2	2.5	10.0	19.0	4.0
r%	13.1		11.6	0.0	8.5	0.3	-0.8	32.8	13.0
				Cognitive complexity					
INTEGRATED	3.2	(13.2)	3.0	3.0	2.1	1.0	0.7	9.0	2.3
ARTICULATED	15.2	(62.3)	15.0	16.0	6.1	1.9	7.9	38.0	6.3
SIMPLE	3.6	(14.9)	3.0	2.0	2.2	0.6	0.1	9.0	3.0
DIFFUSE	1.8	(7.1)	1.0	0.0	1.9	1.4	2.0	8.0	3.0
ARBITRARY	0.6	(2.2)	0.0	0.0	0.9	1.6	1.6	3.0	1.0

Healthy Adults (N = 50) (Continued)

Variable	Mean(%)		Median	Mode	St.dev.	Skew	Kurt	Range	IQ Range
				Justifications and imaginal aspects					
All f	0.4	(1.6)	0.0	0.0	0.7	2.1	4.1	3.0	1.0
All C	3.1	(12.3)	3.0	3.0	2.3	1.2	2.1	10.0	3.0
All Ca	0.1	(0.3)	0.0	0.0	0.3	3.2	8.5	1.0	0.0
All Ci	0.2	(0.6)	0.0	0.0	0.5	3.0	8.8	2.0	0.0
All Cp	0.0	(0.2)	0.0	0.0	0.3	7.1	50.0	2.0	0.0
All C'	1.5	(5.8)	1.0	0.0	1.7	1.0	0.1	6.0	3.0
All F	23.5	(96.4)	23.0	19.0	7.3	2.1	8.1	44.0	8.3
All Sh	1.6	(6.5)	1.0	0.0	1.5	0.8	0.3	6.0	3.0
All AM	2.6	(11.0)	2.0	2.0	2.2	1.0	0.7	9.0	3.0
All HE	0.6	(2.2)	0.0	0.0	0.9	1.8	3.2	4.0	1.0
All HM	3.5	(14.2)	3.0	3.0	2.2	0.6	0.4	10.0	3.0
All OM	0.9	(3.8)	1.0	0.0	1.2	1.4	1.9	5.0	1.3
All T	0.6	(2.5)	0.0	0.0	0.9	1.0	−0.2	3.0	1.0
All V	1.0	(4.3)	1.0	0.0	1.2	1.6	2.8	5.0	2.0
Pure f	0.0	(0.0)	0.0	0.0	0.0	.	.	0.0	0.0
Pure C	0.3	(1.0)	0.0	0.0	0.6	2.6	7.0	3.0	0.0
C·F	2.7	(10.8)	3.0	3.0	1.9	0.9	1.4	9.0	2.3
C'·F	25.0	(102.2)	23.5	19.0	8.1	2.1	7.8	49.0	9.3
Pure F	11.7	(48.4)	11.0	14.0	4.8	1.7	6.9	29.0	5.3
F·Sh	25.1	(102.9)	24.0	21.0	7.8	1.7	5.9	46.0	9.5
F·AM	2.6	(10.8)	2.0	2.0	2.2	1.1	0.8	9.0	3.0
F·HM	3.5	(14.0)	3.0	3.0	2.1	0.7	0.8	10.0	3.0
				Conceptual content					
A	10.4	(44.4)	11.0	11.0	3.4	−0.2	−0.5	14.0	5.0
(A)	0.4	(1.5)	0.0	0.0	0.6	2.1	6.1	3.0	1.0
A$_f$	1.2	(4.8)	1.0	1.0	1.3	1.2	1.1	5.0	2.0

(Ar)	0.0	2.0	22.6	4.6	0.3	0.0	0.0	0.1 (0.2)
Ad + Adx	1.0	3.0	3.0	1.9	0.8	0.0	0.0	0.4 (1.7)
H	2.0	8.0	1.4	1.2	1.8	2.0	2.0	2.2 (9.0)
(H)	2.0	6.0	3.6	1.8	1.4	0.0	1.0	1.1 (4.2)
Hf	1.0	4.0	1.8	1.3	0.9	0.0	1.0	0.8 (3.3)
(Hf)	1.0	2.0	1.4	1.5	0.5	0.0	0.0	0.3 (1.2)
Hd + Hdx	0.3	4.0	14.2	3.3	0.7	0.0	0.0	0.3 (1.2)
Abs	0.0	3.0	19.3	4.3	0.5	0.0	0.0	0.1 (0.6)
Anb	1.0	5.0	3.4	1.9	1.2	0.0	0.5	0.8 (3.2)
Ans	1.0	3.0	0.7	1.2	0.8	0.0	0.0	0.6 (2.1)
Ansx	1.0	2.0	0.3	1.3	0.7	0.0	0.0	0.4 (1.7)
Anx	0.0	1.0	2.7	2.1	0.4	0.0	0.0	0.1 (0.6)
Art	1.0	2.0	1.5	1.5	0.6	0.0	0.0	0.3 (1.4)
Bl	0.3	2.0	2.4	1.8	0.6	0.0	0.0	0.3 (1.2)
Bt	1.3	4.0	0.6	1.2	1.0	0.0	0.0	0.8 (3.3)
Cld	1.0	2.0	0.3	1.2	0.6	0.0	0.0	0.4 (1.8)
Clg								
Dth	0.0	0.0	.	.	0.0	0.0	0.0	0.0 (0.0)
Emb								
Fd	1.0	2.0	1.5	1.5	0.6	0.0	0.0	0.3 (1.2)
Fi	0.0	0.0	.	.	0.0	0.0	0.0	0.0 (0.0)
Geo								
Hh	0.0	0.0	.	.	0.0	0.0	0.0	0.0 (0.0)
Imp								
Ls	1.0	5.0	4.6	1.9	1.1	0.0	0.0	0.7 (2.9)
Mu	0.0	2.0	16.5	4.0	0.4	0.0	0.0	0.1 (0.4)
Rel	0.0	1.0	4.0	2.4	0.3	0.0	0.0	0.1 (0.5)
Sch	0.0	3.0	4.0	2.1	0.7	0.0	0.0	0.3 (1.5)
Sci	0.0	2.0	12.4	3.4	0.4	0.0	0.0	0.1 (0.3)
Tr	0.0	3.0	11.6	3.0	0.6	0.0	0.0	0.2 (1.0)
Ty								
Wp	0.0	2.0	22.6	4.6	0.3	0.0	0.0	0.1 (0.2)

Healthy Adults (N = 50) *(Continued)*

Variable	Mean(%)		Median	Mode	St.dev.	Skew	Kurt	Range	IQ Range
				Human articulation					
HA$_1$	0.1	(0.2)	0.0	0.0	0.2	3.8	13.1	1.0	0.0
HA$_2$	0.3	(1.2)	0.0	0.0	0.7	2.4	5.6	3.0	0.0
HA$_3$	2.5	(10.1)	2.0	1.0	1.7	0.6	−0.2	7.0	3.0
HA$_4$	1.9	(7.5)	1.0	1.0	2.1	1.9	4.0	9.0	2.0
				Motivational articulation					
MA$_1$	0.4	(1.6)	0.0	0.0	0.6	1.9	4.4	3.0	1.0
MA$_2$	1.8	(7.1)	1.0	1.0	1.7	2.3	9.2	10.0	2.0
MA$_3$	1.6	(6.4)	1.0	0.0	1.6	1.2	1.7	7.0	2.3
MA$_4$	0.1	(0.4)	0.0	0.0	0.3	3.2	8.5	1.0	0.0
				Explicit motivational valuation					
M	0.9	(3.5)	0.0	0.0	1.3	2.3	7.6	7.0	1.0
N	1.8	(7.5)	2.0	2.0	1.4	0.5	−0.6	5.0	2.0
B	1.2	(4.8)	1.0	0.0	1.5	1.9	4.0	7.0	2.0
				Implicit motivational valuation					
(M)	3.9	(16.2)	3.5	2.0	2.5	0.7	0.1	10.0	3.3
(N)	15.7	(64.3)	15.0	15.0	5.4	1.6	6.0	32.0	7.0
(B)	0.9	(3.5)	1.0	0.0	1.0	1.2	0.9	4.0	1.0
				Perceptual-cognitive characteristics					
AT	2.0	(7.8)	1.0	1.0	2.1	1.5	1.9	9.0	2.3
BC	0.0	(0.0)	0.0	0.0	0.0	.	.	0.0	0.0

CD	1.8	(8.5)	2.0	0.0	1.8	1.1	0.6	6.0	3.0
CP	0.0	(0.0)	0.0	0.0	0.0	.	.	0.0	0.0
CR	0.7	(2.9)	0.0	0.0	1.1	2.0	4.5	5.0	1.0
CT	0.0	(0.0)	0.0	0.0	0.0	.	.	0.0	0.0
DC	0.0	(0.0)	0.0	0.0	0.0	.	.	0.0	0.0
D_x	0.1	(0.3)	0.0	0.0	0.2	3.8	13.1	1.0	0.0
EJ	0.0	(0.1)	0.0	0.0	0.3	7.1	50.0	2.0	0.0
FCP	0.2	(0.8)	0.0	0.0	0.5	3.8	17.2	3.0	0.0
LR	0.0	(0.0)	0.0	0.0	0.0	.	.	0.0	0.0
P	5.4	(23.3)	5.0	5.0	2.0	-0.2	-0.2	9.0	3.0
PSD	0.1	(0.2)	0.0	0.0	0.3	3.2	8.5	1.0	0.0
PT	0.1	(0.5)	0.0	0.0	0.4	3.4	12.4	2.0	0.0
S	0.6	(2.5)	0.0	0.0	0.9	1.8	3.0	4.0	1.0
(S)	1.5	(5.9)	1.0	1.0	1.2	0.9	0.5	5.0	1.0
SR	1.3	(4.8)	1.0	0.0	2.5	3.6	15.2	14.0	1.0
TR	0.0	(0.1)	0.0	0.0	0.1	7.1	50.0	1.0	0.0
VP	0.1	(0.4)	0.0	0.0	0.3	2.7	5.8	1.0	0.0
(VP)	0.3	(1.1)	0.0	0.0	0.7	2.6	6.2	3.0	0.0

Psychosexual drive and defense effectiveness

Oo P	0.1	(0.2)	0.0	0.0	0.3	5.6	32.4	2.0	0.0
Oo I	1.0	(4.3)	1.0	0.0	1.0	0.6	0.0	4.0	2.0
Oo G	0.0	(0.1)	0.0	0.0	0.1	7.1	50.0	1.0	0.0
Oc P	0.0	(0.0)	0.0	0.0	0.0	.	.	0.0	0.0
Oc I	0.5	(2.1)	0.0	0.0	0.8	1.0	-0.5	2.0	1.0
Oc G	0.0	(0.0)	0.0	0.0	0.0	.	.	0.0	0.0
All Oo	1.1	(4.5)	1.0	0.0	1.2	1.3	1.9	5.0	2.0
All Oc	0.5	(2.1)	0.0	0.0	0.8	1.0	-0.5	2.0	1.0
All Oral	1.6	(6.6)	1.0	0.0	1.5	0.8	0.2	6.0	3.0
Ao P	0.0	(0.0)	0.0	0.0	0.0	.	.	0.0	0.0

Healthy Adults (N = 50) (Continued)

Variable	Mean(%)		Median	Mode	St.dev.	Skew	Kurt	Range	IQ Range
Ao I	0.1	(0.5)	0.0	0.0	0.4	3.4	12.4	2.0	0.0
Ao G	0.0	(0.0)	0.0	0.0	0.0	.	.	0.0	0.0
Ac P	0.0	(0.1)	0.0	0.0	0.2	4.8	22.3	1.0	0.0
Ac I	0.5	(2.1)	0.0	0.0	0.8	1.4	1.2	3.0	1.0
Ac G	0.0	(0.1)	0.0	0.0	0.1	7.1	50.0	1.0	0.0
All Ao	0.1	(0.5)	0.0	0.0	0.4	3.4	12.4	2.0	0.0
All Ac	0.6	(2.4)	0.0	0.0	0.8	1.1	0.3	3.0	1.0
All Anal	0.7	(2.8)	0.0	0.0	0.9	1.2	1.5	4.0	1.0
Po P	0.0	(0.2)	0.0	0.0	0.2	4.8	22.3	1.0	0.0
Po I	0.4	(1.6)	0.0	0.0	0.8	1.9	3.0	3.0	1.0
Po G	0.0	(0.0)	0.0	0.0	0.0	.	.	0.0	0.0
Pc P	0.0	(0.1)	0.0	0.0	0.1	7.1	50.0	1.0	0.0
Pc I	1.5	(6.1)	1.0	1.0	1.4	1.2	1.4	6.0	1.3
Pc G	0.0	(0.2)	0.0	0.0	0.2	4.8	22.3	1.0	0.0
All Po	0.5	(1.7)	0.0	0.0	0.8	1.8	2.1	3.0	1.0
All Pc	1.6	(6.4)	1.0	1.0	1.4	1.2	1.4	6.0	1.0
All Phallic	2.0	(8.1)	2.0	1.0	1.8	0.9	0.0	6.0	2.0

Percentages and ratios

Total R	24.4 (100.0)	24.0	19.0	7.4	2.0	7.5	43.0	9.0
F%	48.4	50.0	50.0	13.6	-0.1	-0.7	56.7	19.9
F+%	76.8	80.0	80.0	13.3	-1.2	1.3	59.5	17.3
B+%	80.9	82.6	100.0	13.4	-0.3	-0.7	50.0	21.3
Afr	68.4	66.7	50.0	24.1	0.5	0.0	114.6	32.0
f%	0.0	0.0	0.0	0.0	.	.	0.0	0.0
r%	6.6	5.1	0.0	6.7	0.7	-0.6	21.7	12.0
PD%	17.5	17.9	25.0	9.0	0.2	-0.7	36.8	14.7
H%	19.0	18.8	14.3	9.9	0.9	1.0	50.0	12.8
A%	52.7	52.6	44.4	15.0	0.1	-0.1	68.0	18.1

Healthy Children (N = 44; Category 1 = 6, 7 Year Olds)

Variable	Mean(%)		Median	Mode	St.dev.	Skew	Kurt	Range	IQ Range
					Location				
W	7.9	(44.0)	9.0	9.0	4.2	0.1	−1.1	14.0	7.0
W̲	0.0	(0.3)	0.0	0.0	0.2	4.5	19.3	1.0	0.0
(W)	0.2	(1.1)	0.0	0.0	0.4	2.8	7.9	2.0	0.0
(W̲)	0.0	(0.0)	0.0	0.0	0.0	.	.	0.0	0.0
TOTAL W	8.1	(45.4)	9.0	9.0	4.2	0.1	−1.1	14.0	7.0
W%	45.4		40.9	6.9	27.1	0.2	−1.3	84.0	51.2
D	9.1	(37.8)	7.0	3.0	7.7	1.1	0.5	28.0	10.8
D̲	2.9	(12.3)	2.0	1.0	2.7	0.9	−0.1	10.0	4.0
D̲+D	12.0	(50.1)	9.5	10.0	9.6	0.9	−0.1	35.0	14.5
D%	50.1		53.6	11.1	24.8	−0.1	−0.9	85.4	36.4
Dd	0.1	(0.5)	0.0	0.0	0.4	4.3	19.6	2.0	0.0
Dd̲	0.5	(2.3)	0.0	0.0	1.3	2.7	6.6	5.0	0.0
Dd̲+Dd	0.6	(2.8)	0.0	0.0	1.4	2.6	6.1	6.0	0.8
Dd%	2.8		0.0	0.0	6.9	2.9	8.2	30.8	1.8
W+(W)+D̲+Dd	3.5	(14.9)	2.0	1.0	3.4	1.3	1.1	13.0	5.0
r%	14.9		11.9	0.0	12.1	0.8	−0.1	46.4	16.8
					Cognitive complexity				
INTEGRATED	2.6	(14.0)	2.5	1.0	1.8	0.7	−0.2	7.0	2.0
ARTICULATED	11.7	(55.2)	10.0	6.0	6.2	1.0	0.5	25.0	8.0
SIMPLE	4.4	(18.3)	2.0	1.0	4.7	1.1	−0.1	15.0	6.8
DIFFUSE	0.9	(4.8)	1.0	0.0	1.2	2.0	5.6	6.0	1.0
ARBITRARY	1.2	(6.5)	1.0	0.0	1.4	1.0	0.1	5.0	2.0
					Justifications and imaginal aspects				
All f	1.1	(4.8)	1.0	0.0	1.8	2.9	9.7	9.0	1.0
All C	3.0	(15.1)	3.0	2.0	2.2	0.9	0.7	9.0	2.8

All Ca	0.0	(0.0)	0.0	0.0	0.0	.	.	0.0	0.0
All Ci	0.8	(3.7)	0.0	0.0	1.0	1.4	1.5	4.0	1.0
All Cp	0.0	(0.3)	0.0	0.0	0.2	4.5	19.3	1.0	0.0
All C'	1.0	(5.3)	0.0	0.0	2.1	2.8	8.5	10.0	1.0
All F	18.4	(86.8)	16.5	11.0	8.0	0.7	-0.2	32.0	12.0
All Sh	0.4	(2.4)	0.0	0.0	1.1	5.1	29.6	7.0	0.0
All AM	2.6	(13.2)	2.0	2.0	2.3	1.3	1.5	10.0	3.0
All HE	0.4	(2.0)	0.0	0.0	0.7	1.9	3.8	3.0	1.0
All HM	2.1	(11.0)	2.0	2.0	1.7	1.1	1.5	7.0	2.0
All OM	1.6	(8.2)	1.0	0.0	1.8	1.3	1.5	7.0	2.8
All T	0.5	(3.2)	0.0	0.0	0.9	1.7	2.0	3.0	1.0
All V	0.4	(1.8)	0.0	0.0	0.8	2.7	8.6	4.0	0.8
Pure f	0.0	(0.0)	0.0	0.0	0.0	.	.	0.0	0.0
Pure C	0.8	(4.1)	0.0	0.0	1.3	1.4	0.9	4.0	1.0
C·F	1.9	(9.7)	2.0	0.0	1.7	0.8	-0.1	6.0	2.8
C'·F	19.4	(92.1)	17.5	14.0	8.4	0.7	-0.4	31.0	12.0
Pure F	10.4	(46.1)	9.0	10.0	7.1	1.1	1.0	31.0	9.0
F·Sh	18.8	(89.2)	16.5	11.0	8.0	0.7	-0.2	32.0	11.8
F·AM	2.4	(12.5)	2.0	1.0	2.3	1.3	0.9	9.0	2.8
F·HM	2.0	(10.5)	2.0	1.0	1.6	1.0	1.1	7.0	2.0

Conceptual content

A	7.6	(36.2)	6.0	4.0	4.2	1.0	0.7	18.0	6.0
(A)	1.2	(6.2)	1.0	0.0	1.2	0.8	0.5	5.0	2.0
Af	1.2	(5.5)	1.0	0.0	1.6	1.6	2.4	6.0	2.0
(Af)	0.2	(0.7)	0.0	0.0	0.4	2.8	7.9	2.0	0.0
Ad+Adx	0.7	(2.7)	0.0	0.0	1.2	2.5	7.7	6.0	1.0
H	1.8	(8.9)	2.0	2.0	1.7	2.0	6.3	9.0	1.8
(H)	1.1	(5.6)	1.0	0.0	1.4	1.9	5.8	7.0	2.0
Hf	0.3	(1.3)	0.0	0.0	0.7	3.7	16.3	4.0	0.0
(Hf)	0.2	(1.4)	0.0	0.0	0.4	1.3	-0.2	1.0	0.0
Hd+Hdx	0.9	(3.6)	0.0	0.0	1.7	2.1	4.2	7.0	1.0

191

Healthy Children (N = 44; Category 1 = 6, 7 Year Olds) *(Continued)*

Variable	Mean(%)		Median	Mode	St.dev.	Skew	Kurt	Range	IQ Range
Abs	0.0	(0.0)	0.0	0.0	0.0	.	.	0.0	0.0
An$_b$	0.4	(2.1)	0.0	0.0	0.7	1.4	0.7	2.0	1.0
An$_s$	0.4	(1.8)	0.0	0.0	0.8	2.6	8.1	4.0	1.0
An$_{sx}$	0.0	(0.0)	0.0	0.0	0.0	.	.	0.0	0.0
An$_x$	0.0	(0.0)	0.0	0.0	0.0	.	.	0.0	0.0
Art	0.2	(1.7)	0.0	0.0	0.5	2.0	3.5	2.0	0.0
Bl	0.3	(1.3)	0.0	0.0	0.5	1.9	3.0	2.0	0.0
Bt	1.3	(6.3)	0.0	0.0	1.3	1.0	0.9	5.0	2.0
Cld	0.3	(1.9)	1.0	0.0	0.6	1.6	1.6	2.0	1.0
Clg	1.0	(4.4)	0.0	0.0	1.0	0.9	0.6	4.0	2.0
Dth	0.2	(1.2)	1.0	0.0	0.5	2.8	7.3	2.0	0.0
Emb	0.0	(0.0)	0.0	0.0	0.0	.	.	0.0	0.0
Fd	0.4	(1.8)	0.0	0.0	0.9	2.5	6.9	4.0	1.0
Fi	0.7	(3.5)	0.0	0.0	1.0	1.2	0.3	3.0	1.0
Geo									
Hh	0.2	(1.0)	0.0	0.0	0.5	2.2	4.6	2.0	0.0
Imp									
Ls	1.4	(7.5)	1.0	0.0	1.2	0.4	−0.8	4.0	2.0
Mu	0.1	(0.5)	0.0	0.0	0.3	2.5	4.6	1.0	0.0
Rel	0.1	(0.6)	0.0	0.0	0.3	2.9	7.0	1.0	0.0
Sch	0.2	(0.7)	0.0	0.0	0.4	2.5	6.0	2.0	0.0
Sci	0.3	(1.3)	0.0	0.0	0.6	2.8	10.0	3.0	0.0
Tr	1.0	(4.6)	0.0	0.0	1.4	1.9	3.9	6.0	1.0
Ty									
Wp	0.1	(0.5)	0.0	0.0	0.4	4.3	19.6	2.0	0.0
				Human articulation					
HA$_1$	1.4	(5.6)	0.0	0.0	2.4	2.5	6.6	11.0	2.0
HA$_2$	0.7	(3.2)	0.0	0.0	1.0	1.5	1.6	4.0	1.0

HA$_3$	0.9 (4.9)	1.0	0.0	1.0	1.1	1.1	4.0	1.0
HA$_4$	1.2 (6.4)	1.0	1.0	1.1	0.7	−0.1	4.0	2.0
Motivational articulation								
MA$_1$	0.1 (0.4)	0.0	0.0	1.0	3.5	11.1	1.0	0.0
MA$_2$	1.7 (7.9)	1.0	1.0	1.5	1.2	2.2	7.0	1.8
MA$_3$	0.7 (4.2)	0.0	0.0	1.0	1.4	1.7	4.0	1.0
MA$_4$	0.0 (0.2)	0.0	0.0	0.2	4.5	19.3	1.0	0.0
Explicit motivational valuation								
M	0.8 (3.9)	0.5	0.0	1.0	1.3	1.1	4.0	1.0
N	1.2 (5.8)	1.0	0.0	1.1	0.8	−0.1	4.0	2.0
B	0.5 (2.9)	0.0	0.0	0.8	2.4	6.9	4.0	1.0
Implicit motivational valuation								
(M)	5.4 (26.3)	5.0	5.0	3.5	1.0	0.3	13.0	3.8
(N)	11.9 (54.4)	9.5	6.0	6.8	0.8	−0.2	25.0	10.0
(B)	1.0 (5.2)	1.0	1.0	1.0	1.1	1.2	4.0	2.0
Perceptual-cognitive characteristics								
AT	2.5 (13.3)	2.0	1.0	2.1	0.4	−1.3	6.0	3.8
BC	0.1 (0.6)	0.0	0.0	0.3	2.5	4.6	1.0	0.0
CD	0.6 (3.6)	0.0	0.0	0.9	1.1	−0.3	3.0	1.0
CP	0.1 (0.2)	0.0	0.0	0.3	3.5	11.1	1.0	0.0
CR	2.3 (11.9)	2.0	3.0	1.9	0.7	0.0	7.0	2.0
CT	0.0 (0.0)	0.0	0.0	0.0	.	.	0.0	0.0
DC	0.0 (0.0)	0.0	0.0	0.0	.	.	0.0	0.0
D$_x$	0.2 (0.8)	0.0	0.0	0.4	2.5	6.0	2.0	0.0
EJ	0.0 (0.3)	0.0	0.0	0.2	4.5	19.3	1.0	0.0
FCP	0.5 (2.4)	0.0	0.0	0.8	1.7	2.1	3.0	1.0

Healthy Children (N = 44; Category 1 = 6, 7 Year Olds) (*Continued*)

Variable	Mean(%)		Median	Mode	St.dev.	Skew	Kurt	Range	IQ Range
LR	0.1	(0.5)	0.0	0.0	0.4	3.7	14.1	2.0	0.0
P	3.8	(19.5)	4.0	4.0	1.8	−0.1	0.0	8.0	2.0
PSD	0.1	(0.7)	0.0	0.0	0.4	3.2	10.5	2.0	0.0
PT	0.5	(2.7)	0.0	0.0	0.9	1.7	1.6	3.0	1.0
S	0.5	(2.4)	0.0	0.0	0.8	2.2	6.6	4.0	1.0
(S)	1.8	(10.0)	2.0	1.0	1.4	0.4	−0.9	5.0	2.0
SR	1.0	(4.9)	0.0	0.0	2.5	5.2	30.3	16.0	1.0
TR	0.2	(0.8)	0.0	0.0	0.4	2.5	6.0	2.0	0.0
VP	0.1	(0.5)	0.0	0.0	0.3	3.5	11.1	1.0	0.0
(VP)	0.5	(2.4)	0.0	0.0	1.1	2.6	7.4	5.0	1.0
Psychosexual drive and defense effectiveness									
Oo P	0.3	(1.2)	0.0	0.0	1.0	4.5	23.5	6.0	0.0
Oo I	1.2	(5.6)	1.0	1.0	1.1	0.9	0.5	4.0	2.0
Oo G	0.2	(0.7)	0.0	0.0	0.4	1.9	1.8	1.0	0.0
Oc P	0.0	(0.1)	0.0	0.0	0.2	6.6	44.0	1.0	0.0
Oc I	0.3	(1.4)	0.0	0.0	0.6	2.3	4.0	2.0	0.0
Oc G	0.0	(0.2)	0.0	0.0	0.2	4.5	19.3	1.0	0.0
All Oo	1.7	(7.5)	1.0	1.0	1.7	1.6	3.0	8.0	1.8
All Oc	0.3	(1.7)	0.0	0.0	0.7	2.3	5.0	3.0	0.0
All Oral	2.0	(9.2)	1.0	1.0	2.0	1.8	4.6	10.0	2.0
Ao P	0.0	(0.0)	0.0	0.0	0.0	.	.	0.0	0.0
Ao I	0.0	(0.1)	0.0	0.0	0.2	6.6	44.0	1.0	0.0
Ao G	0.0	(0.0)	0.0	0.0	0.0	.	.	0.0	0.0
Ac P	0.0	(0.2)	0.0	0.0	0.3	6.6	44.0	2.0	0.0

Ac I	1.0	3.0	1.2	1.3	0.9	0.0	0.5	0.7	(4.0)
Ac G	0.0	1.0	0.3	1.5	0.4	0.0	0.0	0.2	(1.2)
All Ao	0.0	1.0	44.0	6.6	0.2	0.0	0.0	0.0	(0.1)
All Ac	1.0	6.0	6.0	2.2	1.2	1.0	1.0	1.0	(5.5)
All Anal	1.0	6.0	5.6	2.1	1.2	1.0	1.0	1.0	(5.6)
Po P	0.0	0.0	.	.	0.0	0.0	0.0	0.0	(0.0)
Po I	0.0	0.0	.	.	0.0	0.0	0.0	0.0	(0.0)
Po G	0.0	0.0	.	.	0.0	0.0	0.0	0.0	(0.0)
Pc P	0.0	1.0	4.6	2.5	0.3	0.0	0.0	0.1	(0.6)
Pc I	0.0	4.0	−0.3	1.0	1.2	0.0	1.0	1.0	(5.8)
Pc G	0.0	2.0	6.0	2.5	0.4	0.0	0.0	0.2	(0.7)
All Po	0.0	0.0	.	.	0.0	0.0	0.0	0.0	(0.0)
All Pc	2.0	5.0	0.6	1.1	1.4	0.0	1.0	1.3	(7.2)
All Phallic	2.0	5.0	0.6	1.1	1.4	0.0	1.0	1.3	(7.2)
Percentages and ratios									
Total R	14.8	31.0	−0.4	0.7	8.6	13.0	18.0	21.1	
F%	30.2	75.6	−0.6	−0.1	19.3	50.0	46.4	46.1	
F+%	25.2	100.0	1.1	−0.4	22.7	100.0	60.0	60.1	
B+%	19.0	69.5	−0.3	0.3	16.5	55.5	55.5	58.0	
Afr	33.3	82.1	−0.4	0.8	22.5	30.0	45.8	52.6	
f%	0.0	0.0	.	.	0.0	0.0	0.0	0.0	
r%	16.8	46.4	−0.1	0.8	12.1	0.0	11.9	14.9	
PD%	21.7	66.7	0.9	0.9	15.5	25.0	19.8	22.0	
H%	18.0	56.5	0.4	0.8	12.7	0.0	17.2	20.8	
A%	21.1	66.1	−0.2	−0.1	15.5	46.2	53.2	51.4	

Healthy Children (N = 43; Category 2 = 8, 9, 10 Year Olds)

Variable	Mean(%)		Median	Mode	St.dev.	Skew	Kurt	Range	IQ Range
					Location				
W	8.2	(38.2)	8.0	6.0	4.3	0.5	-0.1	18.0	6.0
W̲	0.1	(0.5)	0.0	0.0	0.3	3.5	10.8	1.0	0.0
(W)	0.7	(2.9)	0.0	0.0	1.5	2.9	8.5	7.0	1.0
(W̲)	0.0	(0.0)	0.0	0.0	0.0	.	.	0.0	0.0
TOTAL W	8.9	(41.6)	8.0	6.0	4.7	0.5	-0.4	19.0	7.0
W%	41.6		39.1	40.0	26.9	0.7	-0.3	98.0	36.0
D	11.0	(37.4)	10.0	1.0	8.3	0.7	-0.2	34.0	14.0
D̲	5.6	(16.6)	3.0	0.0	7.4	2.2	5.0	32.0	6.0
D̲+D	16.7	(54.0)	13.0	1.0	14.0	1.3	1.4	56.0	18.0
D%	54.0		60.0	7.1	25.2	-0.7	-0.5	87.1	35.8
Dd	0.1	(0.3)	0.0	0.0	0.3	3.5	10.8	1.0	0.0
Dd̲	1.2	(2.8)	0.0	0.0	2.8	3.6	15.0	15.0	1.0
Dd̲+Dd	1.3	(3.1)	0.0	0.0	2.8	3.5	14.7	15.0	1.0
Dd%	3.1		0.0	0.0	5.1	1.8	2.7	19.5	4.5
W+(W̲)+D+Dd̲	6.9	(19.9)	4.0	1.0	9.7	2.7	8.1	47.0	8.0
r%	19.9		17.1	0.0	16.1	0.8	0.2	61.0	24.9
					Cognitive complexity				
INTEGRATED	2.8	(11.5)	2.0	0.0	2.6	1.3	2.2	12.0	3.0
ARTICULATED	15.6	(56.8)	13.0	13.0	10.6	2.3	7.7	60.0	11.0
SIMPLE	5.7	(19.5)	5.0	1.0	5.5	1.6	2.9	25.0	5.0
DIFFUSE	1.2	(4.5)	1.0	0.0	1.5	1.4	2.0	6.0	2.0
ARBITRARY	1.5	(6.3)	1.0	0.0	2.4	3.2	12.8	13.0	2.0

Justifications and imaginal aspects

All f	1.0 (3.8)	0.0	0.0	2.1	2.9	8.5	9.0	1.0
All C	3.4 (13.3)	2.0	2.0	3.1	1.6	3.5	15.0	4.0
All Ca	0.1 (0.3)	0.0	0.0	0.3	3.5	10.8	1.0	0.0
All Ci	0.3 (1.1)	0.0	0.0	0.8	3.3	11.9	4.0	0.0
All Cp	0.1 (0.5)	0.0	0.0	0.3	2.9	6.7	1.0	0.0
All C'	0.4 (2.0)	0.0	0.0	1.2	3.2	9.2	5.0	0.0
All F	24.6 (89.6)	21.0	12.0	15.2	1.6	2.8	69.0	17.0
All Sh	0.8 (3.7)	0.0	0.0	1.3	2.1	5.1	6.0	1.0
All AM	2.7 (11.0)	2.0	2.0	2.2	1.1	0.7	0.9	3.0
All HE	0.5 (2.2)	0.0	0.0	0.9	2.2	5.2	4.0	1.0
All HM	2.5 (10.0)	2.0	0.0	2.8	1.7	3.2	12.0	3.0
All OM	1.7 (7.5)	1.0	1.0	1.5	1.4	1.7	6.0	1.0
All T	0.5 (2.4)	0.0	0.0	1.0	2.8	9.7	5.0	1.0
All V	0.3 (1.4)	0.0	0.0	0.6	1.6	1.6	2.0	1.0
Pure f	0.0 (0.0)	0.0	0.0	0.0	.	.	0.0	0.0
Pure C	0.5 (2.3)	0.0	0.0	0.9	2.1	4.7	4.0	1.0
C·F	2.4 (9.1)	2.0	2.0	2.5	1.7	4.1	12.0	4.0
C'·F	25.0 (91.5)	23.0	12.0	15.0	1.6	2.8	69.0	17.0
Pure F	15.6 (54.2)	12.1	7.0	12.0	1.7	3.3	57.0	14.0
F·Sh	25.5 (93.2)	23.0	12.0	15.4	1.6	2.7	71.0	17.0
F·AM	2.6 (10.5)	2.0	2.0	2.1	1.1	0.8	9.0	3.0
F·HM	2.4 (9.4)	2.0	0.0	2.6	1.8	4.1	12.0	3.0

Conceptual content

A	10.0 (38.3)	9.0	8.0	5.6	1.0	0.5	24.0	7.0
(A)	1.5 (0.1)	1.0	0.0	1.9	1.6	2.7	8.0	3.0
Af	1.1 (4.5)	1.0	0.0	1.6	2.0	4.2	7.0	1.0
(Af)	0.2 (0.8)	0.0	0.0	0.5	2.5	5.6	2.0	0.0
Ad + Adx	1.0 (2.9)	0.0	0.0	1.6	2.2	4.8	7.0	1.0

Healthy Children (N = 43; Category 2 = 8, 9, 10 Year Olds) *(Continued)*

Variable	Mean(%)		Median	Mode	St.dev.	Skew	Kurt	Range	IQ Range
H	2.3	(8.1)	2.0	0.0	2.7	3.3	15.2	16.0	2.0
(H)	1.1	(4.4)	1.0	0.0	1.6	2.0	4.5	7.0	2.0
Hf	0.5	(1.7)	0.0	0.0	0.8	1.5	1.1	3.0	1.0
(Hf)	0.2	(0.7)	0.0	0.0	0.5	2.5	5.8	2.0	0.0
Hd+Hdx	1.0	(2.8)	0.0	0.0	1.9	2.1	3.3	7.0	1.0
Abs	0.0	(0.3)	0.0	0.0	0.2	4.5	18.8	1.0	0.0
Anb	0.4	(1.5)	0.0	0.0	0.7	1.4	0.9	2.0	1.0
Ans	0.7	(3.3)	0.0	0.0	1.2	1.8	2.3	4.0	1.0
Ansx	0.0	(0.0)	0.0	0.0	0.0	.	.	0.0	0.0
Anx	0.0	(0.1)	0.0	0.0	0.2	6.6	43.0	1.0	0.0
Art	0.2	(0.9)	0.0	0.0	0.6	3.1	10.6	3.0	0.0
Bl	0.3	(1.2)	0.0	0.0	0.7	2.7	7.8	3.0	0.0
Bt	1.5	(5.5)	1.0	0.0	1.9	1.2	0.4	6.0	3.0
Cld	0.6	(2.5)	0.0	0.0	0.8	1.4	1.2	3.0	1.0
Clg	1.1	(4.0)	1.0	0.0	1.3	1.1	0.7	5.0	2.0
Dth	0.3	(1.0)	0.0	0.0	0.5	2.1	3.6	2.0	0.0
Emb									
Fd	0.4	(1.3)	0.0	0.0	0.8	2.0	3.6	3.0	1.0
Fi	0.9	(3.7)	1.0	0.0	1.3	2.9	12.0	7.0	1.0
Geo									
Hh	1.0	(3.4)	1.0	0.0	1.4	2.0	4.4	6.0	1.0
Imp									
Ls	2.3	(9.2)	2.0	1.0	2.0	0.9	0.2	8.0	2.0
Mu	0.1	(0.1)	0.0	0.0	0.3	3.5	10.8	1.0	0.0
Rel	0.2	(0.8)	0.0	0.0	0.4	1.7	0.8	1.0	0.0
Sch	0.7	(2.0)	0.0	0.0	1.4	2.3	5.0	6.0	1.0
Sci	0.1	(0.3)	0.0	0.0	0.6	5.6	33.5	4.0	0.0
Tr	0.7	(3.1)	0.0	0.0	0.8	1.2	1.0	3.0	1.0
Ty									
Wp	0.4	(1.1)	0.0	0.0	1.2	3.5	13.8	6.0	0.0

Human articulation								
HA₁	1.2	(4.0)	1.0	0.0	1.5	1.6	2.2	6.0	2.0
HA₂	1.0	(3.5)	0.0	0.0	1.5	1.8	3.0	6.0	2.0
HA₃	1.2	(4.3)	1.0	0.0	1.6	1.6	3.1	7.0	2.0
HA₄	1.5	(6.2)	1.0	0.0	1.7	1.3	0.8	6.0	2.0
Motivational articulation								
MA₁	0.2	(0.9)	0.0	0.0	0.6	4.0	16.2	3.0	0.0
MA₂	1.7	(7.1)	1.0	0.0	2.0	1.5	2.2	8.0	3.0
MA₃	1.0	(3.7)	0.0	0.0	1.7	3.0	11.4	9.0	1.0
MA₄	0.0	(0.1)	0.0	0.0	0.2	6.6	43.0	1.0	0.0
Explicit motivational valuation								
M	1.0	(4.9)	0.0	0.0	1.6	1.8	3.2	6.0	2.0
N	1.2	(4.4)	1.0	0.0	1.4	1.1	0.2	5.0	2.0
B	0.7	(2.4)	0.0	0.0	1.3	4.3	22.9	8.0	1.0
Implicit motivational valuation								
(M)	7.3	(27.9)	7.0	7.0	4.6	0.5	−0.0	19.0	5.0
(N)	15.6	(54.5)	13.0	10.0	11.4	1.7	3.6	57.0	10.0
(B)	0.9	(4.1)	1.0	0.0	1.0	0.7	−0.8	3.0	2.0
Perceptual-cognitive characteristics								
AT	2.9	(11.9)	2.0	0.0	3.1	1.3	1.5	13.0	5.0
BC	0.1	(1.0)	0.0	0.0	0.4	3.2	10.2	2.0	0.0
CD	0.5	(2.4)	0.0	0.0	1.1	2.4	4.7	4.0	0.0
CP	0.1	(0.2)	0.0	0.0	0.3	2.9	6.7	1.0	0.0
CR	2.9	(11.5)	2.0	0.0	4.7	3.5	14.6	26.0	3.0
CT	0.0	(0.2)	0.0	0.0	0.2	6.6	43.0	1.0	0.0
DC	0.0	(0.1)	0.0	0.0	0.2	6.6	43.0	1.0	0.0

Healthy Children (N = 43; Category 2 = 8, 9, 10 Year Olds) (Continued)

Variable	Mean(%)		Median	Mode	St.dev.	Skew	Kurt	Range	IQ Range
D$_x$	0.2	(0.7)	0.0	0.0	0.6	3.1	10.6	3.0	0.0
EJ	0.1	(0.5)	0.0	0.0	0.5	5.1	28.2	3.0	0.0
FCP	0.5	(2.8)	0.0	0.0	0.8	2.3	7.6	4.0	1.0
LR	0.1	(0.3)	0.0	0.0	0.6	4.3	19.0	3.0	0.0
P	3.7	(15.9)	4.0	4.0	1.9	0.6	0.2	8.0	3.0
PSD	0.2	(0.7)	0.0	0.0	0.4	1.9	1.7	1.0	0.0
PT	0.6	(2.0)	0.0	0.0	0.9	1.5	1.1	3.0	1.0
S	0.3	(1.1)	0.0	0.0	0.6	1.9	2.5	2.0	0.0
(S)	2.1	(9.7)	2.0	2.0	1.9	1.0	0.4	7.0	2.0
SR	0.8	(3.4)	1.0	0.0	1.1	2.4	9.1	6.0	1.0
TR	0.3	(0.9)	0.0	0.0	0.7	2.3	4.1	3.0	0.0
VP	0.0	(0.2)	0.0	0.0	0.2	4.5	18.8	1.0	0.0
(VP)	0.3	(1.0)	0.0	0.0	0.8	3.4	12.8	4.0	0.0
Psychosexual drive and defense effectiveness									
Oo P	0.3	(1.3)	0.0	0.0	0.6	1.9	2.5	2.0	0.0
Oo I	1.1	(4.2)	0.0	0.0	1.9	3.0	12.1	10.0	2.0
Oo G	0.2	(0.7)	0.0	0.0	0.6	2.4	4.7	2.0	0.0
Oc P	0.0	(0.0)	0.0	0.0	0.2	6.6	43.0	1.0	0.0
Oc I	0.4	(1.6)	0.0	0.0	0.7	1.4	0.9	2.0	1.0
Oc G	0.1	(0.3)	0.0	0.0	0.3	3.5	10.8	1.0	0.0
All Oo	1.7	(6.2)	1.0	0.0	2.4	3.0	12.0	13.0	2.0
All Oc	0.5	(2.0)	0.0	0.0	0.7	1.2	-0.1	2.0	1.0
All Oral	2.1	(8.1)	1.0	1.0	2.6	2.8	10.4	14.0	1.0
Ao P	0.0	(0.0)	0.0	0.0	0.0	.	.	0.0	0.0
Ao I	0.0	(0.1)	0.0	0.0	0.2	6.6	43.0	1.0	0.0
Ao G	0.0	(0.0)	0.0	0.0	0.0	.	.	0.0	0.0

Ac P	0.0	(0.2)	0.0	0.0	0.2	4.5	18.8	1.0	0.0
Ac I	0.7	(3.5)	0.0	0.0	1.0	1.6	2.7	4.0	1.0
Ac G	0.1	(0.5)	0.0	0.0	0.3	2.9	6.7	1.0	0.0
All Ao	0.0	(0.1)	0.0	0.0	0.2	6.6	43.0	1.0	0.0
All Ac	0.9	(4.1)	1.0	1.0	1.1	2.1	5.3	5.0	1.0
All Anal	0.9	(4.2)	1.0	0.0	1.1	1.9	4.8	5.0	1.0
Po P	0.0	(0.0)	0.0	0.0	0.0	.	.	0.0	0.0
Po I	0.0	(0.0)	0.0	0.0	0.0	.	.	0.0	0.0
Po G	0.0	(0.0)	0.0	0.0	0.0	.	.	0.0	0.0
Pc P	0.2	(0.7)	0.0	0.0	0.6	3.6	14.0	3.0	0.0
Pc I	1.3	(4.9)	1.0	1.0	1.6	1.8	3.1	7.0	1.0
Pc G	0.3	(1.2)	0.0	0.0	0.7	2.2	5.8	3.0	1.0
All Po	0.0	(0.0)	0.0	0.0	0.0	.	.	0.0	0.0
All Pc	1.8	(6.8)	1.0	1.0	2.4	1.8	3.1	10.0	2.0
All Phallic	1.8	(6.8)	1.0	1.0	2.4	1.8	3.1	10.0	2.0

Percentages and ratios

Total R	27.1	(100.0)	23.0	20.0	15.5	1.7	2.7	67.0	16.0
F%	54.2		55.0	40.0	21.0	-0.3	-0.2	91.3	33.3
F+%	63.7		63.1	75.0	17.0	-0.2	0.1	77.8	19.1
B+%	51.6		50.0	50.0	19.9	-0.3	-0.1	85.7	26.7
Afr	49.1		44.4	33.3	19.2	2.3	9.0	110.7	22.1
f%	0.0		0.0	0.0	0.0	.	.	0.0	0.0
r%	19.9		17.1	0.0	16.1	0.8	0.2	61.0	24.9
PD%	19.1		16.7	16.7	20.5	4.0	20.6	130.0	16.4
H%	17.8		17.6	0.0	10.6	0.4	0.1	44.4	14.4
A%	52.2		54.2	65.0	12.8	0.1	-0.8	49.0	20.1

Healthy Children (N = 43; Category 3 = 11, 12 Year Olds)

Variable	Mean(%)		Median	Mode	St.dev.	Skew	Kurt	Range	IQ Range
				Location					
W	7.9	(48.6)	7.0	6.0	4.1	1.4	2.2	19.0	3.0
W̲	0.2	(1.5)	0.0	0.0	0.4	1.5	0.2	1.0	0.0
(W)	0.1	(0.4)	0.0	0.0	0.3	2.9	6.7	1.0	0.0
(W̲)	0.1	(0.4)	0.0	0.0	0.3	3.5	10.8	1.0	0.0
TOTAL W	8.2	(50.9)	7.0	6.0	4.2	1.5	2.4	20.0	3.0
W%	50.9		50.0	50.0	24.4	-0.1	-0.7	95.2	38.1
D	8.5	(33.9)	5.0	2.0	11.1	2.6	7.4	53.0	6.0
D̲	2.6	(9.3)	1.0	0.0	4.6	3.3	11.1	21.0	2.0
D̲+D̲	11.0	(43.2)	6.0	2.0	15.4	2.9	9.0	74.0	7.0
D%	43.2		45.5	50.0	23.5	0.2	-0.7	92.9	35.7
Dd	0.6	(2.5)	0.0	0.0	1.5	3.1	10.1	7.0	0.0
Dd̲	0.5	(1.5)	0.0	0.0	1.9	5.8	35.7	12.0	0.0
Dd̲+Dd̲	1.1	(4.0)	0.0	0.0	3.0	5.2	30.8	19.0	1.0
Dd%	4.0		0.0	0.0	6.7	1.7	1.8	23.1	7.1
W̲+(W̲)+D̲+Dd̲	3.4	(12.8)	2.0	1.0	6.0	3.8	15.7	33.0	2.0
r%	12.8		10.3	0.0	9.6	0.7	-0.2	33.3	10.2
				Cognitive complexity					
INTEGRATED	3.1	(17.5)	2.0	1.0	2.7	1.0	0.4	11.0	4.0
ARTICULATED	12.9	(61.8)	9.0	8.0	10.5	2.4	6.6	51.0	8.0
SIMPLE	2.3	(6.5)	0.0	0.0	4.8	3.3	12.3	25.0	2.0
DIFFUSE	0.4	(2.5)	0.0	0.0	0.7	1.8	3.0	3.0	1.0
ARBITRARY	1.7	(9.6)	1.0	0.0	2.4	2.9	11.8	13.0	3.0

Justifications and imaginal aspects

All f	0.1	(0.2)	0.0	0.0	0.4	3.6	13.7	2.0	0.0
All C	3.4	(19.6)	3.0	3.0	1.9	1.3	4.4	11.0	2.0
All Ca	0.0	(0.0)	0.0	0.0	0.2	6.6	43.0	1.0	0.0
All Ci	0.2	(1.0)	0.0	0.0	0.5	2.8	7.1	2.0	0.0
All Cp	0.1	(0.4)	0.0	0.0	0.3	3.5	10.8	1.0	0.0
All C'	1.4	(10.3)	1.0	0.0	1.7	1.1	0.4	6.0	3.0
All F	19.7	(95.3)	14.0	13.0	16.0	3.1	11.1	85.0	11.0
All Sh	1.5	(9.8)	1.0	0.0	1.6	1.5	2.4	7.0	2.0
All AM	3.3	(18.5)	3.0	2.0	2.5	0.9	0.9	11.0	2.0
All HE	0.5	(1.7)	0.0	0.0	1.4	3.3	12.2	7.0	0.0
All HM	3.3	(15.1)	2.0	1.0	3.7	2.2	5.2	17.0	3.0
All OM	1.7	(8.7)	1.0	1.0	1.9	2.3	8.0	10.0	2.0
ALL T	0.8	(5.8)	0.0	0.0	1.3	2.2	4.7	5.0	1.0
ALL V	1.0	(7.1)	1.0	0.0	1.2	1.1	0.2	4.0	2.0
Pure f	0.0	(0.0)	0.0	0.0	0.0	·	·	0.0	0.0
Pure C	0.2	(0.7)	0.0	0.0	0.5	2.8	7.1	2.0	0.0
C·F	3.1	(17.8)	3.0	3.0	1.8	1.9	8.9	11.0	2.0
C'·F	21.2	(105.6)	17.0	11.0	15.5	3.1	11.3	85.0	10.0
Pure F	8.8	(37.0)	5.0	2.0	10.2	2.5	6.9	51.0	6.0
F·Sh	21.2	(105.1)	17.0	12.0	16.1	3.2	12.2	89.0	11.0
F·AM	3.3	(18.3)	3.0	2.0	2.5	1.0	1.2	11.0	2.0
F·HM	3.2	(15.0)	2.0	1.0	3.7	2.1	4.7	16.0	3.0

Conceptual content

A	8.3	(42.7)	7.0	6.0	5.7	2.6	8.5	30.0	4.0
(A)	1.3	(7.3)	1.0	1.0	1.5	2.3	8.5	8.0	2.0
A_f	0.9	(5.1)	1.0	0.0	1.3	1.9	3.5	5.0	1.0
(A_f)	0.1	(0.6)	0.0	0.0	0.4	2.2	2.8	1.0	0.0
Ad + Adx	0.6	(1.7)	0.0	0.0	1.7	4.1	17.8	9.0	0.0

Healthy Children (N = 43; Category 3 = 11, 12 Year Olds) (Continued)

Variable	Mean(%)		Median	Mode	St.dev.	Skew	Kurt	Range	IQ Range
H	2.5	(11.2)	1.0	1.0	3.2	2.7	8.5	16.0	2.0
(H)	0.8	(3.7)	0.0	0.0	1.4	2.4	5.9	6.0	1.0
H_f	0.6	(3.4)	0.0	0.0	0.9	1.6	1.6	3.0	1.0
(H_f)	0.4	(2.5)	0.0	0.0	0.8	2.7	8.9	4.0	1.0
Hd + Hdx	0.6	(2.8)	0.0	0.0	1.0	1.8	2.8	4.0	1.0
Abs	0.0	(0.2)	0.0	0.0	0.2	4.5	18.8	1.0	0.0
An_b	0.4	(2.4)	0.0	0.0	0.7	1.2	0.4	2.0	1.0
An_s	0.4	(1.9)	0.0	0.0	0.7	2.1	4.5	3.0	1.0
An_{sx}	0.0	(0.0)	0.0	0.0	0.0	.	.	0.0	0.0
An_x	0.0	(0.0)	0.0	0.0	0.0	.	.	0.0	0.0
Art	0.3	(1.7)	0.0	0.0	0.6	2.4	7.7	3.0	1.0
Bl	0.3	(1.8)	0.0	0.0	0.6	2.0	3.1	2.0	0.0
Bt	1.4	(7.5)	1.0	0.0	1.8	2.2	5.5	8.0	2.0
Cld	0.3	(1.5)	0.0	0.0	0.7	3.9	18.8	4.0	0.0
Clg	0.8	(3.5)	0.0	0.0	1.2	2.3	6.4	6.0	1.0
Dth	0.4	(2.5)	0.0	0.0	0.7	1.8	3.6	3.0	1.0
Emb									
Fd	0.2	(0.9)	0.0	0.0	0.6	3.5	14.5	3.0	0.0
Fi	0.6	(2.9)	0.0	0.0	0.8	1.6	2.4	3.0	1.0
Geo									
Hh	1.0	(4.8)	0.0	0.0	1.4	1.9	3.8	6.0	1.0
Imp									
Ls	1.5	(7.0)	1.0	0.0	2.2	2.6	8.7	11.0	2.0
Mu	0.0	(0.2)	0.0	0.0	0.2	4.5	18.8	1.0	0.0
Rel	0.1	(0.1)	0.0	0.0	0.3	3.5	10.8	1.0	0.0
Sch	0.1	(0.3)	0.0	0.0	0.3	3.5	10.8	1.0	0.0
Sci	0.3	(0.5)	0.0	0.0	1.2	6.0	38.0	8.0	0.0
Tr	0.6	(2.2)	0.0	0.0	1.0	2.5	7.4	5.0	1.0
Ty									
Wp	0.8	(0.7)	0.0	0.0	0.9	4.0	17.0	5.0	0.0

Human articulation

HA₁	1.0	5.0	6.7	2.6	1.2	0.0	0.0	0.6	(2.5)
HA₂	0.0	12.0	32.3	5.4	1.9	0.0	0.0	0.6	(1.6)
HA₃	2.0	9.0	3.7	1.8	2.0	1.0	1.0	1.9	(9.6)
HA₄	2.0	9.0	7.3	2.6	2.0	1.0	1.0	1.4	(6.9)

Motivational articulation

MA₁	0.0	2.0	7.1	2.8	0.5	0.0	0.0	0.2	(0.8)
MA₂	3.0	15.0	10.1	2.9	3.0	1.0	1.0	2.1	(9.0)
MA₃	2.0	8.0	4.0	2.0	2.0	0.0	0.0	1.3	(5.7)
MA₄	0.0	3.0	43.0	6.6	0.5	0.0	0.0	0.1	(0.4)

Explicit motivational valuation

M	1.0	10.0	5.8	2.4	2.3	1.0	1.0	1.3	(5.5)
N	2.0	10.0	6.3	2.2	2.0	1.0	1.0	1.7	(7.7)
B	1.0	4.0	4.5	2.2	1.1	0.0	0.0	0.6	(2.5)

Implicit motivational valuation

[M]	5.0	16.0	0.5	0.6	3.3	4.0	6.0	6.6	(37.8)
[N]	6.0	57.0	9.3	2.8	11.0	3.0	5.0	8.6	(35.5)
[B]	3.0	6.0	0.5	1.0	1.5	0.0	1.0	1.5	(9.1)

Perceptual-cognitive characteristics

AT	3.0	11.0	1.4	1.5	2.8	1.0	2.0	2.7	(14.1)
BC	0.0	2.0	5.6	2.5	0.5	0.0	0.0	0.2	(1.1)
CD	1.0	6.0	4.9	2.0	1.3	0.0	1.0	1.0	(5.6)
CP	0.0	1.0	18.8	4.5	0.2	0.0	0.0	0.0	(0.2)
CR	0.0	16.0	11.3	3.0	2.9	1.0	1.0	2.2	(10.4)
CT	0.0	1.0	43.0	6.6	0.2	0.0	0.0	0.0	(0.1)
DC	0.0	1.0	6.7	2.9	0.3	0.0	0.0	0.1	(0.7)

Healthy Children (N = 43; Category 3 = 11, 12 Year Olds) (Continued)

Variable	Mean(%)		Median	Mode	St.dev.	Skew	Kurt	Range	IQ Range
D$_x$	0.1	(0.5)	0.0	0.0	0.3	3.5	10.8	1.0	0.0
EJ	0.0	(0.1)	0.0	0.0	0.2	6.6	43.0	1.0	0.0
FCP	0.2	(1.3)	0.0	0.0	0.5	2.0	3.3	2.0	0.0
LR	0.0	(0.1)	0.0	0.0	0.2	6.6	43.0	1.0	0.0
P	4.4	(25.5)	4.0	3.0	2.0	0.1	−1.1	7.0	3.0
PSD	0.3	(2.2)	0.0	0.0	0.6	1.4	1.2	2.0	1.0
PT	0.6	(3.2)	0.0	0.0	0.9	1.4	1.0	3.0	1.0
S	0.4	(1.8)	0.0	0.0	0.7	1.6	1.2	2.0	1.0
(S)	2.7	(16.1)	3.0	2.0	1.7	0.1	−0.3	7.0	2.0
SR	0.7	(4.3)	0.0	0.0	1.4	2.3	5.5	6.0	1.0
TR	0.1	(0.7)	0.0	0.0	0.4	3.6	13.7	2.0	0.0
VP	0.1	(0.1)	0.0	0.0	0.3	5.2	27.7	2.0	0.0
(VP)	0.4	(2.5)	0.0	0.0	0.6	1.1	0.2	2.0	1.0
Psychosexual drive and defense effectiveness									
Oo P	0.4	(1.9)	0.0	0.0	0.7	2.1	5.3	3.0	1.0
Oo I	0.9	(4.3)	0.0	0.0	1.3	1.7	2.6	5.0	1.0
Oo G	0.1	(0.3)	0.0	0.0	0.4	3.6	13.7	2.0	0.0
Oc P	0.1	(0.6)	0.0	0.0	0.3	2.5	4.4	1.0	0.0
Oc I	0.4	(2.0)	0.0	0.0	0.7	2.0	4.0	3.0	1.0
Oc G	0.1	(0.5)	0.0	0.0	0.3	2.9	6.7	1.0	0.0
All Oo	1.4	(6.5)	1.0	0.0	1.8	1.6	3.2	8.0	3.0
All Oc	0.6	(3.1)	0.0	0.0	0.8	1.1	0.1	3.0	1.0
All Oral	2.0	(9.6)	1.0	0.0	2.3	1.6	3.0	10.0	3.0
Ao P	0.0	(0.0)	0.0	0.0	0.0	.	.	0.0	0.0
Ao I	0.0	(0.0)	0.0	0.0	0.0	.	.	0.0	0.0
Ao G	0.0	(0.0)	0.0	0.0	0.0	.	.	0.0	0.0

Ac P	0.1 (0.4)	0.0	0.0	0.3	3.5	10.8	1.0	0.0
Ac I	0.5 (2.3)	0.0	0.0	0.9	3.2	13.9	5.0	1.0
Ac G	0.1 (0.6)	0.0	0.0	0.4	3.6	13.7	2.0	0.0
All Ao	0.0 (0.0)	0.0	0.0	0.0	.	.	0.0	0.0
All Ac	0.7 (3.3)	0.0	0.0	1.1	2.5	7.3	5.0	1.0
All Anal	0.7 (3.3)	0.0	0.0	1.1	2.5	7.3	5.0	1.0
Po P	0.0 (0.0)	0.0	0.0	0.0	.	.	0.0	0.0
Po I	0.0 (0.0)	0.0	0.0	0.0	.	.	0.0	0.0
Po G	0.0 (0.0)	0.0	0.0	0.0	.	.	0.0	0.0
Pc P	0.3 (1.6)	0.0	0.0	0.5	1.8	2.5	2.0	0.0
Pc I	1.4 (7.6)	1.0	0.0	1.6	1.2	0.6	5.0	2.0
Pc G	0.2 (0.5)	0.0	0.0	0.6	2.6	5.8	2.0	0.0
All Po	0.0 (0.0)	0.0	0.0	0.0	.	.	0.0	0.0
All Pc	1.8 (9.8)	1.0	0.0	1.8	0.7	−0.6	6.0	3.0
All Phallic	1.8 (9.8)	1.0	0.0	1.8	0.7	−0.6	6.0	3.0

Percentages and ratios

Total R	20.7 (100.0)	14.0	14.0	16.8	3.3	12.2	89.0	11.0
F%	37.0	35.7	14.3	18.8	0.3	−0.6	75.0	26.5
F+%	66.9	66.7	50.0	18.2	0.4	−0.4	66.7	21.7
B+%	59.7	61.5	50.0	19.1	−0.5	−0.2	78.9	27.9
Afr	55.0	42.9	37.5	44.8	4.8	27.0	289.4	32.1
f%	0.0	0.0	0.0	.	.	.	0.0	0.0
r%	12.8	10.3	0.0	9.6	0.7	−0.2	33.3	10.2
PD%	22.7	18.2	0.0	15.5	0.6	−0.2	64.3	25.7
H%	23.6	23.1	14.3	15.5	1.5	4.3	83.3	16.5
A%	57.5	55.6	50.0	16.1	0.4	0.4	75.9	17.6

Foster Adolescents (N = 42)

Variable	Mean(%)		Median	Mode	St.dev.	Skew	Kurt	Range	IQ Range
					Location				
W	6.1	(39.7)	6.5	4	3.0	.3	−.6	12	4
$\overline{W}$	0.0	(0.0)	0	0	0.0	.	.	0	0
(W)	0.0	(0.0)	0	0	0.0	.	.	0	0
$\overline{(W)}$	0.0	(0.0)	0	0	0.0	.	.	0	0
TOTAL W	6.1	(39.7)	6.5	4	3.0	0.3	−0.6	12	4
W%	39.7		39.2	33.3	20.2	0.3	−0.7	80.6	33.3
D	10.0	(54.2)	8	6	7.4	1.4	1.3	31	7
$\overline{D}$	0.0	(0.0)	0	0	0.0	.	.	0	0
$\overline{D}+D$	10.0	(54.2)	8	6	7.4	1.4	1.3	31	7
D%	54.2		54.6	50	20.6	−0.3	−0.8	77.4	34.0
Dd	.5	(2.1)	0	0	.9	2.4	6.1	4	1
$\overline{Dd}$	0.0	(0.0)	0	0	0.0	.	.	0	0
$\overline{Dd}+Dd$	0.5	(2.1)	0	0	0.9	2.4	6.1	4	1
Dd%	2.1		0	0	3.4	1.3	0.3	10.8	4.8
$W+(W)+D+\overline{Dd}$	2.0	(10.5)	1	1	2.1	1.5	2.0	9.0	2.3
r%	10.5		9.5	0	7.9	0.6	0.1	31.8	8.8
					Cognitive complexity				
INTEGRATED	2.5	(16.2)	3	3	1.6	.1	−.6	6	2.3
ARTICULATED	9.8	(54.4)	9	5	6.0	1.0	.3	24	7.3
SIMPLE	2.7	(14.5)	2	1	2.5	1.1	.6	9	3
DIFFUSE	.7	(4.3)	1	0	.9	1.4	3.0	4	1
ARBITRARY	1.0	(7.0)	.5	0	1.3	1.2	.7	5	2

Justifications and imaginal aspects

All f	.4	(2.2)	0	0	1.2	4.4	21.8	7	0
All C	2.0	(11.3)	1.5	1	2.1	1.6	2.8	9	2.3
All Ca	0	(0.0)	0	0	0	.	.	0	0
All Ci	.2	(.8)	0	0	.8	5.6	33.1	5	0
All Cp	.1	(.4)	0	0	.3	5.1	27.0	2	0
All C'	.9	(4.3)	0	0	1.3	2.2	5.2	6	1
All F	15.7	(91.0)	13.0	9	7.5	1.3	1.0	30	7.3
All Sh	1.0	(5.4)	.5	0	1.4	1.6	2.5	6	2
All AM	1.7	(10.8)	2	2	1.2	.5	.1	5	1.3
All HE	.5	(2.7)	0	0	.9	1.7	1.9	3	1
All HM	2.8	(17.0)	2	1	2.2	.8	-.1	9	4
All OM	.8	(3.9)	0	0	1.2	1.6	1.4	4	1
All T	.2	(1.2)	0	0	.5	2.7	6.8	2	0
All V	.4	(2.4)	0	0	.6	1.3	.7	2	1
Pure f	0.0	(0.0)	0.0	0.0	0.0	.	.	0.0	0.0
Pure C	0.2	(1.2)	0.0	0.0	0.5	2.4	5.6	2.0	0.0
C·F	1.8	(9.9)	1.5	0.0	1.8	1.1	0.8	7.0	2.3
C'·F	16.5	(95.4)	13.5	12.0	8.2	1.3	0.9	33.0	8.0
Pure F	8.3	(47.8)	8.0	4.0	5.1	1.4	2.6	24.0	7.0
F·Sh	16.7	(96.4)	14.5	12.0	8.4	1.4	1.1	34.0	7.3
F·AM	1.7	(10.6)	2.0	1.0	1.2	0.3	-0.6	4.0	1.3
F·HM	2.7	(16.9)	2.0	1.0	2.2	0.6	-0.6	8.0	4.0

Conceptual content

A	7.0	(43.5)	6	5	3.2	1.4	2.8	16	4
(A)	0.2	(0.9)	0	0	0.4	2.7	7.4	2	0
Af	0.7	(3.1)	0	0	1.1	2.2	4.7	5	1
(Af)	0.0	(0.2)	0	0	0.2	4.4	18.3	1	0
Ad + Adx	0.6	(2.8)	0	0	1.2	2.9	10.1	6	1

Foster Adolescents (N = 42) (Continued)

Variable	Mean(%)	Median	Mode	St.dev.	Skew	Kurt	Range	IQ Range
H	2.1 (12.9)	2	3	1.6	0.6	-0.0	6	2
(H)	1.2 (7.8)	1	1	1.2	1.3	2.0	5	2
H_f	0.5 (2.7)	0	0	0.8	1.5	1.6	3	1
(H_f)	0.2 (1.3)	0	0	0.6	3.1	10.3	3	0
Hd + Hdx	0.5 (2.3)	0	0	1.0	2.3	5.0	4	1
Abs	0.1 (0.7)	0	0	0.4	4.2	18.6	2	0
An_b	0.4 (2.0)	0	0	0.6	1.1	0.4	2	1
An_s	0.3 (1.2)	0	0	0.6	2.9	9.1	3	0
An_{sx}	0.0 (0.0)	0	0	0.0	.	.	0	0
An_x	0.0 (0.0)	0	0	0.0	.	.	0	0
Art	0.0 (0.1)	0	0	0.2	6.5	42.0	1	0
Bl	0.1 (0.3)	0	0	0.5	5.7	33.6	3	0
Bt	1.1 (7.1)	1	1	1.1	1.3	2.6	5	2
Cld	0.5 (3.0)	0	0	0.6	0.9	-0.1	2	1
Clg								
Dth	0.6 (0.2)	0	0	0.2	4.4	18.3	1	0
Emb								
Fd	0.2 (0.8)	0	0	0.4	1.9	1.5	1	0
Fi	0.3 (1.3)	0	0	0.9	4.4	22.4	5	0
Geo								
Hh	0.0 (0.0)	0	0	0.0	.	.	0	0
Imp								
Ls	1.1 (6.5)	1	1	1.0	0.9	0.7	4	2
Mu	0.0 (0.0)	0	0	0.0	.	.	0	0
Rel	0.1 (0.7)	0	0	0.4	3.1	9.9	2	0
Sch	0.0 (0.0)	0	0	0.0	.	.	0	0
Sci	0.0 (0.2)	0	0	0.2	6.5	42.0	1	0
Tr	0.0 (0.0)	0	0	0.0	.	.	0	0
Ty								
Wp	0.1 (0.5)	0	0	0.5	4.5	22.9	3	0

Human articulation

	Mean	(SD)							
HA₁	.5	(3.1)	0	0	1.5	1.5	.9	3	1
HA₂	.9	(5.4)	1	1	1.1	2.1	.9	4	1
HA₃	1.6	(9.4)	2	2	1.0	1.5	1.4	6	2
HA₄	1.3	(7.4)	1	0	1.1	.8	1.3	5	2

Motivational articulation

	Mean	(SD)							
MA₁	.0	(.4)	0	0	4.4	18.3	.2	1	0
MA₂	1.6	(9.9)	1	0	1.1	.9	1.6	6	2
MA₃	1.2	(7.4)	1	1	1.3	1.1	1.3	5	2
MA₄	0	(0.0)	0	0	.	.	0	0	0

Explicit motivational valuation

	Mean	(SD)							
M	1.0	(7.0)	1	0	.9	-.0	1.2	4	2
N	1.0	(6.0)	1	0	1.1	1.0	1.0	4	1.3
B	.7	(3.8)	0	0	1.5	1.8	1.0	4	1

Implicit motivational valuation

	Mean	(SD)							
(M)	6.2	(35.1)	5	5	1.2	1.0	3.7	16	4.3
(N)	6.1	(35.2)	6	4	2.1	6.7	3.8	21	3
(B)	1.6	(8.7)	1	1	.9	-.1	1.5	5	1.5

Perceptual-cognitive characteristics

	Mean	(SD)							
AT	2.0	(11.6)	1	0	1.3	1.0	2.3	8	4
BC	.1	(.9)	0	0	6.0	36.9	.6	4	0
CD	.3	(1.7)	0	0	2.0	3.0	.6	2	0
CP	0.0	(0.0)	0	0	.	.	0.0	0	0
CR	1.6	(9.8)	1	0	1.2	.5	1.9	7	2.3
CT	0.0	(.1)	0	0	6.5	42.0	.2	1	0
DC	0.0	(0.0)	0	0	.	.	0.0	0	0

Foster Adolescents (N = 42) (Continued)

Variable	Mean(%)		Median	Mode	St.dev.	Skew	Kurt	Range	IQ Range
D_x	0.0	(.2)	0	0	.2	6.5	42.0	1	0
EJ	0.0	(0.0)	0	0	0.0	.	.	0	0
FCP	0.0	(.1)	0	0	.2	6.5	42.0	1	0
LR	0.0	(.3)	0	0	.2	4.4	18.3	1	0
P	4.7	(28.5)	4	5	2.2	1.1	1.6	11	2.3
PSD	0.0	(0.0)	0	0	0.0	.	.	0	0
PT	.2	(1.1)	0	0	.6	3.8	16.4	3	0
S	.1	(.9)	0	0	.4	2.1	2.6	1	0
(S)	1.5	(8.3)	1	0	2.0	2.1	4.9	9	2
SR	.4	(2.6)	0	0	.7	1.8	2.9	3	1
TR	0.0	(.2)	0	0	.2	4.4	18.3	1	0
VP	.1	(.6)	0	0	.3	2.9	6.5	1	0
(VP)	.3	(1.6)	0	0	.7	3.6	15.5	4	0
Psychosexual drive and defense effectiveness									
Oo P	0.1	(0.4)	0.0	0.0	0.4	4.2	18.6	2.0	0.0
Oo I	0.6	(3.4)	0.0	0.0	1.0	1.8	2.7	4.0	1.0
Oo G	0.0	(0.0)	0.0	0.0	0.0	.	.	0.0	0.0
Oc P	0.0	(0.0)	0.0	0.0	0.0	.	.	0.0	0.0
Oc I	0.2	(1.5)	0.0	0.0	0.5	2.2	4.3	2.0	0.0
Oc G	0.0	(0.2)	0.0	0.0	0.2	6.5	42.0	1.0	0.0
All Oo	0.7	(3.8)	0.0	0.0	1.2	2.1	4.3	5.0	1.0
All Oc	0.3	(1.7)	0.0	0.0	0.5	2.0	3.4	2.0	0.0
All Oral	1.0	(5.5)	0.0	0.0	1.3	1.8	4.1	6.0	2.0
Ao P	0.0	(0.2)	0.0	0.0	0.2	6.5	42.0	1.0	0.0
Ao I	0.0	(0.2)	0.0	0.0	0.2	4.4	18.3	1.0	0.0
Ao G	0.0	(0.0)	0.0	0.0	0.0	.	.	0.0	0.0

Ac P	0.0	(0.2)	0.0	0.0	0.2	4.4	18.3	1.0	0.0
Ac I	0.5	(2.4)	0.0	0.0	0.8	1.3	0.1	2.0	1.0
Ac G	0.0	(0.0)	0.0	0.0	0.0	.	.	0.0	0.0
All Ao	0.1	(0.4)	0.0	0.0	0.3	3.5	10.4	1.0	0.0
All Ac	0.5	(2.6)	0.0	0.0	0.9	1.4	0.7	3.0	1.0
All Anal	0.6	(3.0)	0.0	0.0	0.9	1.2	0.0	3.0	1.0
Po P	0.0	(0.0)	0.0	0.0	0.0	.	.	0.0	0.0
Po I	0.0	(0.2)	0.0	0.0	0.2	6.5	42.0	1.0	0.0
Po G	0.0	(0.0)	0.0	0.0	0.0	.	.	0.0	0.0
Pc P	0.0	(0.1)	0.0	0.0	0.2	6.5	42.0	1.0	0.0
Pc I	1.2	(7.3)	0.0	1.0	1.2	1.8	5.4	6.0	2.0
Pc G	0.0	(0.1)	0.0	0.0	0.2	6.5	42.0	1.0	0.0
All Po	0.0	(0.2)	0.0	0.0	0.2	6.5	42.0	1.0	0.0
All Pc	1.3	(7.7)	1.0	1.0	1.3	2.2	7.9	7.0	2.0
All Phallic	1.3	(7.9)	1.0	1.0	1.3	2.1	7.1	7.0	2.0
Percentages and ratios									
Total R	17.1	(100.0)	14.0	11.0	7.6	1.4	0.8	27.0	7.3
F%	47.8		47.2	18.2	18.1	0.1	-0.3	80.0	25.9
F+%	65.9		63.1	50.0	16.4	0.6	-0.3	60.0	25.5
B+%	62.8		63.3	75.0	22.2	-0.5	0.3	100.0	31.5
Afr	50.7		50.0	42.9	15.6	0.9	1.6	78.6	18.0
f%	0.0		0.0	0.0	0.0	.	.	0.0	0.0
r%	0.0		0.0	0.0	0.0	.	.	0.0	0.0
PD%	16.5		16.2	0.0	12.3	0.6	-0.1	45.5	17.1
H%	26.8		28.6	0.0	14.2	-0.2	-0.7	54.5	22.6
A%	50.5		50.0	50.0	16.9	0.3	0.4	73.3	19.0

Talented College Students (N = 67)

Variable	Mean(%)	Median	Mode	St.dev.	Skew	Kurt	Range	IQ Range
				Location				
W	9.2 (39.5)	8	7	4.4	.9	.8	19	6
W̲	2.4 (10.7)	2	0	2.3	.9	1.0	10	4
(W)	.3 (1.3)	0	0	.7	2.4	5.3	3	0
(W)̲	0.0 (0.0)	0	0	0.0	.	.	0	0
TOTAL W	12.0 (51.5)	11	10	5.6	1.2	1.8	26	6
W%	51.5	52.4	47.4	20.3	-0.2	-0.9	79.0	32.9
D	10.8 (38.6)	8	4	8.8	1.7	2.9	40	10
D̲	1.9 (7.4)	1	0	2.0	.9	-.1	7	3
D̲+D	12.7 (46.0)	10	10	9.6	1.6	2.4	44	13
D%	46.0	43.8	52.6	18.4	0.2	-0.9	75.1	31.5
Dd	.7 (1.2)	0	0	4.2	8.0	65.2	34	0
Dd̲	.4 (1.1)	0	0	.8	2.6	6.9	4	0
Dd+Dd̲	1.0 (2.2)	0	0	4.2	7.6	60.4	34	1
Dd%	2.2	0	0	5.8	5.6	38.1	43.0	3.4
W+(W)+D̲+Dd̲	4.0 (14.6)	3	1	3.8	2.0	5.0	19.0	4.0
r%	14.6	13.8	0	10.5	0.9	1.0	47.8	13.4
				Cognitive complexity				
INTEGRATED	5.1 (21.5)	5	3	2.7	.6	-.2	11	4
ARTICULATED	14.5 (55.5)	13	10	8.7	2.1	7.4	-54	9
SIMPLE	2.4 (8.1)	1	0	3.2	1.7	2.2	13	3
DIFFUSE	1.3 (4.5)	1	0	1.8	2.0	3.5	7	1
ARBITRARY	2.5 (10.1)	2	1	2.1	.8	.3	9	3

Justifications and imaginal aspects

All f	.2	(.8)	0	0	.5	2.6	5.5	2	0
All C	5.8	(28.5)	5	4	3.4	.7	−.2	15	5
All Ca	0	(.0)	0	0	0	.	.	0	0
All Ci	.3	(1.4)	0	0	.7	2.1	4.3	3	0
All Cp	.0	(.0)	0	0	.1	8.2	67	1	0
All C'	2.7	(11.6)	2	1	2.1	.5	−.9	8	4
All F	24.6	(96.0)	22	22	12.3	1.9	5.0	70	13
All Sh	3.3	(11.8)	2	0	3.4	2.0	6.0	19	4
All AM	3.6	(15.6)	3	2	2.3	1.3	1.9	11	3
All HE	.8	(3.3)	0	0	1.1	1.8	3.1	5	1
All HM	6.4	(25.4)	6	6	4.2	2.1	7.7	27	4
All OM	2.3	(9.0)	2	1	1.9	.8	−.0	7	3
All T	1.0	(4.1)	1	0	1.4	2.1	5.5	7	1
All V	2.1	(8.7)	1	1	2.0	2.0	6.0	11	2
Pure f	0.0	(0.0)	0.0	0.0	0.0	.	.	0.0	0.0
Pure C	0.2	(0.7)	0.0	0.0	0.5	2.6	6.5	2.0	0.0
C·F	5.3	(21.3)	4.0	4.0	3.3	0.7	−0.4	13.0	4.0
C'·F	27.3	(107.5)	25.0	25.0	13.1	1.9	5.4	74.0	15.0
Pure F	8.1	(29.6)	6.0	6.0	6.3	1.6	2.4	27.0	7.0
F·Sh	28.0	(107.9)	24.0	24.0	14.4	1.6	3.5	77.0	18.0
F·AM	3.6	(15.3)	3.0	2.0	2.3	1.3	1.9	11.0	3.0
F·HM	6.3	(25.0)	6.0	6.0	4.2	2.1	8.1	27.0	4.0

Conceptual content

A	7.7	(31.9)	7	7	3.6	.7	.1	15	4
(A)	0.9	(4.0)	1	0	1.1	2.0	6.2	6	1
Af	1.0	(3.6)	1	0	1.4	2.6	10.1	8	1
(Af)	0.2	(.7)	0	0	.4	2.5	6.0	2	0
Ad+Adx	0.3	(1.0)	0	0	0.7	2.2	4.3	3	0

215

Talented College Students (N = 67) (Continued)

Variable	Mean(%)		Median	Mode	St.dev.	Skew	Kurt	Range	IQ Range
H	4.0	(15.7)	3	4	3.1	1.6	3.8	17	3
(H)	1.6	(5.9)	1	0	1.8	1.4	2.3	8	2
Hr	1.1	(4.2)	1	0	1.6	2.5	8.3	8	2
(Hf)	.7	(2.5)	0	0	1.1	1.8	3.7	5	1
Hd+Hdx	0.6	(2.4)	0	0	0.9	2.2	7.5	5	1
Abs	.1	(.4)	0	0	.4	4.0	15.9	2	0
Anb	.6	(2.5)	0	0	.9	2.4	8.0	5	1
Ans	.4	(1.5)	0	0	.7	2.8	10.0	4	1
Ansx	.3	(1.1)	0	0	1.1	5.5	35.4	8	0
Anx	.1	(.2)	0	0	.3	5.4	31.1	2	0
Art	.3	(.9)	0	0	.6	2.9	9.0	3	0
Bl	.3	(1.0)	0	0	.5	1.9	2.9	2	0
Bt	1.3	(5.3)	1	0	1.3	1.0	.5	5	2
Cld	.7	(3.0)	1	0	.9	1.7	3.1	4	1
Clg									
Dth	.3	(1.2)	0	0	.9	3.1	10.0	4	0
Emb									
Fd	.5	(1.7)	0	0	.9	2.5	8.3	5	1
Fi	.6	(2.5)	0	0	.8	1.2	.6	3	1
Geo									
Hh	.1	(.6)	0	0	.4	3.3	10.9	2	0
Imp									
Ls	1.6	(6.3)	1	1	1.5	1.2	1.3	7	2
Mu	.3	(1.2)	0	0	.6	1.7	1.8	2	1
Rel	.2	(.9)	0	0	.5	2.1	4.0	2	0
Sch	.2	(.7)	0	0	.6	3.5	13.8	3	0
Sci	.1	(.4)	0	0	.3	4.1	17.7	2	0
Tr	.4	(1.6)	0	0	.9	3.0	12.3	5	1
Ty									
Wp	.3	(1.2)	0	0	.5	1.5	1.5	2	1

216

Human articulation

HA$_1$	1	3	2.1	1.6	.7	0	0	.4	(1.7)
HA$_2$	1	5	2.6	1.5	1.1	0	1	.9	(3.4)
HA$_3$	3	18	8.9	2.4	2.9	2	2	3.2	(12.4)
HA$_4$	3	11	.3	1.1	3.0	1	2	3.3	(12.6)

Motivational articulation

MA$_1$	1	7	7.7	2.4	1.3	0	1	.9	(3.4)
MA$_2$	2	12	3.5	1.3	2.1	3	3	3.0	(12.5)
MA$_3$	4	7	-1.0	.5	2.0	0	2	2.3	(9.2)
MA$_4$	0	4	7.3	2.8	.8	0	0	.3	(1.4)

Explicit motivational valuation

M	2	10	1.8	1.2	2.1	1	2	2.3	(9.3)
N	2	9	2.0	1.4	2.2	1	2	2.2	(8.9)
B	3	8	.4	1.0	2.0	0	1	2.0	(7.7)

Implicit motivational valuation

(M)	5	24	4.2	1.5	4.1	4	5	5.9	(23)
(N)	7	32	2.1	1.3	6.5	5	9	9.8	(37.2)
(B)	3	12	2.8	1.5	2.5	1	2	2.9	(11.2)

Perceptual-cognitive characteristics

AT	3	12	1.2	1.2	2.7	0	2	2.7	(11.0)
BC	0	3	16.2	3.8	.5	0	0	.2	(.6)
CD	3	9	1.0	1.4	2.2	0	1	1.8	(7.7)
CP	0	2	67.0	8.2	.2	0	0	.0	(.1)
CR	4	14	8.0	2.2	2.4	0	2	2.2	(8.9)
CT	0	1	67.0	8.2	.1	0	0	.0	(.0)
DC	0	2	67.0	8.2	.2	0	0	.0	(.1)

Talented College Students (N = 67) (Continued)

Variable	Mean(%)		Median	Mode	St.dev.	Skew	Kurt	Range	IQ Range
D$_x$	.1	(.5)	0	0	.4	3.6	13.1	2	0
EJ	.2	(.7)	0	0	.6	3.6	12.9	3	0
FCP	1.1	(3.6)	0	0	1.8	2.7	9.6	10	2
LR	.0	(.1)	0	0	.2	4.5	18.8	1	0
P	5.9	(26.1)	6	5	2.2	.1	.3	12	3
PSD	.2	(1.0)	0	0	.6	3.0	9.6	3	0
PT	.3	(1.3)	0	0	.5	1.8	2.5	2	0
S	1.2	(4.4)	1	0	1.6	2.0	4.7	7	2
(S)	2.9	(11.7)	3	0	2.2	.3	-.7	8	4
SR	2.3	(9.8)	1	0	3.4	2.9	9.6	18	3
TR	.1	(.5)	0	0	.4	3.3	10.9	2	0
VP	.0	(.2)	0	0	.3	6.5	44.0	2	0
(VP)	1.1	(4.7)	1	0	1.5	1.4	1.0	5	2
Psychosexual drive and defense effectiveness									
Oo P	0.1	(0.2)	0.0	0.0	0.5	6.2	42.5	4.0	0.0
Oo I	0.9	(2.8)	0.0	0.0	1.4	1.3	0.6	5.0	2.0
Oo G	0.02	(0.1)	0.0	0.0	0.2	5.7	30.9	1.0	0.0
Oc P	0.0	(0.1)	0.0	0.0	0.2	5.7	30.9	1.0	0.0
Oc I	0.3	(0.8)	0.0	0.0	0.8	3.1	10.1	4.0	0.0
Oc G	0.0	(0.2)	0.0	0.0	0.2	4.5	18.8	1.0	0.0
All Oo	1.1	(3.3)	0.0	0.0	1.7	2.2	6.0	9.0	2.0
All Oc	0.4	(1.2)	0.0	0.0	0.9	2.8	9.3	5.0	1.0
All Oral	1.5	(4.6)	0.0	0.0	2.5	2.6	9.1	14.0	3.0
Ao P	0.0	(0.0)	0.0	0.0	0.0	.	.	0.0	0.0
Ao I	0.1	(0.2)	0.0	0.0	0.3	4.7	23.1	2.0	0.0
Ao G	0.0	(0.0)	0.0	0.0	0.1	8.2	67.0	1.0	0.0

Ac P	0.0	(0.0)	0.0	0.0	0.1	8.2	67.0	1.0	0.0
Ac I	0.6	(2.2)	0.0	0.0	0.9	1.2	0.02	3.0	1.0
Ac G	0.1	(0.5)	0.0	0.0	0.4	3.3	11.1	2.0	0.0
All Ao	0.1	(0.3)	0.0	0.0	0.3	4.1	17.7	2.0	0.0
All Ac	0.8	(2.8)	0.0	0.0	1.1	1.2	0.4	4.0	1.0
All Anal	0.9	(3.1)	0.0	0.0	1.2	1.3	0.6	4.0	2.0
Po P	0.0	(0.0)	0.0	0.0	0.1	8.2	67.0	1.0	0.0
Po I	0.2	(0.8)	0.0	0.0	0.7	4.7	26.4	5.0	0.0
Po G	0.0	(0.0)	0.0	0.0	0.0	.	.	0.0	0.0
Pc P	0.1	(0.4)	0.0	0.0	0.3	2.6	5.2	1.0	0.0
Pc I	1.7	(6.3)	1.0	0.0	2.2	1.1	0.1	8.0	3.0
Pc G	0.2	(1.0)	0.0	0.0	0.5	2.3	4.6	2.0	0.0
All Po	0.3	(0.9)	0.0	0.0	0.8	4.4	24.2	5.0	0.0
All Pc	2.1	(7.9)	2.0	0.0	2.4	0.9	-0.3	9.0	4.0
All Phallic	2.4	(8.8)	2.0	0.0	2.8	1.0	0.2	10.0	4.0
Percentages and ratios									
Total R	25.7	(100.0)	22.0	19.0	12.7	1.7	4.1	69	15
F%	29.6		27.5	27.3	14.2	.3	.1	71.4	21.8
F+%	67.8		66.7	66.7	21.8	-.5	.2	100.0	31.7
B+%	67.7		69.7	75	14.9	-0.1	-.9	60	24.8
Afr	56.7		46.7	45.4	21.9	1.0	.4	88.0	32.7
f%	0		0	0	0.0	.	.	0	0
r%	19.2		19.0	0	11.5	.2	-.3	47.8	17.9
PD%	16.4		18.2	0	15.6	.4	-1.0	52.9	28
H%	30.7		30	27.3	11.4	-.03	-.3	52.1	16.1
A%	41.3		38.5	33.3	13.8	.6	-.01	60	17.9

219

Referred Children (N = 241)

Variable	Mean 5–10	11–13	14–19
Total R	17.7	18.1	15.6
F%	39.5	54.4[b]	53.0[b]
F+%	60.4	67.0	71.9
B+%	61.5[b]	67.2[b]	74.4[b]
Afr	54.4	54.4	54.4
f%	6.4	3.2	2.0
r%	14.0**	14.0**	14.0**
PD%	33.8	28.0	23.0
H%	22.3	22.3	22.3
A%	60.3	60.3	60.3
W	6.4*	5.2*	5.5*
$\overline{W}$	1.2*	0.6*	0.5*
$W+\overline{W}$	7.6	5.8	6.0
W%	42.9	32.0	38.5
(W)	0.3	0.3	0.3
D	7.9	7.9	7.9
$\underline{D}$	1.4	1.4	1.4
$(W)+D+\underline{D}$	9.6	9.6	9.6
D%	56.4	56.4	56.4
Dd	0.6	0.6	0.6
$\underline{Dd}$	0.2	0.2	0.2

Variable	Mean 5–10	11–13	14–19
MA_1	0.1	0.1	0.1
MA_2	1.0	1.0	1.0
MA_3	1.0	1.0	1.0
MA_4	0.1	0.1	0.1
A	8.0	9.2	7.1
(A)	0.8	0.4	0.3
A_f	1.0	1.0	1.0
(A_f)			
Ad + Adx	0.5	0.5	0.5
H	1.7	1.7	1.7
(H)	1.2	0.9	0.4
H_f	0.5	0.8	0.5
(H_f)			
Hd + Hdx	0.4	0.4	0.4
Abs	0.1	0.1	0.1
An_b	0.5	0.5	0.5
An_s	0.6	0.2	0.2
An_{sx}	0.0	0.0	0.0
An_x	0.0	0.0	0.0
Art	0.3	0.1	0.1
Bl	0.5	0.5	0.5
Bt	0.2	0.2	0.2
Cld			

Variable	Mean 5–10	11–13	14–19
Ao P	0.0	0.0	0.0
Ao I	0.0	0.0	0.0
Ao G	0.0	0.0	0.0
Ac P	0.3	0.1	0.0
Ac I	0.6	0.4	0.3
Ac G	0.4	0.4	0.4
All Ao	0.1	0.1	0.1
All Ac	1.3	0.7	0.7
All Anal	1.4	0.8	0.8
Po P	0.0	0.0	0.0
Po I	0.0	0.0	0.0
Po G	0.0	0.0	0.0
Pc P	0.4	0.4	0.4
Pc I	1.0	1.0	1.0
Pc G	0.7	0.7	0.7
All Po	0.0	0.0	0.0
All Pc	2.1	2.1	2.1
All Phallic	2.1	2.1	2.1
AT	2.6	1.8	1.1
BC	0.2	0.2	0.2
CD	0.4	0.4	0.4
CP	0.1	0.1	0.1

Dd+Dd	0.8	0.8	0.8	0.8
Dd%	4.6	4.6	4.6	4.6
W+D+Dd	2.4*	2.4*	2.4*	2.4*
r%	14.0*	14.0*	14.0*	14.0*
Integrated	2.4	2.4	2.4	
(Integrated)	0.0	0.0	0.0	
Articulated	10.7	10.7	10.7	
Simple	2.2	2.2	2.2	
Diffuse	0.6	0.6	0.6	
Arbitrary	1.8	0.9	0.5	
Pure f	0.8	0.4	0.2	
Pure C	0.2	0.2	0.2	
C·F	0.6	0.6	0.6	
C'·F	0.6	0.6		
Pure F	7.5	10.2	8.2	
F·Sh	0.2	0.2	0.2	
F·AM	1.2	1.2	1.2	
F·HM	1.6	1.6	1.6	
HA₁	0.4	0.4	0.4	
HA₂	0.7	1.1	0.6	
HA₃	0.8	0.8	0.8	
HA₄	0.6	0.6	0.6	

Clg			
Dth			
Emb			
Fd	0.3	0.3	0.3
Fi			
Geo			
Hh			
Imp	0.4	0.4	0.4
Ls			
Mu	0.0	0.0	0.0
Rel	0.1	0.1	0.1
Sch	0.1	0.1	0.1
Sci			
Tr			
Ty			
Wp	0.1	0.1	0.1
Oo P	0.2	0.2	0.2
Oo I	0.5	0.5	0.5
Oo G	0.3	0.3	0.3
Oc P	0.1	0.1	0.1
Oc I	0.3	0.3	0.3
Oc G	0.2	0.2	0.2
All Oo	1.0	1.0	1.0
All Oc	0.6	0.6	0.6
All Oral	1.6	1.6	1.6

CR	2.8	1.8	1.3
CT	0.1	0.1	0.1
DC	0.0	0.0	0.0
Dₓ	0.1	0.1	0.1
EJ	0.1c	0.1c	0.1c
FCP	0.8	0.5	0.4
LR			
P	3.9	5.0	4.7
PSD	0.6	0.3	0.2
PT	0.5	0.4	0.2
S	0.3	0.3	0.3
(S)	1.3	1.3	1.3
SR	0.8	0.3	0.4
TR			
VP	0.4	0.2	0.0c
(VP)	1.1	0.8	0.6
M	1.3	0.9	0.7
N	0.8	0.8	0.8
B	0.7	0.7	0.7
(M)	3.4	2.7	1.8
(N)	2.7	2.7	2.7
(B)	0.9	0.9	0.9

**Using Cards III, VIII, IX, and X as rare.

*Using Cards III, IX, and X as rare.

aSignificantly different from healthy adult sample, p ≤ .05

bMales significantly higher p ≤ .05

cFemales significantly higher, p ≤ .05

Hospitalized Adults (N = 20)

Variable	Mean(%)		Median	Mode	St.dev.	Skew	Kurt	Range	IQ Range
				Location					
W	4.6	(35.6)	4.0	4	2.6	.9	2.8	12	2
$\overline{W}$	1.4	(11.6)	1.5	2	1.1	.0	-1.3	3	2
(W)	0.5	(2.7)	0.0	0	1.1	2.6	6.6	4	0
$(\overline{W})$	NA	NA	NA	NA	NA	NA	NA	NA	NA
TOTAL W	6.5	NA	NA	NA	NA	NA	NA	NA	NA
W%	48.5		NA	NA	NA	NA	NA	NA	NA
D	6.2	(44.0)	4.0	2	5.1	1.3	1.0	17	7
$\overline{D}$	0.4	(4.1)	0	0	0.8	2.3	4.9	3	.8
$\overline{D}+\underline{D}$	6.6	NA	NA	NA	NA	NA	NA	NA	NA
D%	49.3		NA	NA	NA	NA	NA	NA	NA
Dd	0.1	(0.2)	0.0	0	0.2	4.5	20.0	1	0
$\overline{Dd}$	0.3	(1.7)	0.0	0	0.6	2.2	4.7	2	0
$\overline{Dd}+\underline{Dd}$	0.3	(1.9)	0.0	0	0.7	2.1	3.2	2	0
Dd%	1.9		0.0	0	4.4	2.6	7.0	17	0
$W+(\underline{W})+\underline{D}+\underline{Dd}$	2.1	(15.8)							
r%	12.0		15.0	0	12.9	1.3	2.5	50	17
				Cognitive complexity					
INTEGRATED	2.4	(17.9)	2	1	2.0	.8	-.0	7	2.8
ARTICULATED	6.0	(42.9)	4	4	4.5	1.2	.4	15	5.8
SIMPLE	2.6	(22.1)	2	1	2.2	.9	.3	8	3
DIFFUSE	1.1	(8.2)	0	0	1.3	.7	-1.4	3	2.8
ARBITRARY	1.3	(8.9)	1	0	1.6	1.6	3.0	6	2

Justifications and imaginal aspects

All f	.5 (4.5)	0	0	0.7	1.3	.5	2	1
All C	2.0 (15.9)	2	1	1.5	.4	−.8	5	2
All Ca	0.0 (0.0)	0	0	0.0	.	.	0	0
All Ci	0.1 (0.6)	0	0	0.2	4.5	20.0	1	0
All Cp	0.1 (0.3)	0	0	0.2	4.5	20.0	1	0
All C'	1.1 (7.1)	1	0	1.5	2.2	5.3	6	1
All F	12.7 (94.9)	11.5	10	6.2	1.2	2.4	27	6
All Sh	0.6 (3.8)	0	0	1.0	2.5	7.2	4	1
All AM	1.4 (9.3)	1	1	1.4	1.1	.9	5	2.8
All HE	0.1 (0.6)	0	0	0.3	2.9	7.0	1	0
All HM	2.2 (16.6)	1.5	0	2.0	.7	−.8	6	3.8
All OM	1.1 (7.8)	1	0	1.1	.5	−1.0	3	2
All T	0.2 (1.4)	0	0	0.5	2.7	7.4	2	0
All V	0.2 (1.7)	0	0	0.4	1.6	.7	1	0

Conceptual content

A	5.9 (45.1)	4	4	4.4	1.4	1.6	17.0	4.0
(A)	0.3 (2.4)	0	0	0.5	.9	−1.2	1.0	1.0
A$_f$	0.3 (1.6)	0	0	0.4	1.3	−.5	1.0	0.8
(A$_f$)	0.0 (0.0)	0	0	0.0	.	.	0.0	0.0
Ad + Adx	0.9 (6.8)	0	0	1.6	2.5	6.2	6.0	1.0
H	1.2 (8.9)	1	0	1.4	1.3	1.6	5.0	2.0
(H)	0.5 (3.2)	0	0	0.8	2.0	4.1	3.0	1.0
H$_f$	0.3 (1.3)	0	0	0.6	2.2	4.7	2.0	0.0
(H$_f$)	0.2 (1.0)	0	0	0.5	3.4	11.9	2.0	0.0
Hd + Hdx	0.5 (4.7)	0	0	0.6	.8	−.2	2.0	1.0
Abs								
An$_b$	0.5 (3.3)	0	0	0.8	1.2	−.0	2.0	1.0
An$_s$	0.6 (4.7)	0	0	1.0	2.5	7.2	4.0	1.0
An$_{sx}$	0.1 (0.6)	0	0	0.3	2.9	7.0	1.0	0.0

Hospitalized Adults (N = 20) (Continued)

Variable	Mean(%)		Median	Mode	St.dev.	Skew	Kurt	Range	IQ Range
An_x	0.1	(0.8)	0	0	0.4	4.5	20.0	2.0	0.0
Art									
Bl	.3	(2.1)	0	0	.7	3.0	10.0	3.0	0.0
				Human articulation					
HA_1	.2	(1.8)	0	0	.4	2.1	2.8	1	0
HA_2	.1	(0.6)	0	0	.3	2.9	7.0	1	0
HA_3	1.2	(8.8)	1	0	1.3	.9	-.3	4	2
HA_4	1.1	(7.9)	1	0	1.1	.6	-1.1	3	2
				Motivational articulation					
MA_1	.3	(2.0)	0	0	.7	2.1	3.2	2	0
MA_2	1.0	(7.8)	1	0	1.1	.7	-.8	3	2
MA_3	1.1	(8.0)	1	1	1.1	1.3	1.2	4	1
MA_4	0.0	(0.0)	0	0	0	.	.	0	0
				Explicit motivational valuation					
M	1.0	(6.6)	1	0	1.2	1.3	1.2	4	1
N	.8	(6.8)	1	0	.9	.9	.2	3	1
B	.5	(4.2)	0	0	1.0	2.6	7.7	4	1
				Implicit motivational valuation					
(M)	5.1	(39.8)	4.5	4	3.0	1.0	1.5	12	3.8
(N)	4.4	(32.3)	3.0	3	3.2	.5	-.9	10	5.5
(B)	1.5	(9.9)	1.5	2	1.6	2.1	6.8	7	2.0

Perceptual-cognitive characteristics

	Mean	(SD)							
AT	.5	(2.1)	0	0	1.0	2.8	8.5	4	0.8
BC	.2	(1.0)	0	0	.5	3.4	11.9	2	0
CD	.6	(6.0)	0	0	1.0	1.7	1.8	3	1
CP									
CR	1.0	(7.8)	1	0	1.3	1.2	.5	4	1
CT	.1	(0.8)	0	0	.3	2.9	7.0	1	0
DC	0.0	(0.0)	0	0	0.0	.	.	0	0
D_x	.3	(2.8)	0	0	.5	.9	-1.2	1	1
EJ	.1	(0.8)	0	0	.3	2.9	7.0	1	0
FCP	1.0	(5.9)	0.5	0	1.4	1.6	2.5	5	1.8
LR	.1	(0.6)	0	0	.2	4.5	20.0	1	0
P	3.6	(27.8)	4.0	4.0	2.1	-0.3	-0.9	7.0	3.0
PSD	.1	(0.4)	0	0	.2	4.5	20.0	1	0
PT	.1	(0.2)	0	0	.2	4.5	20.0	1	0
S	.2	(2.8)	0.0	0.0	.5	3.4	11.9	2.0	0
(S)	1.3	(8.8)	1	0	1.5	1.6	3.5	6	2
SR	.7	(5.8)	0	0	1.3	2.5	6.2	5	1
TR	.1	(0.2)	0	0	.2	4.5	20.0	1	0
VP	.4	(2.8)	0	0	.6	1.2	.8	2	1
(VP)	.3	(1.7)	0	0	.7	3.4	12.3	3	0

Transsexuals (N = 30)

Variable		Mean	Variable	Mean	Variable	Mean
W	8.1*	7.6**	MA_1	0.5	Oc P	0.0
W	1.4*	2.0**	MA_2	2.5	Oc I	0.5
$\overline{(W)}$		0.0	MA_3	2.2	Oc G	0.1^a
TOTAL W		9.6^a	MA_4	0.2		
W%		41.4^a			All Oc	1.8^a
			A	10.1	All Oc	0.6
D		10.6	(A)	0.4	All Oral	2.4
D		0.4	A_f	1.4		
$\overline{D}+D$		11.0^a	(A_f)	0.0	Ao P	0.0
D%		47.4	$Ad+Ad_x$	0.3	Ao I	0.0
dd		2.2	H	2.7	Ao G	0.0
dd		0.5	(H)	1.5		
$\overline{dd}+dd$		2.7	H_f	0.7	Ac P	0.0
dd%		11.6	(H_f)	0.4	Ac I	0.6
			$Hd+Hd_x$	0.4	Ac G	0.1
$W+\overline{D}+dd$	2.3*	2.9**	Abs	0.1		
$\overline{r}\%$	9.9*	12.5**	An_b	0.4	All Ao	0.0
			An_s	0.3	All Ac	0.7
INTEGRATED		4.7^a	An_{sx}	0.4	All Anal	0.8
(INTEGRATED)		0.1	An_x	0.3		
ARTICULATED		15.3	Bl	0.1	Po P	0.1
SIMPLE		3.7	Bt	0.9	Po I	0.3
DIFFUSE		1.1	Cld	0.4	Po G	0.0
ARBITRARY		1.1	Clg			
			Dth		Pc P	0.3^a
Total R		23.2	Emb		Pc I	3.4^a
			Fd	0.6	Pc G	0.3^a
F%		41.0^a	Fi	0.4		
F+%		65.9^a	Geo		All Po	0.4
B+%		74.7^a	Hh		All Pc	3.9^a
Afr		49.6^a	Imp		All Phallic	4.3^a
f%		3.6^a	Ls	0.6		
r%	9.9**	12.5***	Mu		AT	4.4^a
PD%		32.4^a	Rel	0.2	BC	0.1
H%		24.5	Sch	0.0^a	CD	1.0^a
A%		53.4	Sci	0.0	CP	0.1
			Tr		CR	1.4^a
Pure f		0.5	Ty		CT	0.0
Pure C		0.1	Wp	0.1	DC	0.1^a
C·F		1.0			D_x	0.1
C'·F		1.0	M	1.6^a	EJ	0.3^a
Pure F		9.7	N	2.3	F^cP	0.6^a
F·Sh		0.5	B	1.7	LR	0.1
F·AM		2.0			P	5.9

Transsexuals (N = 30) (*Continued*)

Variable	Mean	Variable	Mean	Variable	Mean
F·HM	3.4[a]	(M)	3.3	PSD	0.2
		(N)	12.9[a]	PT	0.2
HA$_1$	0.2[a]	(B)	1.5	S	0.8
HA$_2$	0.4			(S)	1.7
HA$_3$	2.3	Oo P	0.2	SR	1.9
HA$_4$	2.6	Oo I	1.5	TR	0.2[a]
		Oo G	0.0	VP	0.0
				(VP)	1.2[a]

Total of Disordered Perceptual-Cognitive Characteristics 3.2[a]

* Using Cards III, IX, and X as rare.
** and *** Using Cards III, VIII, IX, and X as rare.
[a]Significantly different from healthy adult sample, $p \le .05$.

6
PRACTICE RECORDS

PRACTICE CASE A

7-year-old male

I. 33″	1. Ll a monster.		Uh-huh. (What . . . monster?) I don't know. (I'm not sure where?) points to card. W
			(most people see more than one thing)
	2. A clam.		Just ll (looks like) one. (tell me more?) (I'm not sure where?) points to card. W
II. 12″	3. Sure are hard. A rocket.		(No response) (tell me more) Well, thought it was a rocket 'cause it had fire. (fire?) 'cause it's orange. (I'm not sure where?) points to card. W
III. 6″	This is hard! 4. A butterfly house cause that looks like a butterfly.		Cause it ll a butterfly right there. (tell me more) Don't know cause it ll a butterfly's house (I'm not sure . . . house?) (What . . . house?) Don't know. D1 + D2

IV. 11″	5. Oh that's! (looks at watch) monster	It has feet. (tell me more) It ll those were the arms (what . . . monster?) Don't know. W
V. 1″	6. Oh that one's easy, a bat.	'Cause it ll it's a bat, bat's feet. (bat's feet?) uh-huh, and it has wings. (bats feet?) 'cause they're sorta little. W
VI. 10″	7. Looks—oh—ll an alligator.	'Cause it has eyes like an alligator. (eyes?) 'cause they're little (I'm not sure where?) points to all of blot. W
VII. 3″	8. Smoke.	'Cause it ll it 'cause ???? different things. (What smoke?) 'cause it's brown? W
VIII. 34″	9. Oh—what's this?! A rainbow mix up.	'Cause it has different colors (mix up?) 'cause all the colors mix up together. W
IX. 9″	10. Another one! Slime.	'Cause it ll it was real gooey. (tell me more—gooey?) 'cause of the different colors. W
X. 10″	11. That one look real hard! Birds.	'Cause this ll birds. (What . . . birds?) cause they're yellow and they're little. Dd15

NAME: A   AGE: SEX: EXAMINER: DATE:

Card	Response	Latency	Position	Location	Cognitive complexity	Justifications	Imaginal aspects	Response appropriateness	Content	HA = Articulation of human percepts	MA = Motivational articulation	MV = Explicit motivational valuation	(MV) = Implicit motivational valuation	Inferred psychosexual drives	Defense effectiveness	Perceptual cognitive characteristics
I	1	33"	<	W	SIMP	f	—	+	(H)	HA2			(M)			AT
	2		<	W	SIMP	f	—	−	A				(N)			
II	3	12"	<	W	INTG	C	—	+	Wp, Fi				(M)	Ac		PT, CD
III	4	6"	<	D1+D2	ARB	f	—	−	A, house				(B)		−	PT, CD, P
IV	5	19"	<	W	ARTC	F	—	+	(H)	HA3			(M)			AT
V	6	1"	<	W	ARTC	F	—	+	A				(M)			P, CD
VI	7	10"	<	W	ARTC	F	—	−	A				(M)			PT
VII	8	3"	<	W	DIFF	Cp	—	+	Cld				(N)			(VP), CR
VIII	9	34"	<	W	DIFF	C	—	−	Cld				(B)			
IX	10	9"	<	W	DIFF	C	T	−	Slime				(M)	Ac	−	
X	11	10"	<	Dd15	SIMP	C·F	—	+	A				(N)			CD

Burstein-Loucks scoring sheet: Practice case A

231

NAME: _____ A

AGE: _____ SEX: _____

DATE: _____ TIME: _____

EXAMINER: _____

Responses (R): _____ 11
Additional responses: [ ]
Lost responses:
Precision alternatives:
Card rejection:

EDUCATION: _____
OCCUPATION: _____

LOCATION

W = 9 = 9/11   W% = 82 %
W̲ =
(W) =
D = 1 = 1/11   D% = 9 %
W̲ =
Dd = 1 = 1/11   Dd% = 9 %
D̲d̲ =
Total = 11 = R   rare = r% = 0 %

JUSTIFICATIONS/IMAGINAL ASPECTS

List Justifications in alphabetical order (f
or C, CA, Ci, Cp, C'b,g,w, F &/or Sh)
followed by Imaginal aspects in alphabetical order (AM, HE, HM, OM, T, &/or V)

	Response appropriateness +	−
C·T		1
Cp	1	
C	1	1
F	2	1
C·F	1	
f	1	2

Total = 6 + 5 = R

PERCENTAGES

Afr 3/8 = 38   f% = 3/11 = 27 %
F% = 3/11 = 27 %   PD% = 2/11 = 18 %
F+% = 2/3 = 67 %   H% = /11 =
B+% = 4/5 = 80 %   A% = 4/11 = 18 %

ΣHE + HM = 0 + 0 = 0 %
ΣAM = 0 = 0 %
ΣOM = 0 = 0 %
ΣC = 4 = 36 %
ΣCa + Ci + Cp = 0 + 1 = 9 %

COGNITIVE COMPLEXITY

Intg. 1
Artc. 3
Simp. 3
Diff. 3
Arb. 1
Total 11 = R

PERCEPTUAL-COGNITIVE CHARACTERISTICS

AT 2   P 2
BC   PM
CD 4   PSD
CP   PT 3
CR 1   Rej
CT   S
DC   (S)
Dx   SR
EJ   TR
FCP   VP
LD   (VP) 1
LR

CONTENT

A 4   Abs
(A)   Anb
Af   Ans
(Af)   Ansx
Ad   Anx
Adx   Art
Total 4   Bl
A/R = 4/11   Bt
H   Clg
(H) 2   Cld 2
Hf   Dth
(Hf)   Emb
Hd   Fd
Hdx   Fi 1
Total 2   Hh
H/R = 2/11   Geo
Imp
Ls
Mu
Rel
Sch
Sci
Tr
Wp 1

Other 2
(List)
House
Slime

PSYCHOSEXUAL DRIVES & DEFENSE EFFECTIVENESS

	P	I	G	
Oo			⎱ 0	0
Oc			⎰ 0	
Ao			⎱ 0	2
Ac		2	⎰ 2	
Po			⎱ 0	0
Pc			⎰ 0	
			Total	2

PD% = 2/11 = 18 %

INTERPERSONAL EXPECTATIONS

HA	MA	MV	(MV)
I	I	M	(M) 6
II	II 1	N	(N) 3
III	III 1	B	(B) 2
IV	IV		

Total = 0 + 11 = R

Burstein-Loucks summary sheet: Practice case A

232

Interpretative Note

The overuse of W's and the lack of rare detail, especially in conjunction with a relatively large number of failures to justify suggests a young child whose mental life is primitive, impressionistic, and dominated by subjective meanings (low F%). The record is also remarkable for the absence of fantasy, the use of imagination being restricted to a single reference to Texture. We would infer, then, a minimum of self consciousness and an inner experience that is taken to be a result of outer events whose meaning the observer can see is highly modulated by motivational states. The world is experienced as negative in tone [(MV)], and restrictive or depriving (T, Ac). There may well be uncontrolled impulsivity (Cp, pure C), perhaps motivated by unconscious anger (Ac).

PRACTICE CASE B

6-year-old female

I.	3″	1. Ll that's a bat with a frog head or something. (most people see more than one thing) Ll it has butterfly wings.	Well, its wings (frog head?) Yeah, because it has those bulging eyes. (bulging?) cause they're big. Because see the shapes, prints, see (prints?) you know, like ink prints. W
II.	1″	2. Ll a blackbird with a hole cut in it.	Because it's black, it has a shape kind of like a point, so it ll a bird with wings, and it has a whole cut in it. (a hole?) Because here's the wings and here's the whole part. That's its feet. W
III.	2″	3. Ll 2 people together with a bow-tie in the middle of them or something.	Because here's their legs, and there's where their legs are connected to their bodies, goes up to their chest, their head. (bow-tie?) 'cause it just is the shape of one. D9 + D3
IV.	1″	4. That thing ll a monster with a pogo	Because here's its head, body, arms on the sides, big feet, with some-

stick—really funny, it has big feet, too.

thing sticking up in the middle, that's why I call it a monster with a pogo stick. (funny?) because, just has such a big foot, feet I mean, and such a little head, that it looks funny I guess (pogo stick?) because it's straight and long and has these things to step on. W

V.
1″

5. I know what that ll, ll a butterfly.

Because it has the shape of the wings, the antennas, and the little feet. W

VI.
1″

6. That ll a flying cat, is what it ll, with a horse's mouth, 'cause it has a long mouth, ll it has a big bottom, too.

Because it has these fur things sticking out and the whiskers. (fur?) 'cause it, I just think that this is the cat, I just think it ll a cat. (horse's mouth?) it's kinda long and the shape. (big bottom?) because such, so wide, (traces with finger). W

VII.
1″

7. That ll 2 Indians sitting together, they have things on their heads.

Those are the feathers. (feathers?) Kind of shaped like feathers. (Indians?) because they have a little bit of dark skin and the feathers. (dark skin?) see, right here. (sitting?) because this is their kinda like (points to herself sitting) it's like this part (points to lower torso and upper legs.) W

VIII.
2″

8. That ll walking beavers, they're going to climb-up a tree; bouncing on the hill, they're trying to get the leaves.

They, they're kinda shaped like beavers and a flat tail (a flat tail?) right here. (climbing?) because they have their paws on the thing, like this (imitates with her own body). (tree?) because it's green, with the trunk, straight down the middle, here. (bouncing?) like with their legs, like I bounce on a couch with my bottom. W

IX.   9. That ll 2 witches sit-   Because these are their ugly teeth
1"   ting in green chairs   and pointed hats. (ugly teeth?)
           with pink rocks un-   some big ones sticking out and ll
           der them. They're   this (shows, imitates). I bet they
           trying to decide who   have tartar. (green chair?) because
           is the wickedest   here's the back (imitates sitting).
           'cause they're point-   (pink rocks?) yeah, they're shaped
           ing their fingers at   round. (pointing fingers?) yeah,
           each other, witchy   'cause they're arguing, who is
           hats—I'm always a   going to eat the children, 'cause
           witch on Halloween,   I've head a story about this witch
           I wish I could paint   . . . (witchy hats?) they're
           my cat all back for   pointed. W
           Halloween . . .

X.   10. That ll a rocketship   See, like, the top is like this and
3"   taking off from a plat-   this is the body (demonstrates with
           form with fireworks   her body) It even has the oil tank-
           that are holding cot-   ers. (oil tankers?) here, see, they're
           ton candy.   big and round. (taking off?) be-
                                         cause it has the green smoke com-
                                         ing out of it and anything that
                                         takes off must have smoke com-
                                         ing out of it. (fireworks?) holding
                                         cotton-candy, that's strange, I
                                         know, but it's what it ll. (tell me
                                         more?) Here, these are the rays.
                                         (rays?) These are the rays shooting
                                         out of them, like the sun, it has
                                         rays (demonstrates the sun's rays
                                         using her body). (cotton candy?)
                                         because it's shaped like cotton
                                         candy and it has the stick. (plat-
                                         form?) Here (points along bottom
                                         edge of card.) This is the platform,
                                         here, like this. W

Burstein-Loucks scoring sheet: Practice case B

NAME: B AGE: SEX: EXAMINER: DATE:

Card	Response	Latency	Position	Location	Cognitive complexity	Justifications	Imaginal aspects	Response appropriateness	Content	HA = Articulation of human percepts	MA = Motivational articulation	MV = Explicit motivational valuation	(MV) = Implicit motivational valuation	Inferred psychosexual drives	Defense effectiveness	Perceptual cognitive characteristics
I	1	3″	<	W	ARTC	F		−	(A)				(M)			CR
II	2	1″	<	W	ARTC	C′·F		−	A				(M)			(S), CR
III	3	2″	<	D9+D3	ARB	F		+	H, Clg	HA2			(N)	Pc	G	P, CR
IV	4	1″	<	W	INTG	F		+	(H), Pogo stick	HA3			(M)	Oo, Ao	− −	AT, CR
V	5	1″	<	W	ARTC	F		+	A				(B)			P
VI	6	1″	<	W	ARTC	F	AM	−	(A)				(N)			CR
VII	7	1″	<	W	INTG	F-Sh	HM	+	H	HA4	MA2	N		Pc	−	P
VIII	8	2″	<	W	INTG	C·F	AM	+	A, Bt, Ls				(N)	Oo, Pc	− −	P, SR
IX	9	1″	<	W	INTG	C·Ci·F	HM	+	chairs (H), Ls, Hh	HA4	MA4	M		Ac, Oo	− −	AT, SR, P
X	10	3″	<	W	ARB	Ci·F	OM	−	Tr, Fd, Fi, Cld				(B)		− −	PT, PM, CR, AT

236

NAME: _____ B _____ SEX: _____

AGE: _____

PSYCHOSEXUAL DRIVES & DEFENSE EFFECTIVENESS

	P	I	G	
O_o		3	3	= 3
			0	= 0
O_c		1	1	= 1
			0	= 0
A_o		1	0	= 0
A_c			3	= 3
P_o		2	1	
P_c				

Total 8

PD% = 8 / 10 = 80 %

INTERPERSONAL EXPECTATIONS

HA		MA		MV		(MV)	
I	—	I	—	I	—	(M)	3
II	1	II	1	M	1	(N)	3
III	1	III	1	N	1	(B)	2
IV	2	IV	1	B	—		

Total = 2 + 8 = R

DATE: _____ TIME: _____

EXAMINER: _____

JUSTIFICATIONS/IMAGINAL ASPECTS

List Justifications in alphabetical order (f or C, CA, Ci, Cp, C'b,g,w, F &/or Sh) followed by Imaginal aspects in alphabetical order (AM, HE, HM, OM, T, &/or V)

	Response appropriateness	
	+	−
Ci·F·OM		1
C·Ci·F·HM	1	
C·F·AM	1	
C'·F	3	1
F		1
F·AM		1
F·Sh·HM	1	

Total = 6 + 4 = R

EDUCATION: _____

OCCUPATION: _____

COGNITIVE COMPLEXITY

Intg.	4
Artc.	4
Simp.	—
Diff.	—
Arb.	2
Total	10 = R

CONTENT

A	3	Abs	—
(A)	2	An_b	—
Af	—	An_s	—
(Af)	—	An_{sx}	—
Ad	—	An_x	—
Adx	—	Art	—

Total 5 A/R = 5 / 10

Bl	—
Bt	1
Clg	1
Cld	1
Dth	—
Emb	1
Fd	1
Fi	1
Hh	—
Geo	—
Imp	2
Ls	—
Mu	—
Rel	—
Sch	—
Sci	—
Tr	—
Wp	—

H	3
(H)	1
Hf	—
(Hf)	—
Hd	1
Hdx	—

Total 4 H/R = 4 / 10

Other _3_
(List)
pogo stick
household
transportation

PERCEPTUAL-COGNITIVE CHARACTERISTICS

AT	3	P	5
BC	—	PM	1
CD	—	PSD	1
CP	—	PT	1
CR	6	Rej	—
CT	—	S	—
DC	—	(S)	1
D_x	—	SR	2
EJ	—	TR	—
FCP	—	VP	—
LD	—	(VP)	—
LR	—		

Responses (R): _10_

Additional responses: [   ]

Lost responses: _____

Precision alternatives: _____

Card rejection: _____

LOCATION

W	=	9		
W	=		/ 10	W% = 90 %
(W)	=			
D	=	1		
W	=		/ 10	D% = 10 %
Dd	=			
Dd	=			Dd% = __ %
Total	=	10	= R	
rare	=	0	/ 0	r% = 0 %

PERCENTAGES

Afr = 3 / 7	= 43		f% = 0 / 0	= 0 %
F% = 4 / 10	= 40 %		PD% = 8 / 10	= 80 %
F+% = 3 / 4	= 75 %		H% = 4 / 10	= 40 %
B+% = 3 / 6	= 50 %		A% = 5 / 10	= 50 %

≤ HE + HM = 0 + 2 / 10 = 20 %

≤ AM = 2 / 10 = 20 %

≤ OM = 1 / 10 = 10 %

≤ C = 2 / 10 = 20 %

≤ Ca + Ci + Cp = 0 + 2 + 0 / 10 = 20%

Burstein-Loucks summary sheet: Practice case B

Interpretative Note

A bright and complex child (Intg, number of blends), whose world tilts
only slightly in the connotative direction (F%). The denotative world is
well validated socially (F + %); less so the connotative (B + %). In other
words, emotional responses can be idiosyncratic as well as tempestuous.
There is an unusually high degree of psychosexual conflict (PD%), and it
is not well structuralized. That, especially in the presence of some anxiety
(Sh) and depression (C'), and feelings of living in an unstable world (OM)
suggests response to active environmental stress. Particularly in the presence of the Ci responses coupled with evidence of good ego structure (P,
F + %) one might suggest narcissistic injury with feelings of depersonal-
ization.

PRACTICE CASE C

6-year-old male

I. 1″	1. pumpkin.	Because it's round. (tell me more) There are the 2 eyes and dot for the nose. (eyes?) because they're rectangle. (nose?) because it's a triangle. W
	2. mud	Because it's kind of <u>splattered</u> out and <u>black</u>. (splattered out?) Because it's got this (tell me more) it's all I know, it's just kind of splattered out. (traces outline). W
II. 8″	3. Blood	Cause it's red. <u>D</u>2, <u>D</u>3
III. 2″	4. People	Because they're kinda shaped like 'em. (where?) traces with finger. D1
IV. 1″	5. Monster	Because it's shaped like one and it's kinda big and it's stomping. (stomping?) because it's kinda like this (<u>pantomimes stomping</u>). It's stomping a <u>tree down</u>. (tree-where?) here. (tree?) because it's like this, (traces tree with finger). W
V. 1″	6. Bat	Because it's got wings and the ears are up and it's flying. (flying?) because <u>its wings are moving</u>. (moving?) because they're out (pantomimes wings outspread) (Does it ll it's moving?) Yes. W

VI. 5″	7. Water	Because it's splattered out. (splattered?) because somebody <u>jumped</u> in it. (jumped in it?) because this part is kinda splat-tered-up (tell me more—splattered) be-cause it goes out like this (traces outline with finger). W
VII. 1″	8. Rabbit	Because this ear is kinda large and it ll it's standing on a rock and it's got a tail. (ears?) because they're long (standing?) be-cause it's on a rock (rock?) because it's gray and rectangle. (tail?) because it's kinda up like this (traces tail with fin-ger). <u>D</u>9
VIII. 3″	9. Dragon	Because it's kinda big and it's kinda legs here (tell me more—dragon) cause it's kinda big. D1
	10. Bear	Because it's stomping around. (stomping?) because it's feet are up. (up?) they're not on the grass. D1
IX. 11″	11. Hippopotamus	Because it's kinda shaped like one. (where?) right here. D1
X. 1″	12. Snakes	Because they're kinda long and kinda long (where?) here and here. <u>D</u>9, <u>D</u>4

NAME: C   AGE: SEX: EXAMINER: DATE:

Card	Response	Latency	Position	Location	Cognitive complexity	Justifications	Imaginal aspects	Response appropriateness	Content	HA = Articulation of human percepts	MA = Motivational articulation	MV = Explicit motivational valuation	(MV) = Implicit motivational valuation	Inferred psychosexual drives	Defense effectiveness	Perceptual cognitive characteristics
I	1	1″	∧	W	ARTC	F		+	(Hf)	HA3			(N)			(S)
	2		∧	W	DIFF	C'b·F		−	mud				(M)	Ac	−	
II	3	8″	∧	D2, D3	DIFF	C		+	Bl				(M)			
III	4	2″	∧	D1	SIMP	F		+	H	HA1			(N)			P
IV	5	1″	∧	W	INTG	F	HM	+	(H), Bt	HA2	MA3	M				PM
V	6	1″	∧	W	ARTC	F	AM	+	A				(M)			P
VI	7	5″	∧	W	DIFF	F	HM·OM	−	water		MA2	N		Ac	−	
VII	8	1″	∧	D9	INTG	C'g·F	AM	+	A, rocks				(M)			
VIII	9	3″	∧	DI	ARTC	F		−	(A)				(N)	Pc	−	PT
	10	11″	∧	DI	ARTC	F	AM	+	A				(M)			P, FCP, stomping
IX	11		∧	DI	SIMP	F		+	A				(N)			
X	12	1″	∧	D9, D4	SIMP	F		−	A				(M)	Pc	−	

Burstein-Loucks scoring sheet: Practice case C

NAME: C

AGE: _____ SEX: _____

EDUCATION: _____

OCCUPATION: _____

DATE: _____ TIME: _____

EXAMINER: _____

Responses (R): 12
Additional responses: [ ]
Lost responses: _____
Precision alternatives: _____
Card rejection: _____

LOCATION

W = 5

$\underline{W}$ = 5 /12   W% = 42 %

(W) =

D = 4

$\underline{W}$ = 7/12   D% = 58 %

$\underline{W}$ = 3

Dd = 0

$\underline{Dd}$ = 0/12   Dd% = 0 %

$\underline{Dd}$ =

Total = 12 = R

rare = 3   r% = 3/12 = 25 %

PERCENTAGES

Afr = 4/8 = 50   f% = _____ = 0 %

F% = 5/12 = 42 %   PD% = 4/12 = 33 %

F+% = 3/5 = 60 %   H% = 3/12 = 25 %

B+% = 5/7 = 71 %   A% = 6/12 = 50 %

Σ HE + HM = 0 + 2 = 17 %

Σ AM = 3 = 25 %

Σ OM = 1 = 8 %

Σ C = 1 = 8 %

Σ Ca + Ci + Cp = ___ + ___ + ___ = 0 %

JUSTIFICATIONS/IMAGINAL ASPECTS

List Justifications in alphabetical order (f or C, CA, Ci, Cp, C'b,g,w, F &/or Sh) followed by Imaginal aspects in alphabetical order (AM, HE, HM, OM, T, &/or V)

	Response appropriateness +	−
C'g·F·AM	1	
C	1	
C'b·F		1
F	3	2
F·HM	1	
F·AM	2	
F·HM·OM	1	

Total = 8 + 4 = R

COGNITIVE COMPLEXITY

Intg. 2
Artc. 4
Simp. 3
Diff. 3
Arb. _____
Total 12 = R

PERCEPTUAL-COGNITIVE CHARACTERISTICS

AT	P 3
BC	PM 1
CD	PSD
CP	PT 1
CR	Rej
CT	S 1
DC	(S)
D_x	SR
EJ	TR
FCP 1	VP
LD	(VP)
LR	

CONTENT

A 5	Abs
(A) 1	An_b
Af	An_s
(Af)	An_sx
Ad	An_x
Adx	Art
Total 6	Bl 1
A/R = 6/12	Bt 1
H 1	Clg
(H) 1	Cld
Hf	Dth
(Hf) 1	Emb
Hd	Fd
Hdx	Fi
Total 3	Hh
H/R = 3/12	Geo
	Imp
	Ls
	Mu
	Rel
	Sch
	Sci
	Tr
	Wp

Other 2
(List)
mud
water

PSYCHOSEXUAL DRIVES & DEFENSE EFFECTIVENESS

	P	I	G
O_o			} 0
O_c			} 0
A_o			} 0
A_c		2	} 2
P_o			} 0
P_c		2	} 2

Total 4

PD% = 4/12 = 33 %

INTERPERSONAL EXPECTATIONS

HA	MA	MV	(MV)
I 1	I _____	I _____	(M) 5
II 1	II 2	II 1	(N) 4
III 1	III 1	III _____	(B)
IV _____	IV _____	IV _____	

Total = 3 + 9 = R

Burstein-Loucks summary sheet: Practice case C

241

Interpretative Note

A somewhat depressed child (C') of normal or better intelligence, (Intg, r%). His world is adequately validated, though unpleasant [MV, (MV)]. Psychosexual conflict is active, probably involving phobic symptoms (Ac, Pc), which may be age appropriate.

PRACTICE CASE D

Male adolescent

I. 7"	1. Laughs. A bat. That's it.	Right through here, the way the outside of it is made (bat?) the way it's made. Here's the wings and body. W
II. 26"	2. A heart.	This ll the outline around the heart and this ll the heart (heart?) way it's shaped. (anything else?) No. D3, 6
III. 5"	3. People.	This ll the face, and this ll the body and the hands. D9, 11
	4. Butterflies.	This right here (points) (Ll this?) way it's made—the shape of it. D3
IV. 12"	5. A big man.	It just the whole thing. (A big man?) This ll his head and arms and big old feet and I didn't use this part. (big?) the feet. D
	6. A tree.	This ll the trunk and center ll the covering on the tree—like leaves. (leaves?) the coloring of it. (color?) dark here and light here. W
V. 7"	7. A bat.	The whole thing. (ll this?) the rough edges around it and the points here. W
	8. A caterpillar.	I don't know what made me say that. D3
VI. 8"	9. A bird.	The part here and it ll it was coming out of a cloud. (bird?) the part around the straight line here. D1
	10. A cloud.	The whole area. (ll this?) I guess the, its just the whole thing. A cloud is not formed any specific way. D2

VII. 8″	11. People.	This ll ponytails, this ll the outline of the face and this ll the back part of them and it ll they are laughing at each other. D4
	Rocks.	That's what they are sitting on. (rocks?) I guess the square of 'em with ruff edges.
VIII. 8″	12. Animals.	Right here—ll tigers or something. That's all I see on that one. (tiger?) the shape of it. D1
	13. Sticks.	It's just this here—(ll that?) just straight. Dd21
IX. 22″	14. The sun.	The part here. (sun?) the color. (anything else?) no. D3
X. 15″	15. Bulls.	Right here. (bulls?) way standing up, ll they are up on their legs. (anything else?) no. D8
	16. Crawdads.	Here. (ll this?) it has these pincher type things and ll legs. D10

244

NAME: D AGE: SEX: EXAMINER: DATE:

Card	Response	Latency	Position	Location	Cognitive complexity	Justifications	Imaginal aspects	Response appropriateness	Content	HA = Articulation of human percepts	MA = Motivational articulation	MV = Explicit motivational valuation	(MV) = Implicit motivational valuation	Inferred psychosexual drives	Defense effectiveness	Perceptual cognitive characteristics
I	1	7″	<	W	ARTC	F		+	A				(M)			P
II	2	26″	<	D3, 6	SIMP	F		−	Ans				(M)			P
III	3	5″	<	D9, 11	ARTC	F		+	H	HA2			(N)			P
	4	12″	<	D3	SIMP	F		+	A				(B)			
IV	5		<	D	ARTC	F		+	H	HA3			(N)			P
	6	7″	<	W	ARTC	F·Sh		+	Bt				(N)			LR
V	7		<	W	SIMP	F		+	A				(M)			
VI	8	8″	<	D3	SIMP	F	AM	+	A				(N)			
	9		<	D1	DIFF	F		+	Cld				(N)			
VII	10	8″	<	D2	INTG	F	HM	+	H	HA2	MA2	N				P
	11		<	D4	SIMP	F		+	Ls				(N)			
VIII	12	8″	<	D1	SIMP	F		+	A				(M)			
	13		<	Dd21	SIMP	C		−	Bt				(N)			
IX	14	22″	<	D3	SIMP	F	AM	−	Sun				(B)			
X	15	15″	<	D8	ARTC	F		−	A				(M)			
	16		<	D10	ARTC			−	A				(M)			CR

Burstein-Loucks scoring sheet: Practice case D

NAME: _____ D

AGE: _____ SEX: _____

Responses (R): 16
Additional responses: [ ]
Lost responses: _____
Precision alternatives: _____
Card rejection: _____

DATE: _____ TIME: _____
EXAMINER: _____

EDUCATION: _____
OCCUPATION: _____

LOCATION

W = 2 = 2/16 W% = 13 %
$\underline{W}$ = _____
(W) = _____
D = 12 = 13/16 D% = 81 %
$\underline{W}$ = 1 =
Dd = 0 = 1/16 Dd% = 6 %
$\underline{Dd}$ = 1 =
Total = 16 = R
rare = 2/16 r% = 13 %

PERCENTAGES

Afr = 5/11 = 45   f% = _____ = 0 %
F% = 11/16 = 69 %   PD% = 0 = 0 %
F+% = 8/11 = 73 %   H% = 3/16 = 19 %
B+% = 3/5 = 60 %   A% = 7/16 = 44 %
≤ HE + HM = 0 + 1 = 6 %
≤ AM = 2 = 13 %
≤ OM = ___ = 0 %
≤ C = 1 = 6 %
≤ Ca + Ci + Cp = ___ + ___ + ___ = 0%

JUSTIFICATIONS/IMAGINAL ASPECTS

List Justifications in alphabetical order (f or C, CA, Ci, Cp, C'b,g,w, F &/or Sh) followed by Imaginal aspects in alphabetical order (AM, HE, HM, OM, T, &/or V)

	Response appropriateness +	−
C		1
F	8	3
F-Sh	1	
F-AM	1	
F-HM	1	1

Total = 11 + 5 = R

COGNITIVE COMPLEXITY

Intg. 1
Artc. 6
Simp. 8
Diff. 1
Arb.
Total 16 = R

CONTENT

A	7	Abs	
(A)		An_b	
Af		An_s	1
(Af)		An_{sx}	
Ad		An_x	
Adx		Art	
Total 7	A/R = 16	Bl	
H	3	Bt	1
(H)		Clg	1
Hf		Cld	1
(Hf)		Dth	
Hd		Emb	
Hdx		Fd	
Total 3	H/R = 16	Fi	
		Hh	
		Geo	
		Imp	1
		Ls	1
		Mu	
		Rel	
		Sch	
		Sci	
		Tr	
		Wp	

Other 1 (List) sun

PERCEPTUAL-COGNITIVE CHARACTERISTICS

AT		P	5
BC		PM	
CD		PSD	
CP		PT	
CR	1	Rej	
CT		S	
DC		(S)	
D_x		SR	
EJ		TR	
FCP		VP	
LD	1	(VP)	
LR	1		

PSYCHOSEXUAL DRIVES & DEFENSE EFFECTIVENESS

	P	I	G	
O_o				0/0
O_c				0
A_o				0/0
A_c				0
P_o				0/0
P_c				0

Total 0
PD% = 0 / 0 = 0 %

INTERPERSONAL EXPECTATIONS

HA		MA		MV		(MV)	
I	_	I	_	M	_	(M)	6
II	2	II	1	N	1	(N)	7
III	1	III	_	B	_	(B)	2
IV	3	IV	1				

Total = 1 + 15 = R

Burstein-Loucks summary sheet: Practice case D

Interpretative Note

This adolescent is of average intelligence (Intg) and intellectual energy (r%). He tends to down play the connotative (F%), and assume a world of out there things and events. He appears fairly well socialized (P, B + %, F + %), though capable of emotional overreaction (C, B + %). His repressive stance is clear (LR, PD%). Probably no major symptomatology.

PRACTICE CASE E

Male adolescent

I. 10″	1. A bat.	Ll 2 hands, ll wings—a wing span. W
	2. A space ship.	Ll it's taking off (space ship?) because these are all spread out and that ll fire coming out. (fire?) just look's that way. W
	3. A face mask.	A face mask a samurai would wear (makes it ll this?) this ll where they look out—2 eyes. W (S)
II. 12″	4. Two chickens with their hands pushing away from each other.	Ll they got their hands and them ll chickens. (chickens?) they got red faces and that ll a beak. (pushing?) got their hands together and it ll they're pushing away. D2,6
III. 6″	5. Two men trying to lift a cauldron.	It ll shoes right there and these ll their arms and this ll the caldron. D1
	6. And a frog's face.	Ll 2 eyes and nose right there and that ll a mouth. D3
IV. 7″	7. A giant.	Because it ll big clown here and it's just going up. (ll giant?) just ll one. (W)
	8. And an ant face.	Them ll 2 pinchers that they have and that ll the tongue right here and them ll antenna. W

V. 3"	9. A Butterfly.	It ll 2 antenna and the wing span and the little tail. W
VI. 9"	10. A buffalo hide.	In those books them Indians have buffalo hides hanging on their te-pee and that's what it ll. (hide?) this ll the horns and this ll where they cut it—it is jagged. D1
	11. And a cat.	These ll whiskers (anything else?) just this here. D3
VII. 13"	12. Two African dancers.	2 Kenyan dancers—they fix their hair like that—in an upward motion and these ll dresses and stuff. (African?) because the way they are dressed. (hair?) they fix their hair like that. W
	13. And a flower.	Like a touch-me-not. (ll that?) This bell shape down here. D4
VIII. 4"	14. A Christmas tree.	This part shaped like (anything else?) the colors and stuff. (colors?) ll Christmas colors. D1,8
	15. And 2 bears trying to climb a tree.	These ll bears and this ll a tree. (bears?) got 4 legs. (tree?) this up here shaped like a tree—the top of a pine tree and these ll branches. W
IX. 15"	16. Some deer.	These ll horns up here and these ll the face part and this ll the mouth. (mouth?) it's going out. (face part?) eyes (s) and jaws here. W
	17. And a nuclear bomb exploding.	When the bomb hits, it spreads out and this right here ll the mushroom cloud and this up here ll smoke and stuff. (fire?) up here (fire?) red (cloud?) cause its going up. W

X.   18. Laughs—some bugs   These ll spiders and these ll ter-
10″   have a party.   mites, these ll ants and these ll
                                          lights and this ll all the food here.
                                          (bugs?) these got all these legs (spi-
                                          der) and these have antenna and
                                          stuff (termite) and these got the
                                          head and body shaped like an ant.
                                          (lights?) cause they are yellow.
                                          (food?) this ll the tables they are
                                          sitting at. W

          19. And a King's court.   This ll where the king's throne is
                                          up here and these ll 2 people fan-
                                          ning him—ll fans here and these ll
                                          people down here. (people?) just all
                                          bunches up there. W

NAME: E AGE: SEX: EXAMINER: DATE:

Card	Response	Latency	Position	Location	Cognitive complexity	Justifications	Imaginal aspects	Response appropriateness	Content	HA = Articulation of human percepts	MA = Motivational articulation	MV = Explicit motivational valuation	(MV) = Implicit motivational valuation	Inferred psychosexual drives	Defense effectiveness	Perceptual cognitive characteristics
I	1	10″	∧	W	ARTC	F		+	A				(M)			CR, P
	2		∧	W	ARTC	F	OM	−	Fi, Sci				(N)			(S)
	3	12″	∧	W	ARTC	F	HM	+	(Hf)				(M)			CR
II	4	6″	∧	D2, 6	INTG	C-F	HM	−	A		MA3	N				P
III	5		∧	D1	INTG	F	HM	+	H, clg Caldron	HA3	MA2	N				
	6	7″	∧	D3	ARTC	F		−	Af				(N)			CR
IV	7		∧	(W)	SIMP	F	V	+	(H)	HA4			(M)			P
V	8	3″	∧	W	ARTC	F		−	Af				(M)	Oo	I	P
VI	9	9″	∧	W	ARTC	F		+	A				(B)			PT
	10	9″	∨	D1	ARTC	F		+	Ad				(N)			AT
VII	11	13″	∧	D3	ARTC	F		−	A				(N)			
	12		∧	W	ARTC	F	HM	+	H, clg	HA4	MA3	B		Pc	G	P, CR
VIII	13	4″	∧	D4	SIMP	F		−	Bt				(B)			
IX	14	15″	∧	D1, 8	SIMP	C-F	AM	+	Bt, Rel				(B)			
	15		∧	W	INTG	F		+	A, Bt				(N)			
X	16	1″	∧	W	ARTC	F	OM	−	Af				(N)			P, CR
	17		∧	W	DIFF	C-F	HM	+	Wp, Cld, Fi				(M)	Ac	I	(S)
	18	10″	∧	W	ARB	C-F	HM	+	A, Fd, Lights		MA3	B		Oo	I	AT, CR, P
	19		∧	W	ARB	f	HM	−	H		MA3	B				

Burstein-Loucks scoring sheet: Practice case E

Burstein-Loucks summary sheet: Practice case E

NAME: E

AGE: _____ SEX: _____

EDUCATION: _____

OCCUPATION: _____

DATE: _____ TIME: _____

EXAMINER: _____

Responses (R): 19

Additional responses: [ ]

Lost responses: _____

Precision alternatives: _____

Card rejection: _____

PSYCHOSEXUAL DRIVES & DEFENSE EFFECTIVENESS

	P	I	G	
O₀		2	2	} 2
O_c			0	} 0
A₀			0	} 1
A_c		1	1	
P₀			0	} 1
P_c		1	1	

Total 4

PD% = 4 / 19 = 21 %

INTERPERSONAL EXPECTATIONS

HA	MA	MV	(MV)
I _____	I 1	M _____	(M) 5
II _____	II 1	N 2	(N) 6
III 1	III 4	B 3	(B) 3
IV 2	IV _____		

Total = 5 + 14 = R

COGNITIVE COMPLEXITY

Intg.	3
Artc.	10
Simp.	3
Diff.	1
Arb.	2
Total	19 = R

PERCEPTUAL-COGNITIVE CHARACTERISTICS

AT 2	P 6		
BC	PM		
CD	PSD		
CP	PT 1		
CR 5	Rej		
CT	S 2		
DC	(S)		
D_x	SR		
EJ	TR		
FCP	VP		
LD	(VP)		
LR			

CONTENT

A 7	Abs		
(A)	Anb		
Af 3	Ans		
(Af)	Ansx		
Ad 1	Anx		
Adx	Art		
	Bl	Bt 3	
Total 11		Clg 2	
A/R = 11/19		Cld 1	
H 3	Dth		
(H) 1	Hf		
	Hf	Emb 1	
	(Hf)	Fd 1	
Hd	Fi 2		
Hdx	Hh		
Total 5	Geo		
H/R = 5/19	Imp		
	Ls		
	Mu		
	Rel		
	Sch		
	Sci		
	Tr		
	Wp		

Other 4
(List)
Spaceship 1
Caldron 1
Exhaust 1
Lights 1

JUSTIFICATIONS/IMAGINAL ASPECTS

List Justifications in alphabetical order (f or C, CA, Ci, Cp, C'b,g,w, F &/or Sh) followed by Imaginal aspects in alphabetical order (AM, HE, HM, OM, T, &/or V)

	Response appropriateness +	Response appropriateness −
C·F·OM	1	
C·F	1	
C·F·HM	1	1
F	4	5
F·OM		1
F·HM	2	
F·V	1	
F·AM	1	
F·HM		1

Total = 11 + 8 = R

LOCATION

W = 11 / 19 = 12 | W% = 63 %

W = _____

(W) = 1

D = 6 / 19 = 7 | D% = 37 %

W = 1

Dd = _____ | Dd% = 0 %

Dd = _____

Total = 19 = R

rare = 1 / 19 | r% = 5 %

PERCENTAGES

Afr = 6 / 13 = 46 % | f% = 1 / 19 = 5 %

F% = 9 / 19 = 47 % | PD% = 3 / 19 = 21 %

F+ % = 4 / 9 = 44 % | H% = 5 / 19 = 26 %

B+% = 7 / 10 = 70 % | A% = 11 / 19 = 58 %

≶ HE + HM = 0 + 5 = 26 %

≶ AM = 1 / 19 = 5 %

≶ OM = 2 / 19 = 11 %

≶ C = 4 / 19 = 21 %

≶ Ca + Ci + Cp = ___ + ___ + ___ = 0%

Interpretative Note

A bright adolescent, one whose strengths are analytic rather than synthetic (Intg, Art, r%). His world is well balanced between the denotative and connotative (F%), but with a notable weakness in the consensual validation of the externalities (F + %). The failures seem especially to occur on responses with gender related content. The personalizations are clearly not due to lack of intelligence (vide supra), nor to psychotic process (P, Perceptual Cognitive Section). Given some feelings of vulnerability and helplessness (V, OM), and the relatively strong ego defenses (PD%, P) we may well be dealing with a mild obsessional neurosis in a teenage struggling with age appropriate gender identification issues.

PRACTICE CASE F

Female adolescent

I. 7″	1. Two angels.	Cause of the wing going out—shaped like an angel. (Anything else?) just the shape. D2
	2. A person with 2 heads in between.	Legs, body shape and has 2 heads like this. (LL that?) That's what it ll. D4
II. 21″	3. Two apes on fire.	Ll apes—shaped like apes—has the red like fire. (apes?) the shape. W (Keep it a while—most people see more than one thing). That's all I see.
III. 9″	4. Two girls playing basketball.	Shaped like 2 girls—basketball between 'em—they're bouncing it. (girls?) the thing stuck out right there. (points.) D1
IV. 26″	5. Could be a tree.	The stem ll a tree and shaped like a tree. (anything else?) no. W
	6. Could be Big Foot.	Got 2 arms, 2 big feet. W
V. 4″	7. A big giant fly.	Cause it shaped like a fly and ll a fly. W
VI. 19″	8. Ll a bee.	Cause it's got these 2 things right here and it ll a bee. (anything else?) the tail back here. W

VII. 20" >	9. Ll a butterfly with long wings.	Here's the body and these ll wings. W
VIII. 17"	10. Ll 2 bears climbing up a mountain.	This ll a mountain here and 2 bears on each side (bears?) they got 4 legs (mountains?) goes up like a moun- tain. D1, 4
	11. The inside of a heart.	Ll the heart and the ribs and all. (heart?) shaped like a heart. (ribs?) shaped like that. D2,5
IX. 32"	12. Ll a lady with a big head.	Got legs and a big head shape—got 2 arms. (lady?) I don't know. W
X. 10" 1	13. A volcano exploding.	This ll the lava coming down and this ll the volcano (lava?) cause it's red (volcano?) goes up—shape. D9,11
	14. Fireworks.	Has explosions like fireworks (ll fireworks?) no (explosion?) when it splatters. D1
	15. Two horses.	Ll 2 horses—shape—got 4 legs. Dd7
	16. And rockets.	Shaped, ll a rocket—ll it's going off. (going off?) this ll smoke down here. (smoke?) the gray. D11

NAME: F   AGE: SEX: EXAMINER: DATE:

Card	Response	Latency	Position	Location	Cognitive complexity	Justifications	Imaginal aspects	Response appropriateness	Content	HA = Articulation of human percepts	MA = Motivational articulation	MV = Explicit motivational valuation	(MV) = Implicit motivational valuation	Inferred psychosexual drives	Defense effectiveness	Perceptual cognitive characteristics
I	1	7"	<	D2	ARTC	F		+	(H)	HA4			(B)			P, CR
	2		<	D4	ARTC	F		+	(H)	HA3			(M)			CR
II	3	21"	<	W	ARTC	C·F		+	A, Fi				(M)		G	P
III	4	9"	<	D1	INTG	F	HM	+	H, ball	HA2	MA3	B		Pc		(VP)
IV	5	26"	<	W	ARTC	F		+	Bt				(N)			
	6		<	W	ARTC	F		+	(H)	HA4			(M)			
V	7	4"	<	W	SIMP	F		–	A				(M)			
VI	8	19"	v	W	ARTC	F		–	A				(M)			P
VII	9	20"	<	W	ARTC	F		–	A				(N)			
VIII	10	17"	<	D1, 4	INTG	F	AM	+	A, Ls				(M)			
	11		<	D2, 5	SIMP	F		–	Ans, Anb				(M)			
IX	12	32"	<	W	ARTC	F		–	H	HA3			(M)			
X	13	10"	<	D9, 11	ARTC	C·F	OM	–	Exp				(M)	Ac	P	CR
	14		<	D1	SIMP	F	OM	–	Exp				(M)	Ac	I	
	15		<	Dd7	ARTC	F		–	A				(N)			
	16		<	D11	ARTC	C·F	OM	+	Cld, Rocket				(N)			

Burstein-Loucks scoring sheet: Practice case F

253

Responses (R): 16
Additional responses: [ ]
Lost responses:
Precision alternatives:
Card rejection:

NAME: _____ F
AGE: _____ SEX:

EDUCATION:
OCCUPATION:

DATE: _____ TIME:
EXAMINER:

LOCATION

W = — = 7 — 7/16   W% = 44%
W_ = — =
(W) = —
D = — = 6 — 8/16   D% = 50%
W_ = — = 2
Dd = — = 1 — 1/16   Dd% = 6%
Dd_ = —
Total = 16 = R   rare = 2/16   r% = 13%

PERCENTAGES

Afr = 7/16   f% = —— 0%
F% = 10/16 = 63%   PD% = 3/16 = 19%
F+% = 4/10 = 40%   H% = 5/16 = 31%
B+% = 4/6 = 67%   A% = 6/16 = 38%

≤ HE + HM = 1/6 + 0 = 6%
≤ AM = 1/6 = 6%
≤ OM = 3/16 = 19%
≤ C = 2/16 = 13%
≤ Ca + Ci + Cp = —— + —— + —— = ——%

JUSTIFICATIONS/IMAGINAL ASPECTS

List Justifications in alphabetical order (f or C, CA, Ci, Cp, C'b,g,w, F &/or Sh) followed by Imaginal aspects in alphabetical order (AM, HE, HM, OM, T, &/or V)

	Response appropriateness +	Response appropriateness -
C'·F·OM	1	
C·F·OM		1
F	4	6
C·F	1	
F·HM	1	
F·AM	1	
F·OM		1

Total = 8 + 8 = R

COGNITIVE COMPLEXITY

Intg. 2
Artc. 11
Simp. 3
Diff. —
Arb. —
Total 16 = R

PERCEPTUAL-COGNITIVE CHARACTERISTICS

AT —		P	2
BC —		PM	—
CD —		PSD	—
CP —		PT	—
CR	3	Rej	—
CT —		S	—
DC —		(S)	—
D_x —		SR	—
EJ —		TR	—
FCP —		VP	—
LD —		(VP)	1
LR —			

CONTENT

A	6	Abs	1
(A)	—	An_b	1
Af	—	An_s	1
(Af)	—	An_{sx}	—
Ad	—	An_x	—
Adx	—	Art	—
		Bl	—
Total	6	Bt	1
A/R = 6/16		Clg	1
H	2	Cld	1
(H)	3	Dth	—
Hf	—	Emb	—
(Hf)	1	Fd	—
Hd	—	Fi	1
Hdx	—	Hh	—
Total	5	Geo	—
H/R = 5/16		Imp	1
		Ls	—
		Mu	—
		Rel	—
		Sch	—
		Sci	—
		Tr	—
		Wp	—

Other 4 (List)
Bull 1
Explosion 2
Rocket 1

PSYCHOSEXUAL DRIVES & DEFENSE EFFECTIVENESS

	P	I	G	
O_0				— 0 } — 0
O_c				— 0
A_0				— 0 } — 2
A_c	1	1		— 2
P_0				— 0 } — 1
P_c			1	— 1

Total 3

PD% = 3/16 = 19%

INTERPERSONAL EXPECTATIONS

	HA	MA	MV	(MV)
I	—	—	—	(M) 10
II	1	1	2	(N) 4
III	2	1	1	(B) 1
IV	2	2	—	
	M —	N —	B 1	

Total = 1 + 15 = R

Burstein-Loucks summary sheet: Practice case F

Interpretative Note

This record is in many ways similar to the preceding one (#E). This adolescent is bright, analytic, (r%, Intg, Artc), with similar weaknesses in the validation of the denotative world (F+%), underlined by the low number of populars (P). She is both more idiosyncratic, then, and more guarded (Perceptual Cognitive realm), with psychosexual conflicts structuralized at a somewhat higher level (PD). The failures in appropriateness occur in two runs: responses 7–9, 11–15, suggesting a major vulnerability to stress, with relatively slow recovery, confirmed by poor defense deployed against some anal covert material. The overall picture is of a turbulent adolescent who may stabilize as an anxiety hysteric.

PRACTICE CASE G

Male college student

I.
6"

1. Face, not human, a demon, with ears and horns, eyes nose mouth and a tongue. Yeah, pretty much looks like something like a demon. (?) nothing else.

(demon?) here's 2 horns, and 2 sets of small horns. These are the eyes, they make it look unfriendly. The triangle shape, coming down, to make the eyes slope out. Small nose. Tongue hanging out. The shape of the face is not human and suggests a strange structure or hair here. Looks sort of old, sort of decaying, pieces falling off, either dirt or decomposing, something dead. W

II.
7"

2. The dark spots look like two elephants, facing each other, heads raised trunks in air, front feet up, like standing together.

(Elephants?)—put hands around form—Extended trunk, but not feet, cut off body. This dark spot (on right, dark spot in ink) could be an eye. Left is a light eye. Set of ears here, folded back. D6 (standing?) Yeah, standing together. D6 + 3

Below the elephants, it sort of looks like

(butterfly or moth?) Yeah. (outlines with finger) Better moth

they're standing on a
red butterfly or moth.

than I could draw. Looks kinda
like a monarch butterfly, but it
doesn't have markings like they
do.

III.
12″

3. Two people, maybe
dressed up in tuxedos,
fancy people, maybe
waiters. Bending over
with hands on the head
of an ant or insect, its
got jaws and teeth.

(people?) Feet here, extended.
Like they're trying to keep as far
away as they can. Repulsed, but
trying to keep control of this . . .
(Points) (Head?) Large eyes
(white area), teeth. The jackets, or
whatever, have lapels or collars,
stuffed shirt sort of appearance,
why I thought of tuxedos. Both
have arms extended. The faces
are very angular, short haircut,
not a very human appearance,
but the nose gives a very proper
appearance. D1

4. Looks like on the back,
the two red marks, the
upper torso of an otter,
hanging upside down.
But no bottom of a
body, just head and
front legs, looking be-
hind from where it's
hanging from. Not the
entire beast.

(otter?) D2 points. Something
hanging from the wall. Like
you've cut the poor critter in
half. The head is looking back
up, neck's curved around like
that. Small features, small nose,
small paws. Head with neat features like an otter. D2

5. In between the people,
a moth or butterfly, but
upside down. The red
splotch.

(moth or butterfly?) Yeah right in
there (points) (Upside down?)
Looks upside down because it
seems that generally the wings of
butterflies are larger on top. Oh,
I'd have to . . . it'd be more accu-
rate to turn it over. D3

Those people, they give
the appearance of argu-
ing, fighting over the
head. Their stance
gives the impression

(D1 as in III.1) Cause, they're
standing so they remain as far
apart as possible. Got themselves
angled back, which keeps their
faces from being so close to-

that they're tugging at it, upset at each other.

gether, their heads apart. Angular faces, angling back, give the sense of pulling away instead of helping, tugging or trying to gain control.

6. The picture as a whole an appearance of a deer, with eyes and nostrils, with a red mark upon its nose. It just looks like features, not a whole head.

(deer?) eyes mostly, and upper lip. A red mark on it's nose. Its get the triangular face of a deer, flared back out by nostrils. (points) The face is in here, outlined by the white. W

[Additional Response]
There's a butterfly in here too. (D1). This is it's body (D7) White wings, black circles being camouflage. I don't remember, what kind of butterfly it is that has large circles on its back, like eyes, makes birds think it's eyes to frighten them off.

IV.
23"

7. Looks like a wizard or monk or something. Standing, arms out to sides, wide sleeves, large and open. No hands, giving a ghostly appearance, but like a costume. Like 2 people, like one robe because these legs aren't big enough. One sitting or standing on another's shoulders. Yeah, one is sitting with his legs over the other's shoulders. The one on top is wearing boots. Can see legs over the other's shoulders. Head on top is real small in com-

(person in costume?) Yeah 2 people, this is the toe, hell, wide trousered pants. This person's head extends into a mask, collar of robe. The robe flows down, doesn't close in the middle, the sleeves hang down. (2 people?) The dark central column is one, the light gray shade makes the bell bottom pants, high heel type boots with small toe, sort of disappears here. Sitting on shoulders so legs could come around. (ghostly appearance?) It's all in gray, it's got different shades, swatches and swirls give a gauze like appearance, sort of a spectral type, doesn't have hands or feet. If the robe was closed, you couldn't see the people or feet

parison to robe. Arms not long enough to come out of the costume because its really 2 people; one sitting on top of the other.

because the robe goes to the floor. The mask, or whatever, is not shaped like anything, looks more demonical, not human, takes away from its monk appearance (monk?) Wide sleeves, characteristic of a monk, or a professor, that kind of sleeve, but because of head or lack of hands I think it's less of a priest or monk, more of some supernatural creature. W

V.
21″

8. Looks like a bat—but, it's got antennae, bats don't have antenna. (long pause).

(bat?) It's got a head like a bat, legs like a crane or bat, behind when flying, wings like a bat, not smooth, but ribbed. But the antennae are off. W

9. Which means maybe its a moth,—but moth's wings are not shaped like that. Don't see a lot in that.

And the tendrils on the wing— that's like a moth, but wings are not shaped like a moth and the body's like a bat's. W

VI.
26″

10. Well, I can see 2 people facing each other, a pole in back. An ornamental statue, Indian in nature, sort of a totem pole. They're sort of wearing space suits. Can't see expressions, only eyes can be seen, like a motorcycle helmet. Arms behind backs, each has an identical white circle on chest. They're distorted to a certain extent; legs seem a bit longer than would be proper. Rest of gray could be fog, hazy al-

(2 people?) Heads here, they're just this part, the light. Arms behind their backs. The totem pole is this dark, decorations at the top. People are wearing motorcycle or space type helmets or armor. The triangular indentation is suggestive of a front of motorcycle helmet or cavalier's—It's too dark here to see features. Legs are too long to be proper, would have to chop here—Maybe, I'm not sure. (Indian pole?) It's real thick here, at top flourished like an Indian decoration. (fog?) They have definite front, separate from the darkness behind, but the back, sort of looks like you're looking through water or a fog.

most like looking at them through water. Don't see anything else, once I get a picture in my head it's hard to change.

Distorting, changing the back light-looking through disturbed water or a fog, either could refract the light enough I suppose. W

VII. 11. Two old ladies in rock-
25″   ing chairs, blankets on laps, knee to knee and long hair, mainly in ponytails, sticking straight up, like they're falling. Yeah, hair sticking up all over. Maybe not rocking chairs, wheel chairs, they've got handles to push. No wheels, but that's just sort of cut out. Yeah, 2 old ladies in 2 wheel chairs fall-ing.

(2 old ladies?) Knees here, with shawls. Arms come down, disappear because picture's not complete, maybe they're under the blanket. Have mound of hair here. Here it should be hanging down in a pigtail because falling draws it up (pantomime w/arms as hair) light and dark sort of separates hair from face, either in shadow or black women with lighter hair, which is what suggested since it's gray. (Wheel-chair?) Because old ladies had to be in a rocking chair, but these handles, going back perpendicular rather than curving back. Could be curved back, but looks more like a handle that was jutting back rather than just a curve like a head rest. (no wheels?) It doesn't show the chair at all, except for the extension, the shawl covers the chair, this blanket here, looks like they have something draped over laps. W

12. Down at the bottom, the darker spot looks like a set of lungs and part of sternum in be-tween them.

(lungs?) Right there, a curved shape. Was going to say a moth again, but was bored with moths. Don't know I was thinking of lung, but there they are. Dd 6

VIII. 13. Two badgers trying to
16″   climb up to the top of something. The central

(badgers?) Here, these right here could be badgers. Here's the back left foot (on right "badger") Heres

structure whatever that is. Standing on their back left foot, holding on with front legs. Un huh. Can't do much on that one either.

the back right (on right leg of left badger) Here's the right paw, left paw. The darker spot could be an eye set in the middle of the skull. (Why badger?) Thick form, no tail. (climbing up?) Got their paws, this one's raised. They'd have an awful hard time, because its slanting back. Unless it's wood or something that they can get their claws into. This one looks like it's trying to get this paw up to pull itself on to the upper story. (central structure?) Doesn't resemble anything, but the bottom color resembles sherbet, but it doesn't look like anything. I don't know why badgers are climbing on it. W

IX.
31″

14. I suppose the orange things could be deer. Standing chest to chest, point antlers at each other, as if to buck.

(deer?) (points to D3) here, chest to chest, slanted back, head down on chest. Light part is eyes, Rudolph type of nose, sticks out. Pretty extensive antlers, at each other as if ready to buck. (Buck?) heads drawn back, like ready to crash into each other, ready to do battle. D3

15. Underneath green looks like a pretty good St. Bernard, but they'd have to be wearing chef's hats on their heads to account for the whole green shape. Tongues hanging out, nose to nose. Blue eyes.

(St. Bernards?) Mushroom type chef's hats (Outlines whole dog with finger) Ear, nose, (Blue eye?) This lighter bluish spot. dark spot underneath it, sets off blue, it goes up making almost a circle around it. (tongue?) (points) St. Bernard's tongues always hang out. D11

16. On the bottom, 2 upturned ice cream cones.

(cones?) (outlines w/finger). ice cream, cone, shadow. Light from

Shattered on the bottom. Light shining from on top.

above would make a shadow. They're sort of at an angle, not completely upturned. (Light?) The top of the core is lighter (points to lighter pink on card.) Shadows and blotches suggest a not perfectly circular shape, you know the way ice cream cones ???, it's always misshapen. D6

17. Some green in the middle, looks like the nose of some kind of animal, I can't think of what kind, maybe a pig snout.

(snout?) See this right here, with the vertical where the light green extends. You have to cut out the rest of the picture. The shape of the orange (around it) suggests that it's cut off, like a circle type nose, pig snout. D8

X.
29″

18. Three pairs of funny looking birds, gray set, green set, yellow set. All sitting or standing on branches somewhere.

(birds?) (points to gray D8, green Dd12, yellow Dd15) (gray?) like parrots, dark chest, beak, white eyes and belly. (yellow?) like a cockatoo, large, sharp beak, body, facing away. Orange wings on this back, looking up, a sweep of plumage fans down and back. (green?) like a falcon, wings up forward, here a sharp beak, tuft of feathers on head. (branches?) these blue network of lines. D8, Dd12, Dd15

19. Pink ones almost look like human type faces, but they have bodies like caterpillars, wearing elfish hats, points going down back, instead of up. Not like Merlin's but Santa's elves. Blue faces, blowing into some kind of apparatus. Something

D9 (human faces?) More like child or elves, round, upturned nose, eyes. The purple is the face, pink hats, cloth kind falling back. (caterpillar body?) caterpillar type feet here point inward, sort of like standing up, apparatus leaning against chest. 2 support chambers connected by white spots—mouth piece like a trumpet, against lips, might be against their mouths. Doesn't look like any kind of tool that I've ever seen.

blowing out or breathing. Since they're supported against it, it would explain why they can stand up like that with their backs. They could stand on the very tips. Without the support they couldn't. Like a snake could rise up but not on the tip of its tail, but this way sort of can lean against each apparatus, have more support, (apparatus?) Don't know what it is. Suggestive of a bagpipe, but no pipes, that's the first thing that came to mind, but I don't know. Blowing, anyway, or breathing, could be either. D9

20. Yellow spots, green, give impression of a strung out cat with moustache, green moustache, red eyes, yellow mark around them.

(cat?) orange eye, marks make it look sad. Because eyes drawn down. Moustache drooping down makes it look sad or drugged. Ears coming up are rather small. Face is wide, widens here, make it look fat. D2 + 6

21. I guess underneath the gray birds' legs, looks like eyes, "V", like camel's face with "V" being nose. That's it.

Eyes are white, face white, with large lips, nose is set back on camel's head. Camel that would be used in fighting. Gray metallic helmet with a unicorn peak, to give the appearance of a unicorn. The helmet sits down low, gray goes over eyes, maybe as blinders as if camel was to be used in war. D29 + 11

Card	Response	Latency	Position	Location	Cognitive complexity	Justifications	Imaginal aspects	Response appropriateness	Content	HA = Articulation of human percepts	MA = Motivational articulation	MV = Explicit motivational valuation	(MV) = Implicit motivational valuation	Inferred psychosexual drives	Defense effectiveness	Perceptual cognitive characteristics
I	1	6″	<	W	ARTC	F	HE·HM·OM	+	(Hf), Dth	HA3	MA2	M		Oo	–	(S), AT, BC
II	2	7″	<	D6+3	INTG	C·F·Sh	AM	+	Af, A		MA3	M	(N)	Oo, Pc	– –	P, SR, CR, Dx
III	3	12″	<	D1	ARB	F	HE·HM	–	H, A	HA4	MA3	M				P, (S), AT, CR, (VP)
	4		<	D2	ARTC	F	AM·HM	–	Ad				(N)			AT, BC, (VP)
	5		<	D3	ARTC	F		+	A				(N)			P
	6	23″	<	W	ARTC	C·F		–	Af			M				(S), (VP)
IV	7	21″	<	W	ARB	C'g·F·Sh	HM	–	H, Clg	HA4	MA3		(M)	Pc		AT
V	8		<	W	ARTC	F	T	+	A				(N)			P
	9		<	W	ARTC	F		+	A			M	(N)			P
VI	10	26″	<	W	ARB	C'gw·F·Sh	HM·V	–	totem pole H, fog	HA3	MA2		(N)	Pc	–	AT, CR, (VP)
VII	11	25″	<	W	ARB	C'g·F·Sh	HM	–	H, chairs	HA4	MA2	M				P, CR, PT
	12		<	Dd6	ARB	F		–	Ans, Anb				(N)			
VIII	13	16″	<	W	INTG	F	AM	+	A				(N)	Pc	–	P, (VP), PSD
IX	14	31″	<	D3	INTG	F	AM	+	A			–	(N)			
	15		<	D11	ARB	C·F	AM	+	A, Clg				(M)	Oo		CR
	16		<	D6	ARTC	F·Sh		–	Fd				(B)	Oo	–	
	17		<	D8	SIMP	F		–	Ad				(M)			Dx
X	18	29″	<	D8, Dd12, Dd15	ARB	C·Ci· C'w·f	AM	–	A			M	(N)		–	(S), AT
	19		<	D9	ARB	C·Ci·F	HM	–	(Hf)	HA4	MA3	M	(N)	Oc		AT, CR
	20		<	D2+D6	ARTC	C·Ci·F	HE	–	Af		MA2				–	(S), CR
	21		<	D29+11	ARTC	C'gw·F		–	Af				(M)	Oo		S, CR

Burstein-Loucks scoring sheet: Practice case G

NAME: G

AGE: ___ **SEX:** ___

EDUCATION: ___

OCCUPATION: ___

Responses (R): 21

Additional responses: [ ]

Lost responses: ___

Precision alternatives: ___

Card rejection: ___

DATE: ___ **TIME:** ___

EXAMINER: ___

PSYCHOSEXUAL DRIVES & DEFENSE EFFECTIVENESS

	P	I	G	
O_o		6	6	} 6
O_c			0	0
A_o			0	} 0
A_c			0	
P_o			0	} 3
P_c		3	3	
				Total 9

PD% = 9 /21 = 43 %

INTERPERSONAL EXPECTATIONS

HA	MA	MV	(MV)
I	I	M 7	(M) 4
II 2	II 4	N	(N) 9
III	III 4	B	(B) 1
IV 4	IV 4		

Total = 7 + 14 = R

CONTENT

A 8	Abs	An_b 1
(A)	An_s 1	
Af 4	An_{sx}	
(Af)	An_x	
Ad 2	Art	
Adx	Bl	
Total 14 A/R = 21	Bt	
H 4	Clg 2	
(H) 1	Cld 1	
Hf 1	Dth 1	
(Hf) 1	Emb 1	
Hd	Fd 1	
Hdx	Fi 1	
Total 6 H/R = 21	Hh 1	
	Geo	
	Imp	
	Ls	
	Mu 1	
	Rel 1	
	Sch	
	Sci	
	Tr	
	Wp	

Other ___ (List)

COGNITIVE COMPLEXITY

Intg.	3
Artc.	9
Simp.	1
Diff.	8
Arb.	
Total	21 = R

PERCEPTUAL-COGNITIVE CHARACTERISTICS

AT 7	P 7		
BC 2	PM		
CD	PSD 1		
CP	PT 1		
CR 8	Rej		
CT	S 2		
DC	(S) 4		
D_x 2	SR 1		
EJ	TR		
FCP	VP		
LD	(VP) 5		
LR			

JUSTIFICATIONS/IMAGINAL ASPECTS

List Justifications in alphabetical order (f or C, CA, Ci, Cp, C'b,g,w, F &/or Sh) followed by Imaginal aspects in alphabetical order (AM, HE, HM, OM, T, &/or V)

	Response appropriateness +	−
F·Sh	1	
F·AM	2	
F·T	1	
F	2	2
F·AM·HM		1
F·HE·HM		1
F·HE·HM·OM	1	
C·F·Sh·AM	1	
C·F		1
C'g·F·Sh·HM		2
C'gw·F·Sh·HM·V		1
C·F·AM	1	1
C·Ci·C'w·F·AM		1
C·Ci·F·HM		1
C·Ci·F·HE		1
C'gw·F		1

Total = 9 + 12 = R

LOCATION

W	- 7 -	8/	W% - 38 %
W	- 1 -	/21	
(W)			
D	- 10 -	11/	D% - 52 %
W	- 1 -	/21	
Dd	-	2/	Dd% - 10 %
Dd	- 2 -	/21	
Total	- 21 - R		
rare	- 3/	/21	r% - 14 %

PERCENTAGES

Afr - 9/12 - 57	f% - / - 0 %			
F% - 4/21 - 19 %	PD% - 9/21 - 43 %			
F+% - 2/4 - 50 %	H% - 6/21 - 29 %			
B+% - 7/17 - 41 %	A% - 14/21 - 67 %			

≤HE + HM - 3 + 7 /21 - 48 %

≤AM - 6/21 - 29 %

≤OM - 1/21 - 5 %

≤C - 6/21 - 29 %

≤Ca + Ci + Cp - 0 + 3 + 0 /21 - 14%

Burstein-Loucks summary sheet: Practice case G

Interpretative Note

This college student gives evidence of significant psychological difficulties. Superior integrative ability is deflected by those conflicts (Intg, r%, Arb). There is a significant lack of attention to the denotative (F%), made more serious by weaknesses in consensual validation (F + %, B + %), and a high degree of active conflict (PD%). There is an active fantasy life (HM, HE) but it is negative in tone (MV). The emphasis on oral level conflict (Oo), converge with a potential for suicide (color-shading blends) to suggest significant suicidal potential. Co-occurrence of evidence of adequate socialization (P, MA) and capacity for highly idiosyncratic thinking (BC, SR, PSD), suggest both hysterical conflict and serious narcissistic pathology. Probable diagnosis, hysteria with narcissistic disorder of self.

PRACTICE CASE H

Female college student

I.
8"

1. Ll 2 people, w/another person in the middle, w/hands held up, like that, (pantomime, hands held up alongside head), (pause), a double headed person.

(some people?) Yes. (why?) I don't know. The heads, and arms here, and body. The hands of that person (points to middle). It goes straight down here to the feet. (double-headed?) uh hmn. (why?) (pause) because of the two protrusions on top. W

2. Could be a butterfly. That's about all.

(butterfly?) Symmetry is so it could be a butterfly. W

II.
5"

3. Man, with a very bushy beard, large mouth.

(man?) with a large beard (points D3), large eyes (D30). (Why a man?) His eyes, here's mouth, beard. W

Or a cat.
(precision alternative?)

(cat?) Because of the tuft or hair on the bottom that's like the tuft on a cat's chin—You can almost see whiskers coming out, (shows with fingers). (What made you think of whiskers?) You can imagine the whiskers protruding across the rest of the paper.

III.   Uh, hmn, (long
               pause.) I don't know.
               (long pause)

36″   4. Ll 2 persons facing   (2 persons?) Head, body, legs,
         one another.   they've got on pointed shoes. D1-7

        5. If you turn it upside   (angry person?) Yeah, this would
         down, it ll a very an-   be the eyes and the basic shape of
         gry person, w/big eyes. the face. Angry and ghoulish type
         (did not actually in-   w/the dark eyes. D1
         vert card)

IV.   6. Ll a wizard w/a big,   (wizard?) He's got a very small
5″   long robe, (moves   head, big cloak that drapes, (voice
         arms out imitating   has a melodramatic quality, as if
         robe) getting ready to   play acting), kind of blowing,
         cast some evil spell, ll   (shows w/arms.) (why casting an
         something they'd put   evil spell?) Just because it's black.
         in children's cartoons. I guess I've been playing D and D
         (pushes card back de-   too long. (Dungeons and Dragons)
         cisively.)   (pause) Almost ll a typical wizard
                            casting a spell, imaginary wand,
                            ("lightning bolt" sounds, seems to
                            enjoy it.) W

V.   7. That one ll a butterfly (ll a butterfly or bat?) Yeah, more
1″   or a bat, but looks   like a bat. (why?) Yeah, wings are
         more like a bat   pointed downward, more like a
         (pause), very pointed   bat in flight, not two lobed like a
         ears.   butterfly. W

VI.   Uh, hmn. (long pause)

29″   8. Ll a person standing   (person?) Almost in an eagle cos-
         on top of a hill of   tume, w/wings, standing on top of
         some sort, dressed as a craggy hill. (craggy?) because of
         some sort of bird, like the shape. (like an Indian?) be-
         an Indian.   cause of the costume, Eagle dance.
                            (demo's) W

        9. Or as if someone's   (a brain?) Yeah, kind of like look-
         taken a brain, sort of   ing at top view, see the line going

flattened it (pushes on
table) all the way back
down into the card.

down center. Someone's flattened
it. W

(additional response) Kind of like
a sting ray, too, only tail's not
skinny enough.

VII.   10. 2 genies coming out of
8"   a bottle, facing each
          other. They're girls,
          they have ponytails
          sticking up, out in the
          air. Arms turned out,
          towards sides. (demos)

(2 genies coming out of a bottle?)
Uh huh. (why genies?) I don't
know anything else that comes
out of a bottle. (jokingly) Here it
looks like a bottle, kind of. Steam
raises the genies. (steam?) yeah,
see here the outline could be
steam. (They're girls?) They have
ponytails sticking out, reminds me
of pictures of people in the 50's
w/ponytails. W

VIII.   Uhmn. (long pause)
           Multicolored ink blot.
           It's interesting. (long
           pause)

27"   11. Looks sort of like
          there's 2 sort of mole
          like animals on the
          side. Other than that
          . . . (pushes card back
          decisively).

(moles?) Yeah, the two pink creatures on the side ll moles. (why
moles?) Here's its head, got an
eye, legs, tail, rolled over on its
side. (eye?) the spots where the
eyes should be. D1

IX.   12. Looks as if you're
17"   standing on top of a
          very large object, look-
          ing down into a
          chasm.

          (nervous fidget, but
          keeps looking for over
          1 minute)

(standing on top of an object?)
Looking down into a chasm. Your
eye kind of follows this line
downward—if you're standing
back here. You're up very tall,
looking down.) W

      13. The pink's about the

(blood smear?) Reminds me of the

color of blood in a
blood smear.

color of blood in a blood smear.
It's no longer red, it's pink, like a
smear for a blood count test or
something. D6

X.   Pretty, let's see. (long
            pause)

20″   14. From upside down it
           could be a flower.
           (does not turn card)

(flower?) The stamen, sepal, petals. Yeah, from upside down it
looks like a flower. W

       15. From right side up,
           fireworks.

(fireworks?) Splashes of color like
fireworks in the sky, random figures. W

       16. Or 2 people standing
           (puts hands in a "roof
           shape" fingertips
           touching, palms apart)
           60° angle to each
           other, their foreheads
           are touching, hands
           are touching.

(2 people?) (shows hands again)
At a 60° angle, form an equilib-
rium (sic) triangle. (equilibrium?)
Yeah. Ll their heads are touching
and their hands are touching. D9,
D6, D11

NAME: H   AGE: SEX: EXAMINER: DATE:

Card	Response	Latency	Position	Location	Cognitive complexity	Justifications	Imaginal aspects	Response appropriateness	Content	HA = Articulation of human percepts	MA = Motivational articulation	MV = Explicit motivational valuation	(MV) = Implicit motivational valuation	Inferred psychosexual drives	Defense effectiveness	Perceptual cognitive characteristics
I	1	8″	<	W	ARB	F	HM	–	(H)	HA2	MA1	N				CR
	2		<	W	SIMP	F		+	A				(N)	Oo	I	(S)
II	3	5″	<	W	ARTC	F		–	Hf	HA2			(N)			
				PRECISION ALTERNATIVE												
III	4	36″	<	D1-7	INTG	F	HM	+	H	HA2	MA1	N	(N)			P
	5		<	D1	ARTC	F	HE	–	Hf	HA2	MA2	M				(S)
IV	6	5″	<	W	ARTC	C'b·F	HM	+	(H)	HA4	MA4	M				AT, SR
	7	1″	<	W	ARTC	F	AM	+	A							P
V	8	29″	<	W	INTG	F	HM	+	H	HA4	MA4	N				
VI	9		<	W	ARTC	F	HM	–	Ans			M				
			ADDITIONAL RESPONSE													
VII	10	8″	<	W	[ARTC	F	HM	+	A; Bottle (H), Clg,	HA4	MA4	N	(N)]			P
VIII	11	27″	<	D1	INTG	F	AM	+	A				(N)		I	P, CD
IX	12	17″	<	W	ARTC	F	V	+	Ls				(N)			
	13		<	D6	DIFF	C		–	Bl				(M)	Ac		
X	14	20″	<	W	ARTC	F		+	Bt				(N)	Ac	G	CD
	15		<	W	SIMP	C·F		+	Fireworks				(N)	Oc	G	(VP)
	16		<	D9, 6, 11	INTG	F	HM	+	H	HA2	MA2	N				

Burstein-Loucks scoring sheet: Practice case H

NAME: _____

AGE: _____ SEX: _____

EDUCATION: _____

OCCUPATION: _____

DATE: _____ TIME: _____

EXAMINER: _____

Responses (R): 16

Additional responses: [ ]

Lost responses: _____

Precision alternatives: _____

Card rejection: _____

LOCATION

W = 11 ___ = 11/16 W% = 69 %

W =

(W) =

D = 4 ___ = 5/16 D% = 31 %

W = 1

Dd = 0 ___ = 0/16 Dd% = ___ %

Dd = 0

Total = 16 = R

rare = 1/16 r% = 6 %

PERCENTAGES

Afr = 6/10 = 60 f% = 0/16 = 0 %

F% = 3/16 = 19 % PD% = 4/16 = 25 %

F+% = 2/3 = 67 % H% = 8/16 = 50 %

B+% = 9/13 = 69 % A% = 3/16 = 19 %

≤ HE + HM = 1 + 7/2 = 50 %

≤ AM = 2/16 = 13 %

≤ OM = 0/16 = 0 %

≤ C = 2/16 = 13 %

≤ Ca + Ci + Cp = __ + __ + __ = 0 %

JUSTIFICATIONS/IMAGINAL ASPECTS

List Justifications in alphabetical order (f or C, CA, Ci, Cp, C'b,g,w, F &/or Sh) followed by imaginal aspects in alphabetical order (AM, HE, HM, OM, T, &/or V)

	Response appropriateness	
	+	–
C·F	1	
C		1
C'b·F·HM	1	
F	2	1
F·HM	4	2
F·HE		1
F·AM	2	
F·v	1	

Total = 11 + 5 = R

COGNITIVE COMPLEXITY

Intg. 4

Artc. 8

Simp. 2

Diff. 1

Arb. 1

Total 16 = R

PERCEPTUAL-COGNITIVE CHARACTERISTICS

AT	1	P	4		
BC		PM			
CD	2	PSD			
CP		PT			
CR	1	Rej			
CT		S	2		
DC		(S)	2		
Dx		SR	1		
EJ		TR			
FCP		VP			
LD		(VP)	1		
LR					

CONTENT

A 3 Abs

(A) An_b 1

Af An_s 1

(Af) An_{sx}

Ad An_x

Adx Art

Total 3 Bl 1
A/R = 3/16 Bt 1

H 3 Clg

(H) 3 Cld 1

Hf 2 Dth

(Hf) Emb

Hd Fd

Hdx 1 Fi 1

Total 8 Hh
H/R = 8/16 Imp 1

Ls 1

Mu

Rel

Sch

Sci

Tr

Wp

Other _____
(List)

PSYCHOSEXUAL DRIVES & DEFENSE EFFECTIVENESS

	P	I	G	
O_o		1		} 2
			1	}
O_c			1	}...
A_o				0
		1	1	} 2
A_c		1	1	} 2
P_o				0
P_c				0

Total 4

PD% = 4/16 = 25 %

INTERPERSONAL EXPECTATIONS

HA		MA		MV		MV		(MV)	
II	5	I	2	M	3	(M)	1	
III	3	II	2	N	5	(N)	7	
IV	3	III		B		(B)		
		IV	3					

Total = 8 + 8 = R

Burstein-Loucks summary sheet: Practice case H

Interpretative Note

A very bright but underproductive college student (Intg, R, Arb) with a strong tendency to live in the connotative world (F%). In this case, however, the capacity for social validation is much more intact (F + %, B + %), and there is little to suggest major thought pathology (Perceptual Cognitive Characteristics). Fantasy is human oriented, if negative in tone (HE, HM, MV), and there is evidence of a high degree of sophistication about what activates human behavior (MA). There is suggestion a pregenital neurosis (PD, V), of moderate degree.

7
INTERPRETATION OF THE STRUCTURAL SUMMARY

The following case presentation will illustrate a detailed interpretation of the structural summary of the Rorschach.

Although in practice, psychological testing would include review of individual responses to the Rorschach and analysis of other tests, for didactic purposes only the scoring summary is used here. Information on the clinical picture and clinical outcome is also included.

A CHILD CASE

This 10-year-old boy was referred for evaluation by his pediatrician because of anxiety attacks of two-weeks' duration, accompanied by obsessive fear that he was having or going to have a "heart attack." At the time of the anxiety episodes he would first imagine the heart attack and then hyperventilate, experiencing mild tachycardia and dizziness. However, there was also a chronic obsession with his heart. Neither the boy nor his mother could identify a precipitant to the onset of this symptom. He had been watching television at home when the first episode occurred.

This child was the eldest of four children, with one brother and two sisters. He lived with his working college-educated mother in a modest middle-level income home. He attended fifth grade in the regular curriculum and made average grades. His parents had divorced three years prior to the initial presentation of these symptoms. The divorce reportedly followed years of marital strife and episodic wife abuse caused by the father's alcoholism and paranoid schizophrenia. The mother appeared free of all psychological symptomatology but was quite concerned about the toll the previous strife-torn years and on-going bi-weekly weekend visits took on the children. The father reportedly drank heavily even during visitation.

The subject presented as a bright but interpersonally anxious, mildly agitated, insecure, yet directive child. He spoke rapidly with some pressure of speech and vocalized much worry about the visit, confidentiality, and what the examiner was going to do. It was felt that psychodiagnostic testing would be helpful in illuminating this child's present psychological status and provide additional information for treatment planning.

NAME:

AGE: SEX:

DATE: TIME:

EXAMINER:

EDUCATION:

OCCUPATION:

Responses (R): 71
Additional responses: [ ]
Lost responses:
Precision alternatives:
Card rejection:

LOCATION

W = 0 = 3/71 W% = 4 %
W = 0
(W) = 3
D = 44 = 57/71 D% = 80 %
W = 13
Dd = 6 = 11/71 Dd% = 16 %
Dd = 5
Total = 71 = R r% = 25 %
rare = 18/71

PERCENTAGES

Afr = 28/48 = 48 f% = 4/71 = 6 %
F% = 31/71 = 44 % PD% = 38/71 = 54 %
F+% = 14/31 = 45 % H% = 18/71 = 25 %
B+% = 17/38 = 45 % A% = 29/71 = 41 %
≰HE + HM = 2 + 16/71 = 25 %
≰AM = 4/71 = 6 %
≰OM = 5/71 = 7 %
≰C = 10/71 = 14 %
≰Ca + Ci + Cp = 0/71 + 3/71 + 1/71 = 6 %

JUSTIFICATIONS/IMAGINAL ASPECTS

List Justifications in alphabetical order (f or C, CA, Ci, Cp, C'b,g,w, F &/or Sh) followed by imaginal aspects in alphabetical order (AM, HE, HM, OM, T, &/or V)

	Response appropriateness +	−
f		2
f·HM	1	1
C·F	1	1
Ci·F	2	1
C·F·HM		1
C·F·OM		1
C·F·Sh·HM		1
Cp·F·Sh·HM		
C'b·F	2	1
C'w·F		3
C'w·F·OM	1	1
C'b·C'w·F·OM	1	
F	14	17
F·AM	3	1
F·HM	1	4
F·HM·HE	1	
F·OM	1	
F·Sh·HM	2	1
F·Sh·OM	1	
F·T	1	1
C'·F·Sh·Hm	1	1

Total = 31 + 40 = R

COGNITIVE COMPLEXITY

Intg. 3
Artc. 33
Simp. 24
Diff. 2
Arb. 9
Total 71 = R

PERCEPTUAL-COGNITIVE CHARACTERISTICS

AT 16   P 6
BC 3   PM 2
CD 4   PSD 1
CP   PT 2
CR 14   Rej
CT   S 2
DC   (S) 5
Dx   SR 7
EJ   TR 1
FCP 5   VP
LD   (VP) 3
LR

CONTENT

A 16   Abs
(A) 1   Anb 1
Af 7   Ans 2
(Af)   Ansx
Ad 5   Anx
Adx   Art
Total 29   Bl 1
A/R = 71   Bt 4
H 3   Clg 5
(H) 3   Cld
Hf 2   Dth 2
(Hf) 1   Emb
Hd 9   Fd 6
Hdx   Fi 1
Total 18   Hh 1
H/R = 71   Geo
Imp 9
Ls 1
Mu 1
Rel 3
Sch 1
Sci 1
Tr 3
"Y" 1
Ty
Wp 1   H2O 2

Other FCP-continent/country
(List) mud-slime
sticking out
religion
flying

PSYCHOSEXUAL DRIVES & DEFENSE EFFECTIVENESS

	P	I	G	
Oo	1	7	1	= 8 } =14
Oc		3	2	= 6 }
Ao		2		= 2 } =8
Ac	1	4	1	= 6 }
Po		9		= 0 } =16
Pc	1		6	= 16 }
				Total 38

PD% = 38/71 = 54 %

INTERPERSONAL EXPECTATIONS

HA	MA	MV	(MV)
I 4	I 1	M 8	(M) 8
II 2	II 7	N 2	(N) 40
III 3	III 6	B 6	(B) 7
IV 6	IV 1		
	Total = 16	+ 55	= R

Total = 16 + 55 = R

Burstein-Loucks summary sheet: A child case

275

Interpretation of Structural Summary

Response context

The subject gives 71 responses, a record whose length is over two standard deviations greater than the average for children his age. This heightened productivity indicates above average potential intellectual functioning but also bodes of an over-productivity of mental contents, which may be related to an internalized pressure of thought, as in mania or hypomania, or a pressure to compulsively respond to all blot areas, or, rarely, a playful, creative, productive approach to the blots. Examination of several facets of the summary sheet will shed light on these alternatives. These other quantitative factors should be interpreted in light of an elevated number of responses.

Location/perceptual approach

In the context of a 71 response record, a W% of 4 is extremely low and based upon 3 (W); Dd% is high as is D%. Thus, this child's perceptual approach emphasizes large and small details at the expense of the whole picture. This relative constriction of attention/perception may be due to anxiety, an over-scrupulous need to qualify all responses, and/or a more general disturbance in intellectual functioning. Examination of the proportion of rare responses and of cognitive complexity scorings should further define his intellectual approach.

The proportion of rare responses is high but, because the record is of great length, may not be higher than would be expected, i.e. the increase in proportion of rare responses is in keeping with the overall increase in response total. Nevertheless, this percentage indicates a possibly idiosyncratic or at best novel perceptual approach.

Cognitive complexity

With only three integrated responses out of 71, it appears that this child has difficulty perceiving relationships among the elements of his world in a useful way. The nine arbitrary responses indicate an interest in and attempt to understand relationships, but a relative inability to do so in a socially appropriate, realistic manner. Rather, the attempts to relate perceptual elements that occur appear to result in distortion. The proportion of simple responses is high at the expense of the proportion of articulated responses, indicating a relative lack of perceptual-cognitive analyses and an over-emphasis on easy responses.

Imaginal aspects

This child gave twenty-seven responses containing one or more imaginal aspects; 38% of his responses contained some form of fantasy. He is highly ideational and probably under considerable cognitive pressure. He gave sixteen human movement responses, two of which were paired with human emotion scorings, again indicating above average intelligence and an over-active fantasy life regarding other people. Eleven of sixteen of these fantasies are minuses, i.e. socially inappropriate. Thus, this subject's interpersonal fantasies appear to be problematic or distorted in some way. One out of two fantasies regarding human emotion/motivation are also socially inappropriate. Later review of interpersonal expectations and psychosexual drive content will elucidate these problems. By contrast there are only four animal movement scores; only 6% of all responses contain evidence of drive press (AM). On the other hand, the subject gives five object movement scores, which even in a record of increased length is a larger number than optimal. Thus, he would appear to feel aware of conflict, possibly feeling overwhelmed or threatened by loss of control of drive impulses. He appears to feel threatened by an extreme amount of anxiety, tension, hostility, and/or general frustration. Both texture and vista responses are well within normal limits for a record this size. However, examination of the justification/imaginal aspects list reveals that the vista response co-occurs with a color-shading and human movement response, indicating that the subject evidences a sense of inadequacy and distance in relation to others, coupled with dysphoric affect found to be associated with suicidal risk in adults. Thus, his closest relationships may be problematic.

Justifications

There are four failure to justify responses in this record, indicating occasional lack of awareness and reflectivity in this child. He evidences an excessive number of blend responses, especially in a record of this length where pure F responses are usually heightened. This indicates not only above average intellectual functioning but probable disruption in that functioning. The internal fantasy and emotional operations would appear to be extremely rich and complex and perhaps overly so. F% is moderately low for a child his age, indicating less time spent in the objective, denotative, more neutralized realm of life than in the personal, emotional, fantasy and connotative realm, possibly contributing to a chronic over-taxing of psychological and even physiological resources. There appears to be a tendency to over-personalize. In the affective realm, this subject is experiencing a great deal of sadness and significant anxiety as revealed by the number of achromatic color and shading responses. Color responses show that he is aware of his emotional reactions and often expresses them, but he occasionally reacts inappropriately and expresses these feelings without adequate reality perception. Inappropriate color and minus color responses demonstrate that he has a higher than average tolerance for the non-rational. Thus, he may be affectively unpredictable to others, and somewhat idiosyncratic. There is also an indication of potential hallucinatory or delusional potential as indicated by the use of projected color, associated with increased anxiety, poor reality testing, and sometimes associated with seizure disorder. The presence of color-shading blends suggests an increased risk of suicide and suicidal ideation or impulses when found in adults and, therefore, possibly in this ten-year old's record.

Social appropriateness

F + % of 45 indicates that psychological functioning within the denotative sphere is impaired. Unfortunately, B + % of 45 also indicates significant impairment in the connotative realm. Thus, this child would tend to show major deficits in social appropriateness, reality testing, and judgment in all areas of life, both non-emotional, factual areas, e.g. mathematics, and emotional and fantasy areas, e.g. literature, peer relations.

Perceptual-cognitive characteristics

Six populars are a positive indication of psychological resources in this record, although the number could be higher in a record of 71 responses. These populars indicate an ability to think and respond conventionally, despite indications of problems in reality testing and conventionality elsewhere in the record. Thus, this subject has achieved at least a modicum of psychological structure and socialization from which to build a better integrated personality.

Of greatest concern in this scoring section are the three bizarre content scorings and the fourteen contradictions of reality. Bizarre content is almost exclusively found in schizophrenic patients or other deteriorated psychotic states. These responses speak to the eerie, uncanny experiences to which Harry Stack Sullivan (Kasanin, 1944) referred in his writings and are associated with either preoccupation with or intrusion into awareness of content usually defended against. Thus, bizarre content in this record indicates the breakdown and ineffectiveness of defenses and the ensuing emergence of primitive and socially inappropriate drive content into consciousness. The fourteen contradictions of reality reveal significant impairment in reality testing, as have F + %, B + %, and the nine Arbitrary responses. The three mild verbal peculiarities, two pantomimes, two predicate thinking scores, and one transposition response are not of great concern in a record of this length, but the five fixed concept perseveration scorings are. This child appears to be internally preoccupied or obsessed with certain themes: continent/country, mud-slime, flying, fish. These thought-perception content areas are probably over-cathected drive derivatives, i.e. symbolic and transformed expressions of underlying psychological needs and conflicts.

The subject also uses an over-abundance of affective toning, indicating possible over involvement with the percepts and some mild loss of distance from the task in that, as seven self-reference scorings would also indicate, there is some tendency to personalize the task at hand.

In summary, this child's thinking appears to be problematic. He gives significant evidence of impairment in reality testing, poor judgment, internal preoccupations, or obsessiveness, over-personalization and egocentricity.

Content

Animal percent is low for children and human percent is high, indicating that this child has a keen interest in others but also corroborates other scores in that he tends to view the world in personal terms. The content list reveals that he sees seven animal face responses. This emphasis on animal face responses suggests unconscious fear of attack and a generalized anxiety. The human content area emphasizes human detail at the expense of whole humans. As many humanoids or mythological humans are seen as real humans. This points toward interpersonal anxiety, constriction, and a tendency toward interpersonal criticality.

There is a wide array of content categories used, indicating brightness and a range of interests. Of particular significance are the food, religion, death, and water responses. Food and water responses may be related to dependency conflicts, while themes of religion and death may be evidence of depressive content and problems with aggression and guilt. Examination of psychosexual drives and defense effectiveness will contribute to further understanding of this child's conflicts.

Psychosexual drives and defense effectiveness

Examination of the psychosexual drive percentage reveals an alarmingly high proportion of responses with discernible drive derivative expression. Examination of the psychosexual drive grid shows that there is drive expression at each psychosexual level at a significantly higher rate than expected. This indicates that his psychological conflicts are not well structured at one level but rather involve a multiplicity of conflicts, a range of developmental issues, and probably result in "pan-neurotic" symptomatology, and a range of defenses, from splitting and projection to repression. Drive effectiveness is, for the most part, of intermediate effectiveness, but both good and poor defense effectiveness is evidenced as well. Unfortunately, poor defense effectiveness is in evidence at each level. When the rest of the record is considered, it seems clear that this child's cognitive functioning is being impaired by his psychological conflicts. The degree of conflict experienced appears to result in impaired cognitive functioning with considerable emotional turmoil. Defenses are not sufficient to protect this child from feeling threatened with loss of control and being overwhelmed by his drives.

Interpersonal expectations

Inspection of the levels of human articulation demonstrates that this child's internal representations of other people are appropriately varied in range of investment and detail but with a greater than expected level of highly articulated responses in which a large number of specific attributes are given. His conceptualizations of the activities of others are skewed on both extremes, finding it difficult to understand or identify others' activities with a concomitant greater than average tendency to engage in complex fantasy about others' motives and actions. The quality of these internal representations again consist of two extremes, malevolent and benevolent, with very few neutral in nature. Thus, more conscious internal representations and expectations of others are split between two extremes. This child appears capable of both positive and negative relations but more neutral or casual relatedness does not seem likely. This is reminiscent of a "you're either with me or against me" but never neutral fantasy life. Less conscious and more generalized expectations appear more neutral and positive overall. Malevolent implicit expectations are lower than expected indicating that this child is more aware of the interpersonal nature of his conflicts.

In summary, this Rorschach record is that of a ten-year-old child in severe psychological distress. His ego functioning is being impaired by the overwhelming nature of his psychological conflicts, which involve all psychosexual developmental levels. He is highly ideational but is also experiencing considerable affect, much of a dysphoric nature. There may be increased risk of suicide. Thinking may tend to be obsessive with intrusion of unacceptable, socially inappropriate content of a conflictful nature, which may in turn lead to peculiarities in thought process and poor reality testing. Emotional reactions are sometimes idiosyncratic as well. Thought content is occasionally morose or bizarre.

Fortunately there are indications of above average intellectual functioning, complex internal object representations, and ability to relate positively on an interpersonal level, although there are negative indications here, as well. Despite the affective and cognitive disruption in evidence, this child is still able to react conventionally and to maintain positive involvement with others, i.e. positive object attachments. Although interpersonal distortions do occur, an ability to empathize and relate well remains.

DIAGNOSTIC FORMULATION

Based upon the Rorschach structural summary alone, it appears that a number of diagnostic formulations are possible. Borderline personality disorder, narcissistic behavior disorder (Kohut, 1984), schizotypal personality disorder, or even schizophreniform disorder should be considered. Of course, the symptomatology evidenced in the clinical presentation would greatly influence the final diagnosis made in terms of descriptive psychopathology.

This child was diagnosed as a narcissistic behavior disorder on the basis of his ability to maintain object attachments concurrent with primitive and turbulent psychopathology.

CLINICAL DISPOSITION AND OUTCOME

The child's mother was congratulated for seeking help for her son and given general feedback regarding the test findings. The child was seen in individual psychoanalytically-oriented play therapy for approximately a year, with collateral bi-weekly sessions with his mother. During the course of treatment, the symptom picture quickly shifted. The "heart attacks" quickly abated, within the first three weeks of treatment. However, an obsessive fear of being poisoned with some delusional quality took the place of the "heart attack" as a central concern and remained until well toward the end of therapy, resolving two months prior to termination. Mid-way in the therapy process a hand-washing ritual began, occurring on the average of ten times a day until his hands were raw and bled. This symptom was quickly resolved and meticulousness and tidiness became the order of the day. The last several months of therapy focused on this child's peer relationships and how he could make better friends, relax, and be less controlling in his interpersonal relations. At the time of termination considerable improvements had been made in this child's self structure and in his ability to empathize well with others; his peer and family relations had improved greatly.

The therapeutic process focused on correcting considerable narcissistic injuries, which this child had incurred during his parents' turbulent marriage. After the divorce, his mother had not yet been able to assume a protective, strong, and anxiety-reducing self-object role with her son. Play in the sessions evidenced the expected array of developmental conflicts with demonstrated grandiosity, sadism, and the need for omnipotent control.

Intervention centered on recognizing this child's need for a strong empathic self-object whom he could trust with his most conflictful feelings and thoughts. The child exercised considerable control of the therapy sessions, usually coming in with an agenda of fears he wanted to discuss. Over time he was able to reveal his intensely conflictful feelings toward his alcoholic father which included fear that his father's irresponsibility and "craziness" would kill him. His greatest narcissistic injury lay in the fact that his parents were unable to provide the reasonably predictable and protective "holding environment" he so desperately needed and were so preoccupied with their own turmoil that there was little ability to adequately mirror or empathically nurture their son. As he became older, awareness of his parents, especially father's, inadequacies were glaring and little idealization was possible. His mother, a frequent victim of verbal and sometimes physical abuse, lacked good self-esteem or self-confidence and provided limited opportunity for idealization until after the divorce. With counseling she was able to become more confident, protective, reassuring, and in short, empathic with her son's basic emotional needs. By the end of treatment, his anxiety had abated as had his major symptoms. Reality testing was greatly improved, he had acquired a delightful and appropriate, playful sense of humor, and the grandiosity was no longer in evidence. However, he did continue to be very tidy.

REFERENCES

Applebaum, S. A. & Colson, D. B. A reexamination of the color shading Rorschach test response and suicide attempts. *Journal of Projective Techniques, 37,* 1968, 160–164.

Beck, S. J. Configurational tendencies in Rorschach responses. *American Journal of Psychology,* 1933, *45,* 433–443.

Beck, S. J. Personality disorders by means of the Rorschach test. *American Journal of Orthopsychiatry,* 1930, *1,* 81–88.

Beck, S. J., Beck, A. G., Levitt, E. E., & Molish, H. B. *Rorschach's test, Vol. 1: Basic process.* New York: Grune & Stratton, 1961.

Binet, A. & Henri, V. Psychologie individuelle. *L' Anne'e Psychologigue,* 1895, *2,* pp. 411–465.

Binet, A. & Simon, T. Methodses nouveltes pour las diagnostic du niueau intellectual des anormacy. *Annee Psychologique,* 1905, *11,* p. 191–244.

Blatt, S. J. & Berman, W. H. A methodology for the use of the Rorschach in clinical research. *Journal of Personality Assessment,* 1984, *48*(3), pp. 226–239.

Blatt, S. J., Brenneis, C. B., Schimek, J. G., & Glick, M. Normal development and psychopathological impairment of the concept of the object of the Rorschach. *J. Abnormal Psych,* 1976, *85*(4), pp. 364–373.

Boring, E. G. *A history of experimental psychology (2nd ed.).* New York: Appleton-Century-Crofts, 1950.

Bower, P. A., Testin, R. & Roberts, A. Rorschach diagnosis by a systematic combining of content, thought process and determinant scales. *Genetic Psychology Monographs,* 1960, *62,* pp. 105–183.

Burstein, A. G. Rorschach's test: a review, in Buros, O. K. (ED.). *The eighth mental measurements yearbook, Vol. 1.* Highland Park, N.Y.: Gryphon Press, 1978.

Burstein, A. G. & Loucks, S. A comprehensive scoring manual for Rorschach's test. *The British Journal of Projective Psychology and Personality Study,* 1985, *30*(2), pp. 3–16.

Chapman, L. J. & Chapman, J. P. *Disordered thought in schizophreniz.* Englewood Hills, NJ: Prentice Hall, 1973a.

Cronbach, L. J. Statistical methods applied to Rorschach scores: A review. *Psychological Bulletin,* 1949, *46,* pp. 393–429.

Exner, J. E. *The Rorschach: A comprehensive system.* New York: Wiley, 1974.

Frank, L. K. Projective methods for the study of personality. *Journal of Psychology*, 1939, 8, pp. 389–413.

Friedlander, S. *Measuring hedonic tone in the Rorschach: The implicit motivational value score.* Presented XI International Rorschach Conference. Barcelona, Spain, 1984.

Hertz, M. R. The Rorschach ink-blot test: historical summary. *Psychological Bulletin*, 1935, 32, 33–66.

Hill, E. F. *The Holtzman inkblot technique.* London: Jossey-Bass, 1972.

Holt, R. R. *Manual for the scoring of primary process manifestations in Rorschach responses.* Unpublished manuscript, Research Center for Mental Health, New York University, 1970.

Kasanin, J. S. *Language and thought in schizophrenia.* Los Angeles: University of California Press, 1944.

Kernberg, O. Structured derivatives of object relationships. *International Journal of Psychoanalysis*, 1966, 77, 236–253.

Kernberg, O. *Internal world and external reality.* New York: Aronson, 1980.

Klein, G. A. et al. *Perception, motives and personality.* New York: Knopf, 1970.

Klopfer, B. & Kelley, D. M. *The Rorschach Technique.* Yonkers: World Book, 1942.

Klopfer, B. et al. *Developments in Rorschach technique Vol. 1,* New York, Harcourt Brace, 1954.

Klopfer, B. et al. *Developments in Rorschach technique Vol. 2,* New York, Harcourt Brace, 1956.

Klopfer, W. G. The short history of projective techniques. *Journal of the History of the Behavioral Sciences*, 1973, 9(1), pp. 60–65.

Kohut, H. *How does anaysis cure?.* Chicago: University of Chicago Press, 1984.

Korchin, S. J. *Modern clinical psychology.* New York: Basic Books, 1976.

Lord, F. M. & Novick, M. R. *Statistical theories of mental test scores.* Reading, MA: Addison Wesley, 1968.

Mayman, M. & Krohn, A. Object representations in dreams and projective tests. *Bulletin of the Menninger Clinic*, 1974, 38, 445–466.

Meehl, P. E. *Clinical vs. statistical prediction.* Minneapolis: University of Minnesota, 1954.

Quirk, D. A., Quarrington, M., Neiger, S. & Slemon, A. G. The performance of acute psychotic patients on the indix of pathological thinking and on selected signs of idiosyncrasy on the Rorschach. *Journal of Projective Techniques*, 1962, 26(4), 431–441.

Piotrowski, Z. A. On the Rorschach method and its application in organic disturbances of the central nervous system. *Rorschach Research Exchange*, 1936, 1, 23–40.

Piotrowski, Z. A. *Perceptanalysis.* New York: Macmillan, 1957.

Piotrowski, C. The status of projective techniques: Or, "wishing won't make it go away." *Journal of Clinical Psychology*, 1984a, 40, pp. 1495–1502.

Piotrowski, C. & Keller, J. W. Psychodiagnostic testing in APA approved clinical psychology programs. *Professional Psychology: Research and Practice.* 1984b, 15(3), pp. 450–456.

Piotrowski, C. & Keller, J. W. Attitudes toward clinical assessment by members of AABT. *Psychological Reports*, 1984c, 55, pp. 831–838.

Piotrowski, C., Sherry, D. & Keller, J. W. Psychodiagnostic test usage: A survey of the society for personality assessment. *Journal of Personality Assessment*, 1985, 49(2), pp. 115–119.

Potkay, R. *The Rorschach clinician.* New York: Grune & Stratton, 1971.

Pribram, K. H. The cognitive revolution and mind/brain issues. *American Psychologist*, 1986, 41(5), 507–520.

Rapaport, D., et al. *Diagnostic psychological testing. Vol I and II.* Chicago: Yearbook Publishers, 1945, 1946.

Rorschach, H. (trans: Lemkau & Kronenberg) *Psychodiagnostics*. New York: Grune & Stratton, 1969.

Schafer, R. *Psychoanalytic interpretation in Rorschach testing*. New York: Grune & Stratton, 1954.

Weiss, D. J. *New horizons in testing*. New York: Academic Press, 1983.

Witkin, H. A. et al. *Personality through perception*. New York: Harper, 1954.

INDEX